The CANNON COOKERY BOOK

containing

Valuable aids in the art of cooking, and
RECIPES proved and tested in the
CANNON RESEARCH KITCHEN

(Fourteenth Edition)

Published by

CANNON (G A) LTD.

DEEPFIELDS, BILSTON, STAFFS.

London Office

4 PARK LANE, PICCADILLY, W.1

First Edition .... June, 1932

Second Edition .... April, 1934

Third Edition ...... September, 1935

Fourth Edition .... June, 1936

Fifth Edition .... February, 1937

Sixth Edition ...... November, 1938

Seventh Edition ...... August, 1946

Eighth Edition .... January, 1947

Ninth Edition ...... September, 1947

Tenth Edition .... June, 1948

Eleventh Edition .... May, 1949

Twelfth Edition .... May, 1950

Thirteenth Edition .... October, 1952

Fourteenth Edition .... July, 1953

CONTENTS

INTRODUCTION

A Modern Gas Cooker

THE CANNON COOKERY BOOK has been compiled with the utmost care to enable you to obtain the best results from your A125 Cooker.

The great superiority of gas for cooking is shown by its continued and rapid progress. With your new gas-cooker you can prepare not only every dish and prized recipe which an older generation thought only possible in a coal-oven, but many more of recent invention, and all with a minimum of patience and skill. You will find this cooker easy to use, easy to clean; a constant source of pleasure and of satisfaction in trying out new recipes, in producing appetising meals cooked to perfection. No other source of heat is so certain, so safe to use, and so simple to control as gas.

CANNON, the makers of your gas-cooker, have been established for over a century and a quarter. A long experience of manufacturing processes, coupled with intense research and special attention to design, have resulted in producing the outstanding cooker of the age.

To ensure the utmost satisfaction in use, CANNON cookers are exhaustively tested in specially equipped laboratories and demonstration kitchens.

Adjustment

The Gas Undertaking will leave the cooker correctly adjusted.

Care and cleaning of burners to remove spill-over will ensure that efficiency and economy in use are maintained.

HOW TO GET THE BEST OUT OF YOUR GAS COOKER

READ carefully the card of instructions supplied with your cooker. Hang the card in a convenient place in the kitchen where you can easily refer to it. Always follow its directions closely, together with those in this cookery book.

The Hotplate

Gas passes from the taps to the burners by way of brass "injectors". The aluminium burner caps are removable for cleaning. Always ensure correct location when replacing. Care should be taken when replacing the burners, that the adjustment of the injectors is not disturbed. The top-bar sections are so designed that no flame should impinge directly on to a bar. If this is happening, the burner or the bar is not in its proper position.

Boiling.—Never allow flames to project beyond the base of a kettle or saucepan, as this is wasteful of gas. Most foods (green vegetables are an exception) require only gentle boiling. When boiling-point is reached the gas should be turned down to a small flame. Never use an asbestos mat under a saucepan as this will damage the enamel.

Grilling.—Always heat the fret at full gas-rate for one to two minutes before using, and during this time keep the grill-pan, or an asbestos mat, directly underneath the grill to prevent over-heating the enamelled door tray.

Keep the grill closed when not in use, and stow the grill pan in the drawer, as illustrated.

Frying.—Use a thick metal frying-pan, aluminium or steel, and turn down to a low gas when the fat is sufficiently hot. The thickness of metal distributes the heat and prevents burning. Heavy vessels should be lifted and not dragged across the Hotplate as they tend to damage the enamel.

The Oven

You will probably find that this oven is wider than that of your previous cooker. Use the width to full advantage whenever possible. It may be found convenient, for instance, to place pies or cakes side by side on the same shelf.

Cake tins and baking sheets should not be used if larger than the cake tray supplied with the cooker. The heat circulation of the oven is from back to front, passing over the top of the food. To obtain the best results, food should be positioned centrally within the area occupied by the cake tray. If this area must be exceeded, encroach upon the sides in preference to the front. On no account overhang the burner at the back.

When choosing a shelf height, position the food so that when risen it is no closer to the top of the oven than 3½ in., or midway between the first and second runners. For small cakes, sponges and plate pies a single tray should be placed on the THIRD runner, or two trays on the SECOND and FOURTH. Large cakes should be baked about the CENTRE of the oven. Turkeys and other large birds should be placed on the FOURTH or FIFTH runners, according to size, with head and tail towards the sides. The deep oven shelf is supplied to provide a midway position between normal shelf levels.

The top runner is not intended for baking, but may be used for hanging joints by inverting the deep shelf and suspending the food from the centre.

The sides, back, top and door of the oven are insulated with the best heat-conserving material obtainable. Good insulation confers two advantages of the greatest importance. It reduces the loss of heat and therefore saves gas, and it creates a reserve of heat which acts as a compensator for the loss of temperature which occurs when the door is opened.

In this oven there is no necessity to use a browning shelf. Plate pies should preferably be baked in metal plates or dishes. If it is desired to use earthenware or glass dishes, these should always be stood on a cake tray, which has been preheated. All other foods can be cooked in their customary ways, having regard to the sizes of trays and tins, as already mentioned.

The external enamel is best cleaned with a cloth, using warm soapy water. Use of abrasive powders and pastes should be avoided as far as possible, but when necessary use a mild abrasive.

Caustic solution may be applied to the enamel of the pan supports, boiling burners and oven interior to remove carbonised grease. It should be applied with a rubber mop and contact with the hands avoided. Do not leave on longer than twelve hours. Certain branded products will be found the most satisfactory and should be applied according to the maker's instructions.

When using caustic solutions, or washing soda, avoid application to the following aluminium parts, as it is detrimental to the surface.

(a) Door Handles.

(b) Door Beadings.

(c) Oven Door Seating.

(d) Boiling Burner Caps.

(e) Grill Pan.

(f) Visor around "Autimo" Dial.

A few suggestions—

Before cooking is actually completed it is possible to turn off the gas, sufficient heat being retained by the oven itself to finish off such food as milk puddings, casserole dishes, etc.

Cooking utensils kept free from deposits, i.e., soot, fur, etc., will boil in shorter time and save gas. A correct flame will obviate any deposit on the bottom of a pan or kettle.

Whilst modern detergents will leave the exterior enamel in a resplendent condition, a slightly greasy film on the oven interior enamel acts as a protective and makes for easier cleaning and longer life.

If any technical point arises in connection with the operation of your cooker, seek advice from the local Gas Showroom in preference to experimenting.

FOLD-AWAY, EYE-LEVEL GRILL

THE CANNON Fold-away Eye-level Grill brings to the housewife an entirely new and revolutionary era in Grilled Cookery, for not only does it give visual control, so essential to the cooking of any grilled food in order to produce a perfect result, but, because its design greatly widens the type of grilled dishes which may be prepared and served.

Apart from ease of visual control and operation, the Grill has been designed to give greater capacity in height, as well as width and length, the distance from the heating element to the bottom of the grill pan being greater than that of the normal type of domestic cooker grill.

The Grill Pan is designed to take advantage of this greater variation in height insofar that three positions are obtainable with the grid inside the pan, and two positions with the pan supported on the grid. For example, the Grill is capable of cooking a small joint (of about 3 to 4 lbs. in weight, depending on shape) by placing it on the lowest grid position and sealing each side under full gas for approximately 5 minutes. Remove the joint from the grid and finish cooking either side on half gas rate in the bottom of the grill pan. The total time required is between 25 to 30 minutes, as against 1 hour 10 minutes when using the oven.

Other examples—(1) a mixed grill is best done in the base of the grill pan which is raised by the grill grid.

(2) When preparing Curried Rice, the rice may be dried in the grill pan under the grill instead of in the oven.

When making Toast use the highest position of the grill grid. Four large pieces of toast may be made at the one time by placing two centre pieces in position and leaning the other two to right and left; after a few moments the bread shrinks and the four pieces will fall into position.

THE "AUTIMO" OVEN HEAT CONTROL
WITH COMBINED OVEN TAP

THE "Autimo" is a device for regulating the heat of the Oven as desired.

Numbers inscribed on the dial represent definite temperatures. After lighting the oven burner adjust to the required mark.

Do not anticipate an immediate alteration in the size of the flame. No change is to be expected until the Oven has been closed, and the required heat is attained.

"Autimo" numbers given on the cooking chart have been decided on after exhaustive tests have been carried out with given recipes, but a slight alteration may be required in view of variations in the size of tins, ingredients used, or cooking practice of the individual housewife.

After setting the Dial to the number prescribed in the recipe, allow the oven to heat up for about twenty minutes before inserting the food.

At Mark $\frac{1}{4}$ or $\frac{1}{2}$ the oven will attain in a few minutes a very "slow" heat, sufficient to keep dishes warm or to cook Meringues, etc. Mark 1 represents a "slow" heat sufficient to cook milk puddings, and stews, provided that these are started with hot milk or boiling water and placed not lower than the oven centre. Alternatively, they can be cooked more quickly at Mark 2. Marks 3 and 4 are used for most baked puddings. Mark 5 is suitable for baked fish, and Marks 6 and 7 are used for most kinds of meat. Marks 8 and 9 can be used occasionally when a very strong baking heat is required, but generally a Mark higher than 7 is seldom required.

It should be remembered that the "Autimo" cannot control the time during which the food is to be cooked. When the specified time has elapsed the food must be withdrawn, otherwise it will be cooked too much.

The following notes will assist you to get the best possible results from your "Autimo" Controlled Cooker.

1. Do not regard the numbers given in the recipes as unalterable. It may be that a slight variation of half a mark either way, may produce results more to your liking. The various times and settings given throughout this book will be found correct under normal conditions. Further specific settings are given on the Cooking Chart supplied with each Cooker.

2. Heating up. The time allowed for heating up the oven from cold is very important. 15 minutes preheating is required to attain the correct oven temperature up to Mark 4. For higher settings 20 minutes is advisable.

3. Sometimes you may wish to follow the baking of pastry or other food requiring a high temperature, with a rich fruit cake requiring only Mark 2. In doing so, the following procedure will give the best results. Turn the "Autimo" back to Mark 2, and **open** the oven door. When the flames increase to normal length close the door and allow the temperature to become steady for about five minutes. Then insert the cake and bake for the time required.

"AUTIMO" COOKING CHART

For CANNON A125 GAS COOKERS

FOOD	Mark	SHELF POSITION (from top of Oven)	TIME REQUIRED
STEWS. In closed Casserole	½—1	4th	3—4 hours starting with hot water
MILK PUDDINGS ..	1	4th	1—2 hours starting with hot milk
Custard Puddings		3rd	45 minutes.
FRUIT CAKE (Plain) ..	3	4th	1—2 hours, according to size.
„ „ Rich (Med. size)	2	4th	2—3 hours, according to size.
„ „ Xmas ..	1	5th	4—6 hours, according to size.
Madeira Cake	3—4	4th	1½—2 hours, according to size.
Braised Beef or Mutton ..	3	4th	2 hours.
Meat Pies (Beef Steak, Veal, Ham, etc.)	3—4	4th	2 hours (approx.
Baked Bread Pudding (Lge)	3	4th	50—60 minutes.
Shortbread	3	3rd	40—50 minutes, according to thickness.
Sponge Cake (Mould) ..	3	4th	¾—1¼ hours.
Baked Fish and Fish Steaks	4	4th	30—50 minutes.
Shortbread Biscuits ..	4	2nd & 4th	15—20 minutes.
Victoria Sandwich.. ..	5	2nd & 4th	20—25 minutes.
Queen Cakes		2nd & 4th	15—20 minutes.
Rock Cakes		2nd & 4th	10—20 minutes.
Baked Ham, small ..	6	4th	30 minutes per lb.
„ „ large.. ..	6	5th	20 minutes per lb.
JOINTS, POULTRY AND GAME			
Beef with bone	7	3rd or 4th	15 minutes per lb. and 15 minutes over.
„ without bone.. ..		3rd or 4th	20 minutes per lb. and 20 minutes over.
Veal and Lamb		3rd or 4th	20 minutes per lb. and 20 minutes over.
Pork		3rd or 4th	25 minutes per lb. and 25 minutes over.
Game, Small birds ..		3rd or 4th	35 minutes.
„ Pheasant ..		3rd or 4th	1 hour.
„ Wild Duck..		3rd or 4th	45 minutes.
Turkey		5th	15 minutes per lb. and 15 minutes over.
Roast Rabbit		4th	1½ hours.
Baked Vegetables		5th or Base Plate	1 hour (below joint).
Fruit Tarts and Pies ..		3rd or 4th	40—60 minutes, according to size
„ Tartlets ..		2nd & 4th	35 minutes.
Custard Tarts (large) ..	5	3rd	35—40 minutes.
„ „ (small) ..	6	2nd & 4th	20 minutes.
Yorkshire Pudding ..	7	3rd	30—35 minutes.
„ Tea Cakes ..	7—8	3rd	10—15 minutes.
Scones, Large	6	3rd	20—25 minutes.
„ Small	7	2nd & 4th	10—15 minutes.
Pastry Puff	8	2nd & 4th	15—20 minutes.

15 minutes preheating is required to attain the correct oven temperature up to Mark 4. For higher settings 20 minutes is advisable.

NOTES ON WEIGHING AND MEASURING

ACCURATE weights and measures are essential for success in all cooking, but particularly so when making cakes, puddings, and pastry. Every kitchen should therefore be provided with a pair of scales and weights, and a set of measuring spoons. If scales are not available, however, the following handy measures will be a guide.

N.B. Very Important. When a teaspoonful or tablespoonful is given in a recipe it is understood to mean that the spoon contains as much above the bowl as in it. A level tablespoonful is either given as such or as a half tablespoonful. A heaped tablespoonful contains almost as much as can be piled on it. A quarter teaspoonful denotes half a level teaspoonful.

Dry Foods, such as flour, sugar, rice.

1 teaspoonful containing as much above the bowl as in it	$\frac{1}{4}$ oz.	1 teacup of medium size 4 ozs
1 dessertspoonful, containing as much above the bowl as in it	$\frac{1}{2}$ oz.	1 egg of medium size weighs .. .. 2 ozs.
		1 small egg weighs ..$1\frac{1}{2}$ ozs.
1 tablespoonful, containing as much above the bowl as in it	1 oz.	2 tablespoonfuls (heaped) Breadcrumbs .. 1 oz.
		1 tablespoonful jam or syrup .. .. 2 ozs.

Liquids—

1 tablespoonful .. 1 oz.

Measuring with the aid of a Tumbler

A tumbler holds $\frac{1}{2}$ pint liquid, and the following weights of other ingredients:—

Ground rice ..	.. $6\frac{1}{2}$ ozs.	Medium oatmeal ..	6 ozs.
Rice (whole)..	.. 9 ozs.	Chopped or grated suet	6 ozs.
Flour ..	.. 6 ozs.	Ground Almonds ..	4 ozs.
Raisins, sultanas, currants ..	.. $6\frac{1}{2}$ ozs.	Whole Almonds ..	6 ozs.
		Walnuts	$4\frac{1}{2}$ ozs.
Coconut, desiccated	3 ozs.	Tea	$3\frac{1}{2}$ ozs.
Castor sugar..	.. $8\frac{1}{2}$ ozs.	Coffee	$4\frac{1}{2}$ ozs.
Granulated sugar ..	9 ozs.	Golden Syrup ..	14 ozs.
Brown sugar..	.. $6\frac{1}{2}$ ozs.	Haricot or Butter Beans	8 ozs.
Loaf sugar ..	.. 6 ozs.		
Breadcrumbs	.. 3 ozs.		

Throughout the book, a gill = $\frac{1}{4}$ pint.

THE CANNON **A125** GAS COOKER, complete with "Eye-level" grill, press button ignition, and a combined warming chamber and storage drawer. Finished throughout in gleaming Vitreous Enamel.

The Cannon exclusive "Eye-level" grill, with large capacity grill pan.

Operation

The gas control lever 'A' is shown in the 'off' position.

To turn the gas on.	Move the lever toward you.
To light.	Apply flame beneath radiant fret.
To close.	First turn off the gas then press lever 'A' to right.
To use grill-pan support as utensil or plate stand.	From the closed position, press in 'B' and lower door-shelf.
To reconnect with Radiant fret.	Raise door-shelf approximately three inches.

The grill pan is fitted with a three-position grid.

The highest position is the most suitable for toast.

As with the old type grill, the pan should only be removed for short periods, as it protects the enamel from the fierce heat.

Similarly the back boiling burners should not be left full on when not covered by pans.

The Hotplate

The hotplate has two high-speed burners in the front and two medium simmer burners at the back.

The aluminium alloy caps may be removed for cleaning. As with aluminium cooking utensils, soda should not be used in the water. Ensure that the caps are seated properly on replacing.

Black vitreous enamelled pan supports remove in two sections, as do the enamelled surrounds beneath. It will be noted that the spill-over bowls are integral with the surrounds.

The patented safety taps give a slight initial resistance to turning on, and an audible 'click' on turning off.

'C' shows the handle to the tap which controls the pilot jet of the ignition system.

To light the pilot jet.   First light any one of the four burners.
                                 Turn on tap 'C'.
                                 Press button situated at centre of 'C'.

In use, merely turn on the gas for the required burner or burners and press the button 'C'.

Note. The pilot jet is situated centrally below the hotplate and can be left on indefinitely at negligible cost.

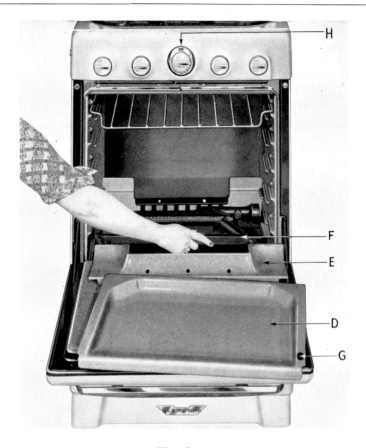

The Oven

The illustration shows how the baseplate 'D', burner duct 'E', and burner 'F' are removed for cleaning. These three components slide along the runner and withdraw from the front of the oven.

Touch hole 'G' is where the flame is applied to light the burner.

The combined oven tap and 'Autimo' control is shown at 'H' (for cooking chart see page xiii).

To turn the gas either on or off, the handle 'H' must first be pressed in.

Always open the oven door before turning on the gas and lighting.

The deep oven grid shelf is shown in position in the oven. Turn shelf upside down on the top runner for hanging food.

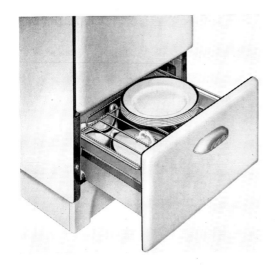

Warming chamber showing deep shelf inserted to take vegetable dishes and gravy boat underneath, with the plates on top.

Warming chamber showing plates inserted between bars of the deep shelf.

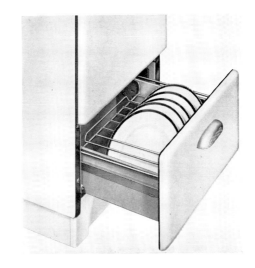

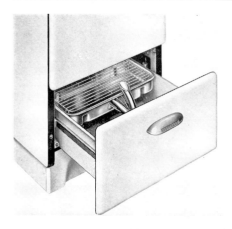

The grill pan stowed at the back of the drawer resting on the sides.

To remove the drawer.

Pull out to furthest extent. Lift first the front and then the back.

To replace drawer.

Insert the rollers into runners at a point four inches along, holding the drawer at the angle shown.

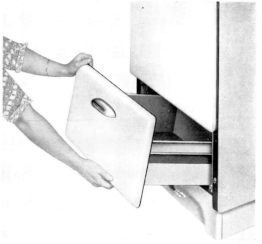

Here the lower part of the cooker is shown with the drawer and front plinth removed for occasional cleaning beneath. The front plinth is secured by the knurled hand screw.

32 small cakes or scones can be baked at one time, with 16 on each tray. 20 may be baked, using a single tray on the second runner from top.

Six 2-lb. (or eight 1-lb.) loaves can be baked simultaneously.

This shows the method used when cooking a three course meal including Fruit Pie (3rd runner), Roast (5th runner), Milk Pudding (base plate). If a shallow plate tart or pie is to be cooked instead of the deep pie shown, it is preferable to raise both shelves by one runner.

If the pie is a large one, or if the fruit is not a good cooking variety, it may be preferred to reverse the position of the pie and the meat. The pie will cook more slowly and should be given longer.

For a more creamy milk pudding place to one side of the base plate with the pie on the opposite side of the 5th runner (thus giving more clearance above). Another way is to place pie and pudding side by side on the 5th runner.

For complete Dinner Menus, see page 139.

STOCK AND SOUP MAKING

STOCK is the liquid in which meat and bones have been boiled for a long time to extract as much of the goodness as possible.

It can be of several kinds, meat stock, bone stock and vegetable stock. Fish and game stocks are made by boiling fish bones and trimmings, and the carcase and giblets of birds.

MEAT STOCK

A meat stock can be either brown or white, depending on the meat used for making it. For white stock, veal or chicken bones must be used; for brown stock, beef and mutton bones.

The advantage of using white stock is that it does not impair the colour of light sauces and soups. For this reason it is chiefly employed for making cream soups and white sauces, and the darker one employed when making brown sauces and dark coloured soups and stews.

In general practice one frequently employs both light and dark meat, or in fact, any meat and bones that may be available.

The making of stock is a very simple process when once the fundamental principles have been mastered, and there is no reason why anyone with even a limited knowledge of cooking should fail to have a supply of good stock always available for the making of soups, sauces, stews and gravies. In hot weather, stock should be brought to the boil every day, otherwise it will not keep.

BONE STOCK

This is made from bones, vegetables, salt and a few herbs, and the same directions should be followed as are given for meat stock, the only difference being that the meat is omitted. When a large quantity of stock is required it proves more economical and is quite suitable for the basis of soups and stews.

VEGETABLE STOCK

Is made without the aid of meat or bones. It is, therefore, less nourishing than either meat or bone stock, but is preferable to water from the point of view of flavour for the making of gravies, soups, etc., the flavour and goodness of the vegetables having been extracted. It is specially suitable for those who for various reasons do not wish to include meat in the diet.

VEGETABLE STOCK

2 *onions.*	1 *leek, if available.*	*Small piece celery.*
1 *carrot.*	1 *turnip.*	1½ *quarts water.*

1½ *ozs. dripping or butter, or 2 tablespoonfuls olive oil.*

(1) Prepare the vegetables in the usual way and slice them rather thickly. (2) Place in saucepan with water and salt. (3) Bring slowly to the boil and simmer gently for 3 or 4 hours. (4) Skim from time to time, and strain when the cooking is completed. (5) Next day, remove any surface fat.

1

SOUPS

POTATO CREAM SOUP

1 *lb. potatoes.*	1 *onion.*	1½ *pints stock.*
½ *pint milk.*	*Pepper and Salt.*	*Small piece mace.*
1 *clove.*	1 *small piece celery, if available.*	
Sprig of parsley.	1 *oz. butter, margarine or dripping.*	
1 *teaspoonful seed pearl tapioca, if desired.*		

(1) Peel and slice the potatoes and onion, and cut the celery into small pieces. (2) Melt the butter or dripping in a saucepan, stir in the vegetables and cook, but do not allow them to fry. (3) Continue to cook over a low gas until the fat has been absorbed. (4) Add the boiling stock or water, pepper, salt, mace and clove, and simmer until the vegetables are tender. The time required is about 40 minutes. (5) Rub the soup through a sieve, return to the saucepan, previously rinsed out, and bring to the boil. (6) Add the milk, and when boiling, sprinkle in the seed pearl tapioca, and allow to simmer very gently for about 15 minutes or until the tapioca is thoroughly cooked. (7) Add more seasoning immediately before serving, if required.

LENTIL SOUP

½ *pint lentils.*	1 *carrot.*	*Small piece celery.*
½ *turnip.*	1 *onion.*	*Bunch of herbs.*
1 *oz. butter or margarine.*		3 *pints stock or water.*

(1) Wash the lentils well, melt the fat, stir in the sliced carrot, onion and celery, and fry until lightly browned. (2) Add the lentils. If necessary, a little additional fat may be added. (3) Pour on the stock or water, add the pepper, salt and herbs, put the lid on the pan, and allow the soup to simmer gently for 1½ to 2 hours, or until the lentils are soft. (4) Rub through a sieve, rinse out the saucepan, return the sieved soup to the pan. (5) Reheat, and if liked, the soup may be further enriched and the flavour improved by adding half a pint of milk or 3 tablespoonfuls unsweetened evaporated milk and an equal quantity of water.

PEA SOUP

Can be made in exactly the same way except that peas, being harder, require considerably longer to cook, and it is advisable to soak them overnight, as this shortens the length of time required for cooking.

TOMATO SOUP

1 *tin or bottle tomatoes.*	1 *onion.*	½ *a carrot.*
2 or 3 *ozs. bacon rinds.*	*Salt.*	*Bunch of Herbs.*
½ *oz. dripping or margarine.*	¾ *oz. flour.*	1 *teaspoonful sugar.*
2½ *pints stock.*	8 *peppercorns.*	

(1) Tie the herbs and spices in a small piece of muslin; these should

consist of a sprig of parsley and thyme, half a bay leaf, small blade of mace, 2 cloves, and the peppercorns, and if celery seeds are available a teaspoonful of these can be tied in the muslin with the other flavourings. (2) Cut the rinds into two or three pieces and fry lightly, but do not overcook. (3) Remove from the saucepan, fry the sliced carrot and onion in the bacon fat, adding the margarine when the bacon fat has been absorbed. (4) Add the contents of a tin or bottle of tomatoes. Fresh tomatoes can be used if liked, and they should be sliced and added after the other vegetables have been fried. At least a pound will be required to replace a moderately sized tin. (5) Add the stock, pepper and salt, put the lid on the pan and simmer gently until the tomatoes and other vegetables are tender. (6) Rub through a sieve, rinse out the saucepan, return the sieved soup. (7) Blend the flour with two or three tablespoonfuls of cold water, stir into the soup, bring to the boil, continuing to stir to prevent lumps forming. (8) Cook for 8 minutes, add more seasoning if necessary and serve with croûtons of toast or fried bread.

CELERY SOUP

1 *head of celery.*   1 *onion.*   1 *oz. butter.*
1 *oz. flour.*   ¾ *pint milk.*   *Salt and pepper.*
1 *pint vegetable or meat stock.*

(1) Wash well the celery, cut in slices, and slice the onion. (2) Melt the butter, stir in the sliced onion and celery, and cook until all the fat is absorbed. (3) Add the stock (if stock is not available, water must be used), and simmer until the celery is tender. (4) Rub the soup through a sieve, return to the saucepan. (5) Add the milk previously blended with the flour, bring to the boil, stirring to prevent lumps forming. (6) Simmer for 10 minutes, add more seasoning if required. (7) Serve with croûtons of fried bread.

PALESTINE PUREE

1 *small head of celery.*   1½ *lbs. Jerusalem artichokes.*
1 *onion.*   *Bunch of herbs.*
2½ *pints stock or water.*   *Pepper and salt.*
½ *pint milk.*   1 *oz. butter.*

(1) Peel and slice the artichokes and celery, and onion. (2) Melt the butter in a saucepan, add the vegetables, and toss until the butter is absorbed. (3) Pour on the boiling stock or water, add the herbs, and simmer until the vegetables are cooked. (4) Rub through a sieve, and return to the saucepan. (5) Add the milk, pepper and salt if necessary, and sprinkle in two tablespoonfuls of breadcrumbs. (6) Pour in a hot soup tureen and serve with croûtons of fried bread or toast.

3

CRESSY SOUP

3 *or* 4 *large carrots.*   1 *small onion.*   2 *ozs. dripping.*
¾ *oz. flour.*   1 *quart of stock.*   *Pepper and salt.*
Bunch of herbs, including parsley.

(1) Melt the fat in a saucepan over a low gas.   (2) Slice the carrots and toss them, with the finely chopped onion, in the fat for 5 or 10 minutes.   (3) Add the stock and the bunch of herbs, and simmer gently for about 20 minutes.   (4) Press the vegetables through a sieve, removing the herbs.   (5) Return to the saucepan, stir in the flour, previously blended with a little cold water, and simmer for 5 minutes.   (6) Serve with dice of toast or fried bread.

OXTAIL SOUP (No. 1)

1 *oxtail.*   2 *ozs. dripping, margarine or butter.*
2 *carrots.*   1 *tablespoonful seasoned flour.*
1 *turnip.*   *Sprig of Parsley, and bay leaf.*
1 *onion.*   2 *quarts of water.*   *Pepper, salt.*

(1) Cut the tail into small joints, and coat with the seasoned flour. (2) Melt the fat in a saucepan, and when quite hot put in the pieces of tail and fry a good brown.   Pour off any fat that may be left.   (3) Add the water, salt, and the parsley and bay leaf tied in a piece of muslin.   (4) Simmer very gently about 2 hours.   (5) Allow to become cold, and carefully remove all fat.   (6) Put in the vegetables cut into small dice, bring to boiling point, and simmer again about 2 hours.   A little more thickening and browning may be added to the soup, if necessary.   A portion of the thicker pieces of oxtail may be used for a separate entrée, if liked.

OXTAIL SOUP (No. 2)

1 *oxtail.*   1 *head celery.*   1 *carrot.*
½ *turnip.*   1 *oz. flour.*   1 *onion.*

(1) Put the oxtail in pan, and cover with cold water.   (2) Simmer gently for 3 or 4 hours.   (3) Allow stock to stand overnight.   (4) Remove all fat, prepare and cut up vegetables, and then put in the stock.   (5) Simmer gently one hour, thicken with flour blended with water.   (6) Add meat from the oxtail, season and serve hot.

MINESTRONE

2 *carrots.*   2 *onions*   ½ *a small cabbage.*
2 *tomatoes.*   2 *potatoes.*   1 *oz. rice or spaghetti.*
4 *or* 5 *stalks of celery.*   2 *tablespoonfuls green peas.*
4 *ozs. haricot beans.*   *Pepper and salt.*
¼ *lb. pickled pork, if liked.*   4 *pints boiling water or stock.*
Grated Parmesan cheese.   *Small piece garlic.*

This Italian soup is a particularly delicious one, but if raw vegetables are used, a good deal of time must be allowed for the cooking. Therefore, tinned vegetables have a definite advantage, and it is an excellent way of using up left-overs, for it is possible to vary the vegetables used and the proportion in which they appear. (1) Cut the pork into small pieces and cook for about 30 minutes. (2) Cut all the vegetables into strips, add them and the cold water and simmer for about 15 minutes. (3) When done, sprinkle in the well washed rice or spaghetti and continue to simmer for about 20 minutes until it is cooked. (4) Pour into a hot soup tureen, and either sprinkle the top with grated Parmesan cheese or serve the cheese separately in a dish.

CREAM OF CORN SOUP

1 *tin of sweet corn.* 1 *small onion.* 3 *peppercorns.*
Pepper and salt. ¾ *pint of stock.* ¼ *pint of milk.*
Small piece of mace. ½ *oz. cornflour.* 1 *oz. dripping or margarine.*

(1) Melt the dripping, add the chopped onion and drained corn. (2) Cook over a low heat for about 5 minutes. (3) Add the stock, mace and peppercorns, and simmer for about half an hour, or until the corn is cooked. (4) Then rub through a sieve, blend the cornflour with the cold milk and stir it into the sieved soup. (5) Return to the saucepan, bring to the boil, stirring to prevent lumps forming. (6) Simmer for 10 minutes and serve with croûtons of toast.

MULLIGATAWNY SOUP

1 *onion.* 1 *carrot.* 2 *ozs. butter or margarine.*
1 *apple.* 2 *ozs. flour.* 1 *teaspoonful curry powder.*
2 *quarts veal stock.* 3 *tablespoonfuls evaporated milk.*
Salt and pepper.

(1) Prepare the vegetables. (2) Fry in fat for 10 minutes. (3) Stir in flour and curry powder, add apple finely chopped, stock and seasoning. (4) Simmer gently for 1 hour, add evaporated milk just before serving.

SHEEP'S HEAD BROTH

1 *sheep's head.* 1 *onion.* 1 *oz. pearl barley.*
1 *sprig parsley.* *Salt and pepper.*

(1) Wash the sheep's head well in salt and water, remove the brains. (2) Put into pan, cover with cold water, add the onion, pearl barley and parsley. (3) Simmer gently for 2 hours. (4) Take out the head, cut off the meat, skin the tongue (the meat may be cut up and returned to the soup or served separately), if necessary dilute with more water or milk. (5) Season and serve. (6) Boil the brains in salted water for 20 minutes. Drain, add small piece of butter or margarine, 1 teaspoonful chopped parsley, mix well and serve with the meat.

SCOTCH BROTH

½ *head celery.* 1 *carrot.* 1 *pound lean beef or mutton.*
¼ *turnip.* 1 *onion.* 2 *tablespoonfuls pearl barley.*
2 *quarts water or stock.* 1 *dessertspoonful chopped parsley.*
Salt and pepper.

(1) Put the meat in pan with cold water. (2) Prepare vegetables and cut into dice, add salt and pepper. (3) Simmer gently for 2-2½ hours, add chopped parsley. (4) Serve at once.

CHICKEN BROTH

1 *chicken.* 1 *onion.* 1 *teaspoonful chopped parsley.*
Salt and pepper. 1 *blade of mace.*
½ *oz. cornflour.* 1 *teacupful milk.*

(1) Cut up chicken, wash the gizzard, liver and neck. (2) Put into a saucepan, cover with cold water. (3) Bring to the boil, then simmer until the chicken is tender. (4) Remove scum, strain, take out gizzard, etc.; return to the pan, adding to the stock an onion cut up finely, mace and seasoning. (5) Simmer gently for a further half hour. (6) Add the flour blended with the milk, cook for a few minutes longer, sprinkle chopped parsley on the top of the broth before serving.
N.B.—The pieces of cooked chicken can be served in white sauce with dried vegetables or carrots, as a separate entrée.

GRAVY SOUP

1 *quart good stock.* 1 *onion.* 1 *carrot.*
1 *oz. dripping or margarine.* 1 *slice turnip.* 1 *oz. flour.*
½ *lb. gravy beef.*

(1) Melt the dripping in a pan. (2) Cut up vegetables and fry until golden brown. (3) Add flour, then stock, and the meat cut up finely. (4) Simmer gently for 1½ hours, season and serve hot.

MUSHROOM SOUP

½ *lb. mushrooms.* 1 *small onion.* 1 *pint stock.*
½ *pint milk.* ½ *oz. cornflour.* *Seasoning.*

(1) Put the stock in a pan with mushrooms cut up small, and the onion whole. (2) Simmer gently for ½ hour, then remove the onion. (3) Thicken with flour blended with milk. (4) Stir until it boils, season, and serve.

MUTTON BROTH

1 *oz. pearl barley.* 1 *onion.* 1 *carrot.*
¼ *turnip.* *A little celery.* *Salt and pepper.*
1 *lb. scrag end neck of mutton.*

(1) Cut up the meat, taking off most of the fat. (2) Prepare and cut up vegetables, put all together in the stewpan with 1 quart of water, add pearl barley and seasoning. (3) Simmer for about 2 hours, skim off the fat. (4) Take out the bones before serving.

VEGETABLE SOUP (with bones)

2 *shin bones* (*cut up*).   1 *carrot.*   1 *head celery.*
2 *potatoes.*   1 *onion.*   1 *slice turnip.*
2 *ozs. rice, macaroni or spaghetti.*   *Salt and pepper.*

(1) Put bones in the pan with sufficient water to cover. (2) Simmer gently for 4 or 5 hours keeping the bones well covered with water. (3) Allow stock to stand overnight. (4) Remove all fat, add to the stock the vegetables cut into dice, rice or alternatives, salt and pepper. (5) Simmer gently for 1½ hours, and serve.

LEEK SOUP

6 *leeks* (*of moderate size*).   1 *quart stock.*   1 *stick celery.*
½ *pint milk.*   1 *oz. cornflour.*   *Salt and pepper.*

(1) Cut off the roots of leeks and celery and remove unwanted tops. (2) Wash and cut up into small pieces. (3) Put into the stewpan with the stock, simmer gently for 1 hour, add salt and pepper to taste. (4) Rub through a sieve, blend cornflour with the milk, and add to the soup. (5) Stir until it boils.

GIBLET SOUP

2 *sets giblets.*   1 *onion.*   1 *carrot.*   ¼ *turnip.*
1 *head celery.*   1 *oz. flour.*   1 *oz. dripping.*
1 *quart water.*   *Salt and pepper.*

(1) Wash giblets and cut them up. (2) Put into a stewpan with vegetables prepared and cut up in small pieces. (3) Simmer for about 1½ hours, until giblets are cooked. (4) Melt the dripping in a pan, add the flour, mixing well. (5) Add the soup gradually, stir until it boils, removing any scum which arises. (6) Season, add meat cut up in small pieces before serving.

FISH

All fish decomposes quickly; it should therefore be purchased only when required.

When buying small fish see that the heads are not cut off. This applies to fresh haddock, whiting, herring, mackerel, sprats, plaice, lemon soles, and eels. The eye should not be sunk deeply in the socket. Examine the gills, they should be red inside. The firmer the flesh, the fresher the fish.

For general purposes FISH can be placed in
THREE CLASSES, viz.:—OILY, WHITE FISH and SHELL FISH.

OILY FISH

HERRINGS, SALMON, MACKEREL, etc.

With these types, oil is distributed through the body, and the food is very nourishing. It is not, however, suitable for invalids.

WHITE FISH
HALIBUT, PLAICE, COD, HAKE, etc.
As the fat is in the internal organs, this class of fish is not so nourishing, but it is, however, easily digested and very suitable for invalids. To clean fish, wash in salted water and drain on a cloth. Do not leave fish in water for too long a time.

SHELL FISH
OYSTERS, CRABS, LOBSTERS, COCKLES, etc.

FISH BOILED
2 lbs. cod or hake.
(1) Place in a pan with sufficient water to cover, add a teaspoonful of salt, and 1 teaspoonful of vinegar; allow 10 minutes to the lb. and 10 minutes over. (2) Remove carefully from the pan, drain and serve with parsley sauce. (3) Garnish with slices of lemon and parsley.

SOLE À LA BLANCHE
1 sole.   *½ pt. milk.*   *1 bay leaf.*   *Pepper and salt.*
1 oz. flour.   *1 oz. butter or margarine.*
Parsley, lemon or beetroot.
(1) Fillet and wash one sole, remove dark skin, roll and tie up the fillets. (2) Put bones, washed and broken up, into a pan with half a pint of milk, add a little mace, 1 bay leaf, salt and pepper. (3) Simmer gently half an hour, strain the liquid. (4) Put into the pan 1 ounce of butter or margarine and melt, and 1 ounce of flour, mix well. (5) Add the liquid gradually, stir until it boils, add rolls of fish: simmer very gently for 10 minutes. (6) Arrange neatly on a dish, pour sauce over, decorate with parsley, lemon or beetroot.

SALMON (BOILED)
1 salmon (minimum 2 lb.).
(1) Place the salmon in a coarse cloth, using a fish pan, or an enamelled plate in bottom of pan. (2) Hold the corners of cloth in place with the lid of the pan, this enables the fish to be lifted easily. (3) Place in boiling salted water, simmer very gently; add 1 tablespoonful of salt and 1 tablespoonful of vinegar to 1 quart of water. (4) Allow 10 minutes for each lb. and 10 minutes over. (5) Serve with any piquant sauce, and garnish with cucumber and parsley.

DRESSED CRAB
1 crab (boiled).   *Salad dressing (see page 24).*
(1) Remove the meat from the claws and shell, flake it and mix well with the dressing. (2) Wash the shell, and insert the mixture. (3) Garnish with hard-boiled egg, parsley and sliced lemon.

FISH À LA CREME

2 *lbs. potatoes.*	*A little milk.*	*Salt and pepper.*
¾ *lb. fish.*	1 *egg (optional).*	1 *oz. butter or margarine.*

(1) Boil and mash the potatoes. (2) Add beaten egg, milk, fat, salt, and pepper. (3) Beat well, arrange in border around a plate, make a few balls to place around the top. (4) Put in oven to brown. (5) Boil the fish, remove skin and bones, chop finely. (6) Make half a pint of white sauce (see recipe, page 131). (7) Mix with the fish. (8) Pile in the centre of potatoes, sprinkle with brown breadcrumbs, and serve hot.

FISH STEAMED

(1) Wash and dry the fish in a cloth. (2) Place on a buttered plate, and put a few small pieces of butter on the fish, cover with a plate, place two plates over a pan of water. (3) Allow the water to simmer 20 minutes, then remove the fish. (4) Serve garnished with parsley and slices of lemon. This method is suitable for invalids.

PLAICE (Steamed for an Invalid)

(1) Wash and dry one or two fillets of plaice. (2) Place between two buttered plates; put over pan of boiling water. (3) Steam for 20 minutes. (4) Serve with small sprinkling of salt, and a little lemon juice.

FISH STEWED

EELS (Stewed)

(1) Wash and cut up fish. (2) Cover with cold water, add 1 sliced onion, a little parsley and dried herbs, salt and pepper. (3) Simmer gently for half hour, remove fish. (4) Thicken gravy with flour and water, stir until it boils; pour over the fish and serve.

STEWED FINNAN HADDOCK

Mark 5—10-15 minutes

1 *Finnan haddock.*	1 *dessertspoonful flour.*
Pepper and salt.	1 *dessertspoonful chopped parsley.*
1 *oz. butter.*	½ *pint milk.*

(1) Pour boiling water over the haddock, allow to stand a few minutes. (2) Remove into a cooking dish, cover with milk and cook slowly for 10 to 15 minutes. (3) Take haddock from cooking dish and put on a hot dish. (4) Mix flour with a little milk, stir this into the sauce; add butter, parsley, pepper and salt, and pour over the haddock.

FISH BAKED

BAKED HADDOCK WITH MUSHROOM STUFFING AND MUSHROOM SAUCE (see page 132)

Mark 5—45-60 minutes

1 *moderately large fresh haddock.*	1 *small rasher of bacon.*
4 *tablespoonfuls breadcrumbs.*	4 *mushrooms.*
Pepper, salt. 1 *egg.*	1 *teaspoonful parsley.*

(1) Clean and scrape the haddock to remove the scales. (2) Prepare the stuffing thus:—Fry the mushrooms slightly, and chop them up finely. (3) Chop the rasher, put the breadcrumbs, mushrooms, rasher, pepper and salt, and parsley into a basin, and mix up with sufficient beaten egg to bind. (4) Fill the cavity in the haddock with the stuffing, and sew it up with trussing needle and fine white thread. Truss the haddock in the shape of the letter "S", tying tightly to keep it in position. (5) Place in a baking tin, put a little dripping on top for basting, and bake for 45 minutes to 1 hour with the "Autimo" set at 5. Any surplus stuffing can be made into savoury balls and baked with the fish.

HADDOCK AND POTATO PIE

Mark 5—45 minutes

1 *Finnan haddock.* 4 *potatoes.* 2 *eggs. Pepper. Milk.*

(1) Well butter a baking dish. (2) Peel, wash and thinly slice the potatoes, remove the bones and shred the fish. (3) Put into the dish a layer of potatoes, a layer of fish and a sprinkle of pepper. (4) Repeat the layers. (5) Beat the eggs and pour over the mixture, adding enough milk to cover. (6) Bake in the oven for 45 minutes with the "Autimo" at mark 5.

FISH SCALLOPS

Mark 5—15 minutes

Cooked white fish.	*Breadcrumbs.*	*White sauce.*
Seasonings.	*Lemon juice.*	*Butter or margarine.*

(1) Grease the scallop shells and sprinkle with breadcrumbs. (2) Spread some white sauce over, then put on layers of fish: season well. (3) Continue with the layers until well filled, squeeze lemon juice over, cover with sauce, sprinkle with breadcrumbs, placing small pieces of fat on top. (4) Bake in a moderate oven 15 minutes with "Autimo" set at 5.

STUFFED PLAICE (BAKED)

Mark 5—20 minutes

1 *plaice.* 1 *oz. breadcrumbs.* $\frac{1}{2}$ *oz. dripping. Yolk of egg.*
$\frac{1}{2}$ *teaspoonful chopped parsley. Seasoning.* 1 *oz. butter.*

(1) Cut open the fish from head to tail with a pointed knife, lifting the flesh from the bones. (2) Mix together the crumbs, dripping, parsley, seasoning and yolk of egg. (3) Put stuffing inside slit of fish, brush

over with the white of egg; sprinkle with breadcrumbs and a few small pieces of butter. (4) Bake in a moderate oven about 20 minutes with "Autimo" set at 5.

HALIBUT, BAKED WITH TOMATOES

Mark 4—20 minutes

(1) Take a slice of halibut, wash in salted water and dry in a cloth. (2) Put into a well buttered pie dish, lay sliced tomatoes over, sprinkle with salt and pepper, and add a few pieces of butter. (3) Bake in a moderate oven with the "Autimo" set at 4 for 20 minutes. (4) Place fish and tomatoes on to a hot dish. (5) Blend one teaspoonful of cornflour with milk, add to the liquid, and allow to boil. A few drops of carmine may be added to improve the colour of the sauce. (6) Pour around the fish and serve.

LEMON SOLE AU GRATIN

Mark 5—20 minutes

1 *lemon sole.*	1 *teacupful milk.*
Cheese sauce (see page 130).	*Breadcrumbs.*

(1) Wash the sole, place in a buttered pie dish with the milk. (2) Cover with greased paper and bake for 20 minutes with "Autimo" set at 5. (3) Take out the fish, make cheese sauce using the milk (see recipe page 130). (4) Pour sauce over the fish, sprinkle with browned breadcrumbs, garnish and serve.

BAKED STUFFED HERRINGS

Mark 6—30 minutes

4 *herrings.*	2 *tablespoonfuls oatmeal.*
1 *onion (par boiled).*	*A little tomato pulp for binding stuffing.*
Salt and pepper.	1 *teaspoonful chopped parsley.*

(1) Prepare the herrings, remove the back bone, wash thoroughly and spread a portion of stuffing on each herring. (2) Roll or fold up, place close together in a greased dish, add a quarter pint vinegar and water, or lemon juice and water: place a few pieces of dripping or margarine on the top. (3) Cover with greased paper, baking about half an hour in the oven at Mark 6.

GRILLED HERRINGS
with Mustard Sauce (see page 132)

4 *herrings.*	1 *oz. butter.*	1 *tablespoonful vinegar.*
¾ *oz. flour.*	¼ *pint water.*	1 *teaspoonful mustard.*
Little pepper, flour and salt.		

(1) To grill the fish, wash well, trim off the fins and scrape to remove all the scales, and remove any roe. (2) Wipe the fish dry and score. (That is, split the skin in one or two places with a sharp knife.) (3) Brush over with a little melted butter, dredge with flour, and sprinkle

11

with a little pepper and salt. (4) Place on the grid of the grill pan, which should be put in position under the grill when red hot, and cook for 4 minutes on one side; then turn and cook for the same length of time on the other side. Continue until the fish is thoroughly cooked. It is impossible to say how long this will take as it depends on the size and thickness of the fish.

GRILLED COD CUTLETS
with Maitre d'Hotel Butter (see page 131)
(1) Select four or five cod cutlets of even thickness, so that they will take about the same time to cook. After wiping, brush them over with a little melted butter or margarine, and tie them with string to keep in shape. (2) Place under a red hot grill and cook for about 4 minutes on one side, turn and cook on the other. Then complete the cooking. (3) Place on a hot dish, put a small pat of Maitre d'Hotel butter on each—this must be done immediately they come from the grill in order to form a sauce.

GRILLED FINNAN HADDOCK
1 *Finnan haddock.*   2 *ozs. butter or margarine.*
(1) Pour boiling water over Finnan haddock, and allow to stand a few minutes. (2) Drain off the water, put fish into a shallow tin, with butter or margarine on top. (3) Place tin under red hot grill, cook for 5 minutes, garnish with parsley.

KIPPERS
Prepare the kippers by snipping the tail bone, this avoids curling up toward the flame. Grill in the same manner as for haddock.

FISH FRIED
(See Section on Frying, pages 49 to 51).

EELS FRIED
(1) Skin and cut up 2 lbs. eels, wash and dry in cloth, covering with flour. (2) Fry in hot fat until brown and crisp. (3) Dish up, garnish with parsley and serve.

FRIED FILLETS OF FISH
(Egged and Crumbed)
4 *to 6 fillets of fish. Breadcrumbs. Beaten egg. Frying fat.*
SEASONED FLOUR:
1 *level tablespoonful flour.* 1 *teaspoonful salt.* ¼ *teaspoonful pepper.*
Wipe the fillets and pass them through the seasoned flour. Have ready plenty of dry white breadcrumbs on a sheet of paper, and some beaten egg on a plate. Dip the fillets into the egg, brushing over with

a pastry brush, drain off surplus egg, toss in the breadcrumbs, then press on the crumbs with a flat knife or with the hand. Place in the frying basket. When the fat has reached the required temperature, i.e., 360°F.—or, if a thermometer is not available, when a faint blue smoke can be seen rising from the pan, lower the basket so that the fish is covered with fat, and leave it for one minute. Then raise it gently, and if golden brown and firm to the touch it is cooked and can be removed. There is no need to turn food cooked in deep fat, as being entirely immersed it cooks evenly. Drain the fillets on kitchen paper, fry a small sprig of parsley in the fat after it has cooled slightly, serve the fillets on fish paper and garnish with the parsley. The parsley should be washed and well dried before attempting to fry it.

FRIED LEMON SOLE IN BATTER

1 *lemon sole.*   *Seasoned flour.*

BATTER:
    4 *ozs. flour.*   1 *egg.*   1 *tablespoonful melted butter.*
    Pinch of salt.   4 *tablespoonfuls tepid water.*

First prepare the batter; sieve the flour and salt into a basin, separate the yolk from the white of the egg. Make a well in the centre of the flour, stir in the yolk of egg, butter and tepid water, then beat hard to make the batter as smooth as possible, and allow to stand whilst preparing the fish. Fillet the fish, divide the fillets in halves or three according to size, pass through seasoned flour, then whip up the white of egg stiffly and fold as lightly as possible into the batter. With the aid of a skewer, lower each fillet into the batter, coat it evenly, allow surplus batter to drop off and then lower it gently into a deep pan of fat from which a faint blue smoke is rising. If a thermometer is available, the temperature should be 360°F. Allow the fillets to cook until the batter is crisp and golden brown. They should not be removed from the pan until all the batter is firmly set, otherwise it becomes sodden and moist after removal from the pan. Drain on kitchen paper, serve on a hot dish with a fish paper, and garnish with a little fried parsley.

WHITEBAIT (Fried)

½ *lb. whitebait.*   ½ *oz. flour.*   *Lemon.*   *Parsley.*
(1) Wash and dry the fish. Sprinkle with flour. (2) Fry in boiling fat for three to five minutes. (3) Strain, and serve garnished with parsley and lemon.

SHRIMP RISSOLES

½ *pint shrimps.*   ½ *lb. short pastry.*
SAUCE:
    1 *oz. margarine.*   1 *oz. flour.*   1 *gill milk and water.*
(1) Make a thick sauce with the margarine, flour and milk and water, add ½ pint shrimps to the sauce. (2) Prepare ½ lb. short pastry, then

cut into very thin rounds. (3) Put 1 teaspoonful of mixture in each, close up, brush over with egg, toss in breadcrumbs. (4) Fry in deep, hot fat. (5) Drain on crumpled paper before dishing up.

FRIED SKATE

1½ *lb. of skate.*	1 *gill vinegar.*	1 *oz. breadcrumbs.*
1 *onion.*	1 *egg.*	*Salt and pepper.*

(1) Wash the skate and leave it to soak for two hours in a dish of vinegar and water, covered with sliced onion. (2) Drain well, brush with beaten egg, dip in breadcrumbs, and dust with salt and pepper. (3) Fry to a nice brown and serve with chipped potatoes.

FISH COOKED EN CASSEROLE
WHITING EN CASSEROLE

Mark 5—40-50 minutes

3 *whiting.*	*Milk to cover.*	*Small piece of mace.*
1 *oz. butter.*	*Pepper and salt.*	*Very small piece of lemon rind.*

(1) Fillet the whiting, sprinkle with pepper, salt and flour. (2) Place them in the bottom of a buttered pie dish, cover with the milk: add the piece of mace and a very small piece of lemon rind. (3) Cover with greased paper, and cook with the "Autimo" set at 5 for 40 to 50 minutes.

COD STEAKS

Mark 5—45 minutes

2½ *lbs. cod.*	1 *oz. butter.*	1 *teaspoonful parsley.*
Lemon juice.	*Pepper and salt.*	

(1) Cut the cod into steaks and place in greased baking tin. (2) Sprinkle with pepper, salt, parsley and lemon juice. (3) Spread butter on the fish, and cover with greaseproof paper. (4) Cook in centre of the oven 45 minutes. The liquid from the fish may be used for making sauce to serve with the fish. Baked tomatoes with the fish improve the appearance and flavour.

(Complete Dinner No. 24).

SOUSED HERRINGS

Mark 5—1 hour

6 *medium-sized fresh herrings.*	1 *Spanish onion.*	2 *cloves.*
1 *teaspoonful salt.*	12 *peppercorns.*	2 *chillies.*
Enough vinegar and water,	*A blade of mace.*	2 *bay-leaves.*
equal quantities to cover.		

(1) Wash, scale and clean, behead, bone and fillet the herrings. (2) Take out the roes, which can be used for savoury, then roll up the herring slices. (3) Slice the Spanish onion finely. Set the slices of onion in a baking dish and season with salt. (4) Scatter the spices over and lay the bay-leaves in the corner of the dish. (5) Put in the herrings and cover with vinegar and water. (6) Bake for 1 hour at Mark 5. Serve cold.

BAKED FISH EN CASSEROLE

Mark 5—¾ hour.
   4 *cutlets of cod or similar quantity of white fish.*
   2 *shallots.*   ½ *oz. butter.*
SHRIMP SAUCE: (See page 133).

(1) Wipe the cutlets and skewer into position or tie with thin white string.   (2) Rub the casserole or au gratin dish with butter, place the cutlets in the dish and sprinkle with the very finely chopped shallot.   (3) Put a small nut of butter on the top of each cutlet, and sprinkle with pepper and salt.   (4) Cover with greased paper and bake in a very moderate oven until the fish is cooked.   (5) Pour the shrimp sauce over the baked fish and brown under the grill.

FISH RÉCHAUFFÉ
A FISH RÉCHAUFFÉ

   8 *oz. cooked fish.*   1 *teaspoonful finely chopped parsley.*
   2 *eggs.*   *Few drops anchovy essence.*
   5 *or* 6 *tablespoonfuls thick white sauce* (see page 131)

(1) Flake the fish well, put the sauce on to warm over a very low gas, then beat hard with a whisk to make it smooth and creamy.   If unsweetened evaporated milk is available a tablespoonful can be added to the sauce to enrich it.   (2) Stir the fish into the sauce, add the parsley and anchovy essence.   (3) Put into a pie-dish or au gratin dish, and reheat in a slow oven.   (4) Poach the eggs in the usual way and serve on top of the fish.

FISH CAKES

   1 *lb. cooked fish.*   ¾ *lb. mashed potatoes.*
   Little anchovy essence.   1 *oz. butter or margarine.*
   1 *tablespoonful milk.*   1 *teaspoonful finely chopped parsley.* .
   1 *egg.*   *Pepper and a pinch of ground mace.*

(1) Flake the fish finely, removing all skin and bones.   (2) Cook the potatoes, and when quite tender strain off the water, mash with a fork, stir in the butter and milk.   (3) Add the flaked fish, parsley, pepper, anchovy essence and the mace.   (4) Beat well, add just sufficient egg to bind the mixture.   (5) Turn on to a plate; when cold, divide into equal parts, the number depending on the size preferred.   (6) Shape into flat cakes, brush over with egg, coat with breadcrumbs and fry in a pan of deep fat from which a faint blue smoke is rising. For details of frying, see pages 49-51.

CRAB CUTLETS

   1 *small tin of crab.*   4 *potatoes, boiled and mashed.*
   Salt and pepper.   *Egg and breadcrumbs for coating.*

(1) Turn crab out of tin on to a plate, cut up finely, mix together with mashed potatoes, add salt and pepper.   (2) Form into cutlet shapes on a floured board, coat with egg, and toss in breadcrumbs.   (3) Fry in a hot fat a few minutes until golden brown.

SALMON SAVOURIES

1 *small tin of salmon.* *Equal part mashed potatoes.*
Salt and pepper. *Egg and breadcrumbs for coating.*

(1) Mix together salmon, finely chopped, and mashed potatoes, season to taste; a little chopped parsley may be added. (2) Turn mixture on a floured board, form into rolls, brush over with egg, toss in breadcrumbs. (3) Fry in hot fat.

CURRY OF COLD FISH

1 *lb. cooked fish, flaked* *Curry Sauce (see page 130).*
 roughly. *Boiled rice, if available.*

(1) Add fish to the sauce, mix well. (2) Place in a pan, reheat for about half an hour. (3) Serve with boiled rice, and garnish with parsley and slices of lemon.

MISCELLANEOUS

FISH PASTE

½ *lb. cooked fish.* ½ *oz. butter.*
1 *teaspoonful mayonnaise sauce* (see recipe page 132).

(1) Remove the skin and bone from the cooked fish. (2) Add seasonings, butter, and mayonnaise sauce. (3) Pound well together, press into a jar, covering with melted butter. This paste will only keep for a few days. White fish or salmon may be used.

FISH SALAD

Lobster, or any other *Lettuce.* *Cress.*
 cooked fish. *Tomatoes.* *Salad Dressing* (page 24)

(1) Prepare and cut up vegetables, arrange in a salad bowl. (2) Remove bones from the fish. (3) Display in suitable pieces on the salad, and serve with dressing.

SALMON SALAD AND MAYONNAISE

Boiled salmon (cold). *Hard boiled eggs.* *Lettuce.*
Thin slices of tomato. *Cucumber.* *Gherkins.*
Anchovies (boned). *Beetroot.* *Capers.*
Mayonnaise sauce (see page 132).

(1) Remove all skin and bone from salmon, and cut into pieces suitable for serving. (2) Place each serving of salmon in well shaped lettuce leaf. Mask salmon neatly with thick mayonnaise. (3) Place on a large dish, and garnish with small lettuce leaves, slices of cucumber and beetroot cut into attractive shapes; tomatoes, capers, anchovies, gherkins cut into thin strips, and hard-boiled eggs in slices. Create as artistic an effect as possible as this is essentially a dish to tempt jaded appetites in hot weather.

16

BOILING

BOILING is cooking food at a temperature of 212°F. in water, milk or stock. It is a suitable method of cooking meat which might otherwise be tough, although best joints such as leg or shoulder of mutton are frequently boiled. The object in boiling food should be to keep in as much of the goodness as possible. In this respect it differs from stewing, where the goodness is drawn into the liquid.

When making stock and soups, however, the object is exactly the reverse, namely, to draw out as much of the goodness as possible from the meat and bones. This is, however, the exception which proves the rule, for when boiling potatoes, vegetables, greens, meats, and fish, the object should be to conserve the goodness.

Boiling is an economical method of cooking, for very little gas is required when once boiling point has been reached, the low flame of a small burner being sufficient to keep a large saucepan at boiling point. The impression which exists amongst many inexperienced cooks that by boiling hard they will shorten the time of cooking is difficult to understand, for when once boiling point is reached the temperature cannot rise, all surplus heat being utilised in changing the water into steam. Therefore, it is a useless waste of gas when once the contents of the pan have reached 212°F. to allow the flames to lick round the sides of the pan, the lowest flame will be sufficient to maintain this temperature.

In order to understand the theory of boiling it is necessary to know that protein, which is contained in meat, fish and poultry, coagulates or hardens on exposure to heat. It is common knowledge that if a piece of raw beef be plunged into boiling water it immediately changes colour and becomes firm on the outside. The protein in egg also sets firmly when heated. This hardening or coagulation of protein is very important, since it forms a protective coat on the outside of the meat and prevents the juices from escaping. It is obvious therefore that when it is desired to retain the goodness of the food it should be put into fast boiling water and allowed to remain at this temperature for a short time, until a firm surface has been formed on the outside. Therefore, with the exception of the boiling of salt meats when it is sometimes necessary to draw out some of the salt, all meat, poultry and fish should be put into boiling water for about 10 minutes. The gas should then be lowered until the liquid is just boiling. Fast boiling is not necessary. If a joint of meat such as a round of beef were put into cold water and the water brought up to boiling point a good deal of the juices would be drawn out before the outside had time to harden. This would not of course matter if the liquid were to be utilised for soup making, but frequently it is discarded. Although vegetables do not contain protein in large quantities, as they consist mainly of cellulose and starch,

17

they should also be plunged into fast boiling water in order that cooking may be completed in the shortest possible time so that there need be no unnecessary loss of goodness.

Boiling Meat.

The time to allow for boiling meat depends to some extent on the size and thickness of the joint, but as a general rule it will be found that 20 minutes to the pound and 20 minutes over is sufficient time to allow when boiling a solid piece of mutton or beef. A bony joint, such as neck of mutton, would be cooked in less time than this. Salt meat—the fibres of which are rather tougher—requires longer cooking, and 25 minutes to the pound and 25 minutes over should be allowed, and as already mentioned, salt meat should be put in **cold** water and brought to the boil in order that some of the excess salt may be extracted. Fish cooks very much more quickly, and approximately 10 minutes to the pound and 10 minutes over is sufficient.

Cooking of Puddings

Meat puddings, sweet puddings containing fruit, and ordinary suet puddings also require to be cooked throughout the whole time in fast boiling water, If the water is allowed to go off the boil the liquid soaks into the pudding and makes it sodden.

Cooking by Pressure

During recent years a new type of cooking utensil, the Pressure Cooker, has gained in popularity. In pressure cookers the food is cooked at a temperature considerably higher than that of boiling water. This is made possible by using a saucepan, the lid of which is clamped on tightly. This prevents the steam from escaping and in consequence pressure is increased and the temperature thereby raised. As a result of various tests it has been proved that pressure cooking is a very satisfactory way of dealing with a number of foods, particularly dried beans, peas, lentils, cereals, and for jam making. One great advantage of pressure cooking is that the time of cooking is reduced very considerably, the greater heat rendering the cellulose and fibres soft more rapidly.

Boiling Potatoes

Although there is nothing difficult in the cooking of potatoes, many people find it impossible to serve them whole and in an attractive condition. This is chiefly due to the fact that they are frequently boiled far too rapidly causing the outside to be over-cooked before the inside is tender. Different varieties of potatoes cook differently, and for this reason it is advisable to choose a potato that one knows boils satisfactorily. It is also advisable not to mix potatoes when boiling them. Another rule which must be observed, and one that is well worth the little trouble involved, is to select potatoes carefully, choosing as near as possible all of the same size, so that one day medium sized potatoes could be cooked, the next day small, and the next day large. When the potatoes are extra large and there is only a limited time in which to cook them they should be divided either into half or four. Potatoes and root vegetables should be boiled with the lid on saucepan.

It is undoubtedly more economical to boil potatoes in their skins, and there is no doubt that nothing quite compares with potatoes cooked in this way. The chief drawback is the trouble of peeling on the plate, and the fact that if they are peeled by the cook after being dished they are very liable to get cold. Moreover, dishing-up time is always rather busy and it is not always convenient to find time for skinning potatoes.

Whether the potatoes are cooked in their skins or after peeling is immaterial, but it is important, whichever way is selected, that boiling should be carried out very slowly, and after straining, the cooking should be completed in the steam from the potatoes themselves; this makes them floury and dry, rather than "mushy" and wet, as is so often the case.

Have a pan of cold water ready with sufficient salt to season when cooking old potatoes, and boiling water for new potatoes. The boiling should be continued until almost cooked. To test, put a skewer in the largest potato in the pan. When almost cooked, pour off the water, getting rid of as much as possible, then return the saucepan, with the lid on, to the stove and place over the gas jet. This dries the saucepan, completes the cooking and makes the potatoes floury,

New potatoes should be put into boiling water, boiled for 25 minutes with a sprig of mint and strained when tender, then tossed in a very little butter and a teaspoonful of finely chopped parsley to every two pounds of potatoes.

Boiled Greens

In order to reduce the time of cooking so that no unnecessary loss of mineral salts and goodness will occur, greens should be shredded and Brussels sprouts cut into four. After thoroughly washing and soaking they should be put into fast boiling salted water and boiled rapidly until tender. A little sugar added to the water will help to preserve the colour of green vegetables, without destroying food values. As soon as the vegetables are cooked, strain immediately through a colander, press out all surplus moisture with a saucer or vegetable press, place in a hot dish and send to table at once.

VEGETABLES, SALADS, ETC.

Vegetables are of great importance in the diet. They contain mineral salts which purify the blood, and also have properties and supply materials which build up the bones and teeth.

19

A mistake is often made by boiling vegetables in too much water then draining and pouring away the water which contains most food value. Green vegetables boiled in a little water with the lid on the saucepan retain a larger proportion of the vitamins so beneficial to health. This method of cooking also reduces the time required for cooking.

Four Classes

1. ROOTS, *i.e.*, Carrots, Turnips, Parsnips, etc.
2. TUBERS, *i.e.*, Potatoes, Artichokes, etc.
3. GREEN, *i.e.*, Cabbage, Brussels Sprouts, Cauliflower, etc.
4. DRIED, *i.e.*, Peas, Beans and Lentils.

Choice of Vegetables

Roots and tubers should be firm, not shrivelled, and of a good shape. Greens should be green, crisp and firm. When bent, the leaves should snap.

Dried vegetables should be of the best quality.

Cauliflower and Broccoli should be white, with outer leaves fresh in appearance.

The following vegetables may be cooked with the dinner in the oven:

Carrots (thinly sliced or diced)	Brussels Sprouts
Turnips (thinly sliced or diced)	Potatoes
Celery (cut into lengths)	Artichokes (cut up)
Beetroot	Parsnips (diced)
Leeks	Runner Beans (cut up)
Green Peas	Onions (cut up)
Cabbage	Whole onions can be wrapped in
Cauliflower	greaseproof paper with a nut of dripping on each, placed in a meat tin or casserole.

Put the vegetables into a casserole dish, add one teaspoonful butter and salt. Pour boiling water over. Cover the dish with a lid or greaseproof paper. Cook in the oven underneath the meat.

Boiling Vegetables

	Approximate time required
Artichokes	30-40 minutes
Asparagus	20-30 ,,
Beans, Broad	30-35 ,,
Beans, Scarlet Runner	25 ,,
Beetroot	1-2 hours
Brussels Sprouts	15-20 minutes
Cabbage	20-30 ,,
Carrots (according to age)..	30-50 ,,
Cauliflower	30 ,,
Celery	20-30 ,,
Leeks	20-30 ,,
Onions, Whole	45-50 ,,
Onion, Sliced	20 ,,
Parsnips	40-50 ,,

Peas, Green	20-30	minutes
Peas, Dried (after soaking)	1-2	hours
Potatoes, New	25	minutes
Potatoes, Old	20	,,
Rice (for curries)	15-20	,,
Spinach	15	,,
Turnips	40-50	,,
Vegetable Marrow	30	,,
Vegetables, Parboiled ..	Bring to boil, and boil for 5 minutes	

CABBAGE

(1) Remove discoloured leaves, wash the cabbage, and divide into 4 pieces. (2) Allow to soak in salted water for half an hour. (3) Put into boiling salted water, and cook for about 20-30 minutes. (4) Strain in colander, press and chop well, add a little butter and seasonings if required.

BRUSSELS SPROUTS

METHOD 1.

(1) Trim the sprouts and wash well in cold water. (2) Cook in boiling salted water for about 15 minutes. (3) Drain thoroughly, and serve in a hot dish.

METHOD 2.

(1) Wash and clean the vegetables, and drain well. Have sufficient water boiling to cover the greens. (2) Put the sprouts in the boiling water with 1 tablespoonful salt. Boil for 5 minutes. (3) Place sprouts in a colander to drain, press the moisture out well. (4) Replace in a saucepan with 1 oz. butter, 1 teaspoonful salt, a pinch of pepper, and if available, a little stock. (5) Bring quickly to the boil, and allow to simmer for 45 minutes. NOTE—In cooking vegetables in this manner, see that your stock or water has simmered away by the time they are cooked, for your vegetables should on no account be sloppy. This should be borne in mind with other recipes also.

CARROT CREAM

Mark 4—15 minutes

> 1 *lb. carrots.*   1½ *ozs. dripping or margarine.*
> 1 *tablespoonful flour.*   ¼ *pint vegetable water, or milk and water.*
> *Pepper, salt, nutmeg.*   1 *tablespoonful dried breadcrumbs.*

(1) Wash and scrape the carrots, cut into small pieces and cook in a little salted water until quite soft, this usually takes about 40 minutes. (2) Strain off the water and reserve for the sauce. Mash or chop the carrots finely and place in a greased pie dish. (3) Melt 1 oz. fat in saucepan, mix in flour. Stir in the vegetable water, adding a little milk if necessary. Cook on a low gas 3 or 4 minutes. Season with

21

a little pepper and grated nutmeg. (4) Pour over the carrots, sprinkle top with a spoonful of dry breadcrumbs, dot with tiny pieces of fat, and place in the oven for fifteen minutes on 3rd runner from top, with "Autimo" set at mark 4.

CAULIFLOWER (BOILED)

(1) Wash well, remove outside leaves, cut off stalk. (2) Leave in salt and water about half an hour. (3) Place in boiling salted water with stalk upwards, cook gently about half an hour, or according to size. (4) Drain carefully in a colander; place in a dish, cover with white sauce and serve. (See recipe White Sauce on page 131).

CAULIFLOWER au GRATIN

Prepare cauliflower as above and cook until tender. Drain, and set in a dish with flower upwards.

Cheese Sauce will be found on page 130.

Pour the sauce over cauliflower, sprinkle over remainder of the cheese, also a few breadcrumbs. If desired, place in the oven to brown slightly.

CELERY (BOILED)

(1) Wash celery and cut in even lengths, and tie together. (2) Place in boiling salted water, simmer gently about 45 minutes. (3) Strain and serve, coated with white sauce. (See recipe White Sauce page 131).

CREAMED CELERY WITH CHEESE

(1) Wash celery and cut into short lengths, cook until tender in boiling salted water, to which a tablespoonful of vinegar can be added. (2) Strain off the water, to three cups of celery add 1½ cups of white sauce (see page 131). (3) Put into casserole, sprinkle with one third of a cup of grated cheese. (4) Place in hot oven until the cheese melts.

ONIONS (BOILED)

(1) Peel onions and cut across lightly at one end. (2) Place whole in a pan of boiling salted water, continue to boil for 45-50 minutes. NOTE—Sliced onions put into a pan with a little cold water will cook in 20 minutes, with the lid on the pan.

LEEKS (BOILED)

METHOD 1.

(1) Peel off outer skin, remove root fibres and any top parts not required. Wash well. Cut leeks in halves, lengthways. (2) Place in a saucepan with 1 oz. dripping, ½ teacupful stock or water, 1 teaspoonful salt, and 1 saltspoonful pepper. (3) Bring quickly to the

boil, replace lid on saucepan and simmer for 1 hour. (4) Drain and serve. If preferred, serve with White Sauce poured over.

METHOD 2.

(1) As page 22. (2) Place in a pan of salted boiling water. (3) Boil for 20-30 minutes. (4) As above.

PARSNIPS

(1) Wash the parsnips and pare thinly. (2) Put into a pan of boiling water with a little salt, and boil until tender, 40-50 minutes. (A small piece of dripping added to the water will improve the flavour.) (3) Serve whole, or mashed, with butter, pepper and salt.

BEETROOT (SERVED HOT)

METHOD 1.

(1) Wash well, the skin must not be broken. (2) Place in a pan of boiling water and cook until tender (one or two hours according to size). (3) Peel the beetroots, cut into cubes, serve in a hot dish, pour over them the White Sauce.

METHOD 2.

Proceed as 1, 2, 3 above. (4) Melt 1 oz. butter in saucepan, toss in the cubes of cooked beetroot. (5) Heat thoroughly, season, and serve hot.

BROAD BEANS

(1) Shell the beans, and cook in boiling salted water with a piece of fat bacon added, for 30-35 minutes. (2) Strain and serve with parsley sauce. (See recipe page 132).

FRENCH BEANS

(1) Wash beans, cut off ends and remove strings. Slice lengthways in thin strips. (2) Put into boiling salted water. Cook gently for 20-25 minutes. (3) Drain, and serve in a hot dish, with a little butter, and salt and pepper.

ASPARAGUS

(1) Wash well in cold water, cut off the hard end of asparagus—the tops should not be broken—tie in bundles. (2) Put in boiling (salted) water and simmer for about half an hour with lid on saucepan. (3) Drain, and serve with white sauce.

MASHED POTATOES

(1) Prepare and boil potatoes. (2) Drain and dry well, mash with a fork, adding salt and pepper, also a piece of butter or margarine, and sufficient milk to make them creamy. (3) Beat until white, serve hot.
(Recipe for Duchess Potatoes, page 53).

SPINACH

(1) Wash well, and remove the stalks. (2) Put into a saucepan with 1 tablespoonful of water. Cook gently until tender, about 15 minutes. (3) Drain well, chop finely; serve with a little butter, salt and pepper.

GREEN PEAS

(1) Shell the peas, and cook in boiling water with salt added. A sprig of mint and half a teaspoonful of sugar will improve the taste. (2) Boil from 20 to 30 minutes according to age. (3) Strain, and add a piece of butter when serving.

GREEN PEAS AND LETTUCE

1 *head lettuce.*	1 *tablespoonful butter.*	$\frac{1}{8}$ *teaspoonful pepper.*
1 *lb. peas.*	1 *teaspoonful sugar.*	$\frac{3}{4}$ *teaspoonful salt.*
1 *sprig mint.*	1 *tablespoonful flour.*	$\frac{1}{2}$ *cup stock or water.*

(1) Wash the lettuce, drain and chop. Place in saucepan with the peas and mint. (2) Add stock and salt, and boil gently for 20-30 minutes. (3) Add pepper and sugar, and thicken with butter and flour blended together. (4) Strain and remove the mint before serving.

LETTUCE WITH FRENCH SALAD DRESSING

1 *good crisp cabbage lettuce.*	2 *tablespoonfuls oil.*
1 *tablespoonful vinegar.*	1 *teaspoonful salt.*
Little made mustard.	*Sprinkling of pepper.*

The lettuce should be soaked for a short time in cold water, if it is not freshly pulled. (1) Wash well and separate the leaves. Drain free from water and shake well. The large leaves can be broken if desired. (2) The French Dressing (made by blending oil, vinegar, salt, made mustard and pepper together) should be poured over the leaves, immediately before serving.

VEGETABLE MARROW

(1) Divide the marrow in four or more pieces according to size; peel and remove all seeds. (2) Place in a pan of boiling water containing a little salt, and a squeeze of lemon juice. (3) Boil gently for 30-35 minutes. (4) Serve with White Sauce (see page 131). If preferred, dish up on toasted bread.

SCRAMBLED EGGS

4 *eggs.*	1 *or* 2 *tablespoonfuls milk.*
Salt, pepper.	1 *oz. butter, or margarine.*

(1) Break eggs into a basin, add pepper and salt, and beat lightly. (2) Melt butter in a pan. (3) Put in the eggs and milk, and stir gently over low heat until eggs begin to set. (4) Pile the egg mixture on prepared rounds of buttered toast, serving immediately.

POACHED EGGS

(1) Break a new laid egg carefully into a cup. (2) Into about 1¼ inches of water in a saucepan, add a little vinegar and salt, and bring to the boil. (3) Pour the egg carefully into the water and simmer gently until the egg is just set, then lift out with a slice. (4) Serve on a round of buttered toast.

SAVOURY TRIPE

1 *lb. dressed tripe.*   4 *spring onions.*   *Bayleaf.*
Pepper, salt.   ½ *pt. hot milk.*   2 *ozs. margarine.*
2 *ozs. flour.*   1 *dessertspoonful vinegar.*
2 *tablespoonfuls chopped capers or nasturtium seeds.*
1 *dessertspoonful gravy powder.*

(1) Cut the dressed tripe into small portions, and spring onions into ½in. lengths, using all the green part also. (2) Bring to the boil in sufficient water to cover, with a bayleaf, salt and pepper. (3) Cook gently for 1½ hours. (4) Melt 1½ ozs. margarine, stir into it 2 ozs. flour and 1 dessertspoonful gravy powder. (5) Blend thoroughly, add gradually ½ pint of tripe liquor, and ½ pint of hot milk. (6) Stir smoothly until the cream thickens, season well with pepper and salt, then add 1 dessertspoonful of vinegar and 2 tablespoonfuls of chopped capers or nasturtium seeds. (7) Add the tripe and small pieces of onion to the thick sauce. (8) Serve very hot.

BOILED CALF'S HEAD WITH STUFFING

1 *calf's head.*
STUFFING:

2 *streaky rashers.*   6 *tablespoonfuls breadcrumbs.*
½ *an onion.*   1 *tablespoonful finely chopped suet.*
Pepper and salt.   1 *teaspoonful chopped parsley.*
Pinch of thyme.

Put the breadcrumbs and other ingredients for the stuffing into a basin and mix with a small quantity of beaten egg. It is then ready to use. Wash the head well, remove the tongue and brains. Put the stuffing inside the mouth and tie the head together with a piece of muslin. Place in a saucepan of fast boiling water, add salt, allowing about a tablespoonful to two quarts, and see that there is sufficient water to cover it completely. Bring to the boil and remove any scum that arises. Continue to boil for three hours. Put the brains and tongue into the saucepan about one hour before the cooking is completed. To serve, put the calf's head on a dish, pour over parsley sauce and garnish with the tongue and brains cut into small pieces. If desired, the stuffing may be omitted.

25

BOILED MUTTON WITH CAPER SAUCE

1 joint of mutton: leg, shoulder or breast.   *4 or 5 onions.*
Pepper and salt.   *3 carrots.*   *3 turnips.*
Caper sauce (see page 130).

Wash the mutton well, put into a saucepan of fast boiling water, add the salt and a little pepper, bring to the boil again, remove any scum that rises.   Scrape and peel the carrots and turnips, cut the carrots into four lengthwise and the turnips into two or four according to their size.   Peel the onions but leave them whole.   Put the vegetables into the boiling liquor and cook the joint for the required length of time.   For example, allowing 20 minutes to the pound and 20 minutes over, a joint weighing 4½ lbs. would take 1 hour 50 minutes. If the vegetables are cooked before the meat they may be removed and returned to the saucepan in time to get thoroughly heated through before serving.   To serve, place the joint on a dish, place the carrots, turnips and onions at either end and pour the caper sauce over.

STEAK AND KIDNEY PUDDING

1 lb. steak.   *¼ lb. kidney.*   *Seasoned flour.*   *Cold water.*

Suet Pastry:

8 ozs. flour.   *Level teaspoonful baking powder.*
4 ozs. suet (chopped).   *Good pinch of salt.*
Cold water to mix.

First prepare the meat, cut into pieces of even size, pass through seasoned flour; this is made by mixing one tablespoonful flour, one teaspoonful salt and a quarter of a teaspoonful of pepper.   Then prepare the pastry.   Sieve the flour, salt and baking powder into a basin, add the suet, mixing to a soft paste with the cold water.   Turn on to a floured board, cut off one third for the top, flour the hands lightly and shape both pieces of dough into a neat ball.   Flour a rolling pin and roll out the large piece into a round, the diameter of which should be rather more than twice that of the basin.   Grease the basin and line it with the pastry, put in the prepared meat and any seasoned flour that may remain, cover with cold water, roll out the small piece of pastry for the top, moisten the edge of the pastry and press the top in position.   Cover with a floured pudding cloth and plunge into fast boiling water.   See that the water remains boiling hard the whole time the pudding is cooking, and if the water boils away fill up with more.   The time to allow is 2 hours.   Remove the cloth and serve with a clean table napkin folded round the basin.

STEAMING

S TEAMING is cooking food in the steam from fast boiling water—a particularly economical method, as little if any of the goodness of the food is lost, and moreover, a minimum of gas is required. It is, in fact, possible to cook a full dinner in a tier-steamer using one small gas burner.

The usual mistake made in steaming is that of not allowing sufficient time for the cooking, and consequently dissatisfaction often results. Steaming can be carried out in an ordinary saucepan, as when steaming a pudding, the basin being placed on a pastry cutter or patty pan, and the water allowed to come only half way up the basin. The use of a specially constructed steamer is, however, recommended, for with its aid there is no risk of the water boiling into the food, or of the food being spoilt by the saucepan boiling dry.

The following are the simple rules which must be observed.

1. When steaming puddings the basin or mould should only be three parts filled, for steaming produces very light mixtures, and none of the goodness is lost as in boiling.

2. It is essential to protect food from condensed steam whilst cooking, otherwise it will make it sodden. Therefore, the basins and food being cooked should be covered with one or two thicknesses of greased paper. No pudding cloth is necessary.

3. When using a saucepan for steaming, the water must be renewed fairly frequently, otherwise it is liable to boil dry. It is therefore necessary to keep a kettle of boiling water handy. Cold water must not be used for replenishing.

4. No special steamer is required for cooking fish, but an old soup plate is excellent for the purpose. This should be well buttered, the fish placed on it, after being prepared in the usual way by washing and trimming. Pepper and salt should then be sprinkled over it, a little lemon juice and small pieces of butter on top. The soup plate containing the fish should be placed on a saucepan into which the deep part of the plate fits. Well greased paper should be placed over the fish and the saucepan lid over it. This is a very excellent way of cooking fish for an invalid, as it contains all the nourishment and flavour and is more easily digested than fried fish.

The use of a 3-tier steamer may necessitate the closing of the Griller Door Shelf.

Choice recipes for Steamed Puddings will be found on pages 123-129.

RABBIT AND BACON PUDDING

1 *small or half a large rabbit.*	2 *rashers*
Seasoned flour.	2 *teaspoonfuls parsley.*

SUET CRUST PASTRY:

3 *ozs. chopped suet.*	*Pinch of salt.*
6 *ozs. flour.*	*Cold water to mix.*

Wash the rabbit well, cut into neat joints, and pass through seasoned flour made by mixing the tablespoonful of flour with pepper and salt. Cut the rashers into fairly small pieces. Prepare the suet crust pastry in the usual way, by mixing the flour, baking powder and salt together and blending with cold water. Turn on to a floured board, cut off one-third, roll out, and line the basin with the large piece of pastry, arrange the rabbit and bacon inside the basin, sprinkle with the parsley and the remainder of the seasoned flour. Three parts fill the basin with water or stock, place the small round of pastry on the top, cover with greased paper and steam for 3 hours.

MEAT AND VEGETABLE PUDDING.

$\frac{1}{2}$ *lb. plain flour.* 1 *teaspoonful baking powder, pinch salt.*
Small onion. 2 *ozs. dripping or suet.*
$\frac{1}{2}$ *tin mixed diced vegetables, or piece diced carrot and turnip.*
4 *ozs. diced cooked meat or corned beef, or* 4 *ozs. uncooked minced beef.* *About* 1 *teacupful gravy or water.*

Mix flour, baking powder and salt together. Rub in the dripping (or chopped suet, if used). Put the diced vegetables, chopped onion and meat into the dry ingredients. Mix to a fairly stiff consistency with the gravy or water. Turn into a greased pudding basin, cover with greased paper and steam for 2 hours. Serve with gravy and vegetables.

STEWING

STEWING is cooking food slowly in a small quantity of liquid, such as water, stock, milk or syrup, and occasionally wine and stock.

It is a particularly economical method, and therefore deserves to be used far more than it is, for not only can the cheap and coarser cuts of meat be used, but very little heat is required, and consequently a stewed dinner can be cooked with a consumption of very few cubic feet of gas.

The process can be carried out either in a saucepan or casserole on the top of the stove, or in a glass, china or earthenware casserole, marmite, etc., in the oven.

In stewing, the object is to extract the nourishment from the meat and bones being cooked, and to render tough coarser fibres digestible and tender. This is achieved by cooking or simmering slowly in liquid at a temperature of 180°F.

Other points to note are that (1) no goodness from the meat is lost, for the liquid in which it is cooked is served with it. (2) It is a very convenient method of cooking, particularly when facilities are rather inadequate, as a good supply of vegetables can be cooked with the meat in the same saucepan or casserole. (3) It is a suitable dish to choose when meal hours are uncertain, for stews can be kept hot for a long time without in any way impairing their palatability. It can also be reheated without detriment. (4) A stewed dish need not be dull and unappetising if trouble be taken to learn the correct methods of making the foundation, and a little effort made to serve the dish attractively. Ordinary dishes made from cheap parts of veal, middle neck and scrag, and shin of beef can be enriched and piquancy added by introducing foods of definite flavour, such as mushrooms, tomatoes, onions, and by the skilful use of herbs and seasonings. Discrimination must always, however, be exercised with the use of such things as mace, cinnamon, thyme, parsley, lemon rind, cloves and allspice, for whilst the use of too generous a quantity would spoil the dish, the use of just the right amount transforms an otherwise dull dish into an extremely palatable one.

Far greater use should be made of such things as Worcester Sauce, mushroom ketchup, celery salt, vegetable and meat extracts, for these are very valuable aids when used in moderation, and they simplify the cook's task considerably, as a variety of flavours are blended in a teaspoonful of sauce, etc.

The colour of a stewed dish is also of very great importance, for whilst one of ugly fawn colour is unappetising, the same dish is transformed if carefully browned. Care, however, is necessary in browning the roux or foundation, for if the cooking is hurried, the flour is inclined to burn.

The Preparation of the Foundation or Roux

Practically all stews are thickened with flour, which is generally introduced at the commencement of cooking, but occasionally, a few minutes before serving. Certain stews, such as Irish Stew have no additional thickening, the starch from the potatoes that are cooked with the meat being considered sufficient.
The following is a recipe for roux:—

1 oz. flour,
1 oz. butter,

and this is sufficient for thickening a pint of liquid. If required, stews can be made thinner or thicker by using more or less.

Roux may be of three kinds—white, fawn and brown, according to the kind of food to be cooked. For example, a white roux is used for white meats and fish, fawn for veal and rabbit, and brown for beef, mutton and game. To make the roux, melt the butter, stir in the flour until it is well blended, then place over a very low heat and cook the flour and butter slowly, stirring constantly, otherwise it is very liable to burn. If cooked slowly and stirring is almost continuous, the roux changes colour very gradually from white to cream, pale fawn, light brown and then to deep brown. Too rapid cooking scorches the flour and produces a strong and burnt flavour. This is one of the most common and frequent faults made by amateurs when preparing stews. There is little, however, to learn in preparing roux, except that cooking must be very slow and gradual, and the stirring must not be neglected. When the roux is of the correct colour—this will depend, as already explained, on the meat which is to be cooked in it—add the liquid, water, stock, milk, stock and wine whichever is to be used. Raise the gas and continue to stir until the liquid reaches boiling point, in order to prevent lumps forming by the uneven bursting of the starch grains. The meat, vegetables, etc. may then be added to the roux as well as the necessary seasonings and flavourings.

The flavour of most stews is improved if the meat and vegetables are fried before being added. This gives a more savoury flavour and, moreover, improves the colour. Onions, when merely added for flavouring purposes, should be chopped finely and fried in a little dripping or butter before the roux is made. Here again it is wise to practise economy in the use of gas, for too high a flame invariably results in burnt particles of onion, which may entirely spoil the flavour of the dish. When golden brown they should be removed from the pan, the flour stirred into the fat, and the roux made according to the directions already given.

STEWED MUTTON AND GREEN PEAS

1½ lbs. middle neck of mutton.   1 oz. dripping or butter.
1 oz. flour.   1 pint stock or water.   2 onions of moderate size.
1 carrot.   Sprig of parsley.   Pepper and Salt.
1 teaspoonful Worcester sauce.

Chop the onion finely; melt the dripping and fry the onion very slowly until golden brown, then strain to separate the fat. Remove the onions, put on to a plate, return the fat to the saucepan. Meanwhile, cut the neck of mutton into neat joints, trim off surplus fat and remove the spinal cord. Fry each cutlet or joint golden brown on both sides. Unless a large pan is being used, one or two only can be fried at the same time. When the cutlets are cooked remove from the pan, add a little more dripping if necessary (there should be about an ounce in the pan as this is the correct amount to absorb the flour and to make the roux). During the frying of the meat some fat is likely to come from it. Stir in the flour, and cook very slowly until a bright golden brown. Add the liquid, bring to the boil fairly slowly, stirring meanwhile, then return the fried onion, add pepper, salt, sauce and parsley, add the sliced carrot and place the joints of meat on top. Cover with a lid, bring to simmering point and allow it to simmer slowly until the meat and vegetables are tender; about 1¾ to 2 hours will be sufficient. When fresh peas are in season, these should be cooked in fast boiling water to which a little salt has been added, so that they are tender when the stew is ready to be served. When fresh peas are not obtainable, a can of English peas should be selected instead. Melt half an ounce of butter in a saucepan, but do not allow it to get hot; open the tin of peas, strain off all the liquid in which they have been canned and add to the melted butter. Heat over a very low gas until the peas are hot. To serve, place the joints or cutlets of meat as neatly as possible down the centre of the dish, with the carrot and peas at either side. The gravy can be poured over the meat, but keeps hotter if served separately in a tureen or sauceboat.

STEWED RABBIT (1)

1 *rabbit*.	1 *carrot, turnip and onion*.	¼ *head celery*.
1 *oz. flour*.	*Sprig of parsley and thyme*.	½ *pint milk*.
½ *pint water*.	*Juice of half a lemon*.	*Small piece mace*
Pepper and salt.	*Bread for frying or toast*	1½ *ozs. butter*.

Wash the rabbit well and cut into neat joints. Slice the vegetables thinly; put the herbs and mace with a tiny piece of lemon rind in a small piece of muslin and tie tightly. Arrange the joints of rabbit with the sliced vegetables in a casserole or saucepan, add the herbs, pepper and salt, cover with the milk and water, bring to the boil slowly either in the oven or on top of the stove and simmer very gently for 2½ hours. When the rabbit is cooked, melt the butter in a saucepan, stir in the flour and add the strained liquid in which the rabbit has been cooked. Bring to the boil, simmer very gently for about 8 minutes, then pour over the rabbit, reheat in the oven for a few minutes. If cooked in a casserole, the food can be served in the utensil in which it has been cooked, or "en casserole". If cooked in a saucepan, it should be dished neatly and garnished with small croûtons of fried bread or toast. One or two slices of fairly thin bread should be toasted, cut into small squares and then each cut across diagonally. The dish is improved if the diagonals of fried toast or bread are placed round the edge of the stew.

STEWED RABBIT (2)

1 *rabbit (jointed)*.	4 *ozs. bacon*.	1 *large onion*.
1 *clove*.	½ *teaspoonful mixed herbs*.	*Salt and pepper*.
1½ *pts. water*.	1 *oz. flour*.	

Wash and joint the rabbit. Place in covered stew-jar or casserole, with cut up onion and bacon, seasoning herbs and clove. Cover with water. Cook either in the oven with Autimo set at Mark 3, for 2 to 2½ hours, or simmer gently on top of the stove. When almost cooked, thicken with the flour mixed to a paste with a little cold water. Simmer for 10 minutes. A little milk may be added to the rabbit if desired.

IRISH STEW

1½ lbs. middle neck or scrag of mutton. 2½ lbs. potatoes.
¾ lb. onions.   Pepper and salt.

Cut the meat into neat joints, remove the spinal cord and cut off surplus fat. Put the meat into a saucepan, cover with cold water, add pepper and salt—about a level teaspoonful salt should be sufficient—bring slowly to the boil, skim carefully, add the onions cut into slices, and simmer gently for 1 hour. Add the potatoes cut into four and continue to simmer for another 40 minutes, or until the potatoes are thoroughly cooked. To serve, arrange the meat in the centre of the dish with the potatoes and onions around.

STEWED MUSHROOMS

Wash and remove the skin from mushrooms, cut up into small pieces; put in a pan, just cover with milk, simmer gently 20 minutes; thicken with 1 teaspoonful cornflour blended with milk, add seasonings, also piece of butter or margarine, boil up and serve.

STEWED SWEETBREADS

1 or 2 sweetbreads.   Rasher of bacon.   ½ pint of stock.
½ pint milk.   1 oz. butter.   ¾ oz. flour.
Small piece of mace.   Lemon juice.   Spray of parsley.
Pepper, salt.

Wash the sweetbreads and soak them. Put them into a saucepan of cold water and bring to the boil, then strain off the water. Add the stock and milk, pepper, salt, mace, parsley, a very tiny piece of lemon rind if liked, and a squeeze of lemon juice. Simmer for ¾ hour, thicken with flour, and simmer for a further 10 minutes. Blend the flour with a very little cold milk, and strain it into the sweetbread. Stir whilst coming to the boil. Continue to simmer slowly for 50 minutes or until the sweetbreads are quite tender. In the meantime fry the rasher of bacon in a frying pan. Serve together on a croûton of buttered toast with a rasher of freshly fried bacon.

STEWED STEAK AND SAVOURY DUMPLINGS

1 *lb. stewing steak.*   *Salt and pepper.*   *Water.*

SAVOURY DUMPLINGS:

6 *ozs. flour.*   *Cold water for mixing.*
¼ *teaspoonful baking powder.*   ½ *teaspoonful salt.*
3 *ozs. chopped suet.*   1 *small onion, grated finely.*

(1) Cut the steak into neat pieces, just cover with water, add the seasoning, and stew gently for one hour. (2) Prepare the dumplings by mixing the dry ingredients, adding the onion, and mixing to a soft paste with cold water. (3) Roll into balls, with floured hands, and place them on top of the meat. (4) Continue cooking for another half-hour.

STEWED TRIPE AND ONIONS

1 *lb. tripe.*   2 *large onions.*   ½ *pint water.*   ½ *pint milk.*
1 *oz. butter.*   1 *oz. cornflour.*   *Salt and pepper.*

(1) Peel and cut up onions, put in a stewpan with cold water, bring to the boil, drain off the water. (2) Add tripe cut up into neat pieces, pour over the ½ pint water, simmer gently for ¾ hour. (3) Blend cornflour with milk, add to the stew and allow to cook ten minutes. (4) Add butter and seasonings to taste, and serve.

POTTED MEAT (No. 1)

Mark 2—3 hours

2 *lbs. shin beef.*   *Pepper and salt, according to taste.*
Gelatine, if liked.

(1) Cut up meat into fairly small pieces. (2) Put into stew jar with pepper and salt, and cover with cold water. (3) Place in oven and stew gently for three hours, or longer, until the meat is quite tender. (4) Allow to cool slightly, then put meat through a fine mincer. (5) Add the gravy from the meat and thoroughly mix together, with a fork or whisk. (6) Put into moulds, or a glass dish, turn out when cold. NOTE.—If liked, a little prepared gelatine with one or two drops of cochineal may be added before putting into moulds, or the moulds may be covered with melted butter when cold.

POTTED MEAT (No. 2)

Mark 2—3 hours

2 *lbs. lean beef.*   1 *cow heel.*   *Pepper and salt, according to taste.*

METHOD AS ABOVE.

33

STEWED FRUIT

The same principle applies to fruit as to other stewed foods. The cooking should be carried out very slowly in a limited amount of liquid. The liquid in which fruit is cooked is a syrup made from water and sugar or from fruit juice and sugar (the latter is preferable if available). Care should be taken to avoid overcooking or mashing of fruit. The aim is to serve a dish in which the fruit remains whole and the liquid clear, but nicely flavoured and coloured.

To do this the following method should be adopted:—

Dissolve 2 to 3 ozs. of sugar, or Golden Syrup and sugar, as available, in ½ pint water. Boil gently about 5 minutes. Place the fruit carefully in the syrup and cook very slowly to allow fruit to remain whole. Or, the fruit may be placed on a fireproof dish with the syrup poured over and then cooked in the oven. One or two drops of pink colouring added to the syrup will greatly improve its appearance.

Stewing Dried Fruit

All dried fruit should be well washed to remove any dust. It should then be soaked for several hours, adding sufficient water to cover well, Next day, pour off any of the water remaining—or, if necessary, add more—to make up to half a pint. Add sugar to taste, bring to the boil and simmer until of a syrupy consistency. Then add the soaked fruit and cook very gently until it is tender.

ROASTING AND BAKING

STRICTLY speaking, roasting is cooking food by direct rays of heat and should be carried out in front of a clear steady fire on a roasting jack. This method of cooking is little practised now, except in large country houses and hotels, for it has long been superseded by oven cooking, and the terms "roasting" and "baking" have become almost synonymous.

In baking, or oven cookery, food is cooked largely by convected hot air, and to a small extent, by conduction. It is not considered a very economical method of cooking meat, as the cheaper and tougher joints cannot be cooked satisfactorily in this way, because the fibres are rendered tough, hard and indigestible. The prime parts such as leg, shoulder, ribs, sirloin, etc., are the joints usually baked. Baking is, of course, the method by which a very large number of puddings, all cakes and pastries, are cooked. It is therefore important that the elements of baking, and the method of using the oven should be thoroughly understood, so that full advantage of gas cooking may be obtained.

Baking Meat

The object when roasting or baking meat should be to conserve as much of the goodness as possible, and to render fibres soft and tender. In order to do this the oven must be preheated for 20 minutes before the food is put in so that the heat may be sufficiently intense to coagulate the albumen on the outside to form a hard surface through which the juice cannot escape.

There are two methods of baking. (1) in a meat tin. (2) by hanging the joint in a well-ventilated oven or by placing it directly on one of the grid shelves. The disadvantage of suspending the joint in the dome of the oven is that other food cannot be cooked at the same time. This disadvantage can, of course, be overcome by placing the joint on the grid shelf, and if potatoes are being roasted place in meat tin directly below the joint, thus collecting meat juices and dripping.

Although as already explained it is important to subject a joint to almost fierce heat to begin with, cooking should be completed at a lower temperature, otherwise an unnecessary loss of moisture and fat takes place. In order to reduce the loss of moisture some people prefer to use a covered roaster; this also has the advantage of preventing splashing the oven sides with fat, but the meat takes slightly longer to cook.

One can purchase from Hardware Stores a meat tin with a special pourer and strainer to keep back the meat particles when straining off the dripping.

The flavour and appearance of all roast poultry and game is improved if, before placing in the oven, dripping or fat bacon is spread thickly over the breast of birds, and then covered with greased paper.

Time for Cooking

To give absolutely definite time for cooking is almost impossible, as this naturally depends on the size of the joint, and the temperature of the oven. As a general rule, however, beef requires 15 minutes to the pound and 15 minutes over if it is required slightly under-done; and 20 minutes to the pound and 20 minutes over if it is required well-done. As mutton should not be served under-done, 20 minutes to the pound and 20 minutes over should always be allowed. The same time should also be allowed for lamb and veal.

The fibres of pork are finer and of closer texture than those of other meat, it therefore requires more thorough cooking, 25 minutes to the pound and 25 minutes over is the time to allow.

A rabbit requires from 1 to 1½ hours, and other times to allow for the more common foodstuffs are:

Heat up Joints stuffed with force-
and cook meat, such as shoulder of
at Mark 7. mutton ..   ..   ..   25 minutes to the pound and 25 minutes over.

Hare	1 hour 40 minutes to 2 hours.
Chicken	1-1½ hours.
Duck	1½ to 1¾ hours.
Goose	2-3 hours, according to size.
Grouse and Ptarmigan	¾ to 1 hour.
Partridge and Pheasant	50 minutes to 1¼ hours.

Time required for roasting English Turkeys.
A 24lb. English bird requires about 3 hours.
An 18lb. English bird requires about 2 hours 20 mins.
A 12lb. English bird requires about 1 hour 45 mins.
A 6lb. English bird requires about 1 hour 15 mins.

If the Turkey appears to be cooking too quickly, the heat may be reduced to Mark 4 or 5 after the first hour.

The "Autimo" Oven Heat Controller simplifies the use of the oven very considerably, for it is only necessary to set it at a required number and to allow the oven to heat up for 20 minutes before cooking is commenced.   The food can then safely be left as the flow of gas is automatically regulated.   For full description see pages xi-xii.

ROAST BEEF WITH YORKSHIRE PUDDING

Mark 7—Time depending on weight

The usual accompaniments to Roast Beef are Yorkshire Pudding, Clear Gravy and Horse-radish Sauce.

Joints can be either boned or not, as liked.   Boning simplifies carving, and the bones can be used for gravy and soup making.   The meat should not be washed before cooking, but merely wiped with a damp cloth, afterwards sprinkled with pepper and salt; flour is not necessary.   If the butcher has not already done so, it should be skewered into position and tied with string.   When the correct temperature has been reached—that is by setting the "Autimo" to mark 7 and preheating for 20 minutes—the joint should be put in the oven, slightly below the centre, and left the required length of time with the indicator at Mark 7.

Frozen or chilled meat should be thoroughly thawed before placing in the oven for cooking.

When cooked remove from the oven on to a hot dish.

A common mistake with amateurs is to serve a greasy gravy. Owing to its unpalatability this should be avoided at all costs. Any particles of fat seen on the gravy can be removed by passing a piece of clean unglazed kitchen paper over the surface.

The Yorkshire Pudding can be cooked in the meat tin under the joint, it then becomes impregnated with particles from the meat, or it can be cooked in a separate tin above the joint. The flavour of the pudding if cooked underneath the joint is very delicious, but there are then, of course, no meat particles with which to make the gravy.

MEAT GRAVY (Clear)

Remove meat from tin, pour off the fat, allowing about one tablespoonful of meat particles and juices to remain. Add ½ to ¾ pint boiling stock or vegetable water, and boil with a little pepper and salt. Strain, and serve in a sauceboat.

MEAT GRAVY (Thick)

Mix one tablespoonful of flour to meat juices, and proceed as for Meat Gravy (clear) as above.

YORKSHIRE PUDDING

Mark 7—20-30 minutes

4 *ozs. flour.*	1 *egg.*	½ *pint liquid (½ milk, ½ water).*
Good pinch of salt.		2 *tablespoonfuls dripping.*

Sieve the flour and salt into a basin, stir in the beaten egg and the milk slowly, in order to mix the batter as smoothly as possible. When half the milk has been added, beat hard to introduce as much air as possible, then stir in the remainder of the milk. Put the dripping in the pan, placing it in the oven or on the top of the stove over a low gas jet until it is really smoking hot. Then quickly pour in the batter and return to the oven, having previously set the "Autimo" at 7. The time required for cooking varies from 20 to 30 minutes, according to the thickness of the pudding; the larger the tin the shallower the batter, and the quicker it cooks, so that the same quantity of batter will take longer to cook in a small tin than in a large one.

BAKED HAM

Mark 7—Time depending on weight

1 *ham weighing about* 10 *lbs.*		*Brown breadcrumbs.*
3 *lbs. flour.*	*Water.*	6 *apples.*

The popular accompaniments to baked ham are baked unsweetened apples and a rich brown sauce, flavoured with cider. Owing to the difficulty of accommodating very large hams in an ordinary domestic gas oven it is not advisable to attempt to bake them whole. A large one can, however, be divided into two, and one half baked and the other half boiled.

Weigh, wash and soak the ham for about 10 hours. Then calculate the length of time required for cooking, allow 20 minutes to the pound and 20 minutes over, so that a ten pound ham requires 200 plus 20 minutes, or 3 hours 40 minutes. The first half of the cooking is done by boiling in water in order to draw out some of the salt from the meat, for if the complete cooking is done by baking there would be a chance that the ham would be too salt and unpalatable. Put the ham into cold water, bring to the boil—this should take about 50 minutes to 1 hour—and allow to simmer gently for 1½ hours. Then take up, remove the skin and allow to cool slightly. Meanwhile, mix the flour with sufficient cold water to form a paste, flour a board and roll out until it is sufficiently large to cover the ham. Wrap the pastry round the ham, keeping it in position with string, then put into an oven of which the "Autimo" has been set for 20 minutes at "7" and continue to bake for the required length of time, that is 2 hours and 10 minutes. Remove from the oven, take off the paste, brush over with a little butter and return to the oven for about 10 to 20 minutes to crisp the outside, then remove, sprinkle with brown crumbs, place on a hot dish and send to table with baked apples and brown or cider sauce.

BOILED AND BAKED HAM

Mark 7—30 minutes

Soak the ham in water overnight. Place ham in pan, cover with water. Bring to the boil and then boil for 30 minutes. Turn off the gas and put lid tightly on pan and allow to stand until cool. Take the ham out of the water and remove the skin. Cover with breadcrumbs and place in oven that has been preheated for 20 minutes at Mark 7, and bake for 30 minutes.

PORK PIES

¾ *lb. lean pork.*   1 *small apple—chopped* (*if wished*).
A little onion (*if liked*)   ·   1 *clove* (*optional*) *Pepper. Salt.*

HOT WATER CRUST:
Beaten egg for brushing over the pie.   ½ *lb. flour.*
¾ *gill milk and water.*   2½ *ozs. lard.*

Cut up the pork into small dice, and sprinkle with pepper and salt. Put any bones and the sliced onion in a saucepan, with a little salt and simmer slowly whilst the pastry is being prepared. The introduction of a very little apple and 1 clove is a matter of personal taste, and optional, and can be omitted if wished. Sieve the flour and salt into a warmed basin, put the milk or milk and water, whichever is being used, on to boil, then add the lard to the milk. As soon as it has melted, make a well in the centre of the flour, and pour in the boiling liquid and lard. Mix with a knife until the pastry is cool enough to be handled. If necessary, a little more hot water or milk can be added. Knead the pastry until it is very pliable and smooth, then mould it. The easiest way is to use a raised pie mould, as the pastry can be rolled out, and the pie case lined as a piedish is lined. It is possible, however, to make excellent pies raised by hand with the aid only of a band of stiff paper, or experienced people can make raised pies without even the help of paper. If moulding by hand, cut off $\frac{1}{4}$ of the pastry for the top, put the left hand in the middle of the pastry, and with the right hand work it up until it forms a round or oval case. Put the pork in the middle of the pastry, add 3 or 4 tablespoonfuls of the prepared stock, according to the size of the pie, cover with a lid of pastry rolled out until it is about $\frac{1}{4}$ inch thick, and decorate with leaves of pastry, and mark the top edge. Brush over with beaten egg. Tie a band of greased paper around the side of the pie, to keep it a good shape, and bake in the oven with the "Autimo" set at "5" until the pastry is nicely browned, then lower it to "4" and continue to cook until the pie has been in the oven for $1\frac{1}{2}$ hours. When cooked, fill up the pie with more of the hot, seasoned stock. Leave the pie in the mould until it is cold. Decorate with a little parsley, and send to table.

SAVOURY SQUARES

1 *tin diced mixed vegetables.*	1 *small onion.*
3 *or* 4 *ozs. cold meat or corned beef.*	
2 *tablespoonfuls thick gravy or sauce.*	

PASTRY:—

2 *teaspoonfuls baking powder.*	$\frac{1}{2}$ *lb. plain flour.*
3 *ozs. cooking fat or dripping.*	$\frac{1}{2}$ *teaspoonful salt.*
Milk and water for mixing.	

Mix flour, baking powder and salt together. Rub in the fat, or if very hard, grate on coarse part of suet grater. Mix to a stiff paste with cold milk and water. Line a shallow tin 8in. by 7in. with half the pastry. Strain liquor from the tin of diced vegetables, add onion and meat chopped finely, also about 2 tablespoonfuls thick gravy or sauce and seasoning to taste. Spread the mixture over the prepared tin. Cover with remaining pastry rolled out to fit, and pinch edges together. Mark pastry across in squares. Bake for 40 minutes on 3rd runner from top of oven with "Autimo" set at Mark 5.

ROAST PHEASANT

Mark 7

Accompaniments: Brown Crumbs, Bread Sauce, Clear Gravy and Fried Potatoes.

The success of game depends very largely on the quality and age of the bird, old birds being inclined to be tough even if carefully roasted. The length of time to hang birds depends entirely on personal taste, the idea once prevalent that unless "high", game is hardly worth eating is not so deeply rooted in the mind of the modern housewife as it was formerly. It is always regarded as a good test to see whether the feathers may be plucked easily from the inside of the leg. If they come away easily without tearing the flesh the bird is considered to be in good condition for cooking.

Water birds, such as Wild Duck should be eaten quite fresh, for the oil contained in them is very apt to become rancid. When plucking the bird, a few of the best tail feathers should be retained for garnishing. The bird must then be drawn, trussed, and singed. The gizzard, liver, heart and neck—called the giblets—should be used for making the gravy. They should be covered with water, salt added, and simmered for one hour.

After trussing, cover the breast of the bird with a piece of fat bacon. Special bacon called "larding bacon" is obtainable and is ideal for the purpose, giving an excellent flavour to the bird and preventing it from becoming dry. When butter is cheap, the cook should be excused the extravagance of inserting a small lump inside the bird, as this keeps the inside moist and imparts a good flavour. Put the bird in a baking tin, and put in an oven at which the "Autimo" has been set at "7" for 20 minutes, allowing it to cook at this temperature for the time required. It should be basted once or twice during cooking if the bird has not been larded, that is, covered with fat bacon. Moreover, should the bird show signs of scorching it should be covered with one or two thicknesses of well greased paper.

Whilst the pheasants are cooking, the accompaniments must be prepared.

BROWN CRUMBS

1½ to 2 ozs. fine dry breadcrumbs.   *1 oz. butter.*

As the breadcrumbs are specially required, fine stale bread only should be used, and the crumbs should be rubbed through a fine sieve. Melt the butter in a shallow frying pan or in a saucepan, and when melted, sprinkle in the breadcrumbs and cook over a very low gas until golden and evenly browned. An even colour is only obtained by shaking and tossing the crumbs frequently during cooking, and by having the gas very low. Serve the crumbs on lace paper on a hot plate.

Recipe for Bread Sauce appears on page 129.

FRIED POTATOES

Fried sliced potatoes are the correct accompaniment to game, and as they take a good time to prepare, the potatoes should be cut some time before they are required. Considerable saving of time is effected if a special potato or vegetable cutter is used. Immediately they are cut, put into cold water to prevent their discolouring. Put on a deep pan of fat to get hot, and when a deep blue smoke is rising, have ready a frying basket containing two handfuls of well-dried sliced potatoes. Lower into the pan and allow them to fry until evenly browned. Full directions for frying are to be found on pages 49-51.

Two important points to remember when frying potatoes are (1) they must be sliced very thinly so that they will cook quickly and evenly, and (2) they must be thoroughly well dried in a cloth before being put into the fat, otherwise they cause it to splutter badly and boil over. When brown, lift the basket from the fat, allow it to drip for a few minutes, then put the potatoes on to kitchen paper to drain for a few minutes. To serve. Place in a vegetable dish on a paper d'oyley.

TO PREPARE BROWN GRAVY

¾ *to* 1 *pint stock, made from the giblets.*　　*Pepper and salt.*

When the birds are cooked, pour off the fat from the baking tin, taking care to drain off as much as possible. Then pour in the stock and bring to the boil, dissolving the brown particles. Pour into a sauce-boat, removing any particles of the fat from the surface by passing over a piece of unglazed kitchen paper.

ROAST CHICKEN

Mark 7—1-1½ hours

1 *chicken.*　　　　　2 *rashers of bacon.*
Bacon fat or dripping for basting.

For roasting, always choose a young bird. If old, it should be stewed, boiled or steamed. Prepare and truss in the usual way. Brush over with a little melted butter, if wished, and dredge lightly with flour. Put bacon fat across over the breast of the bird. Place in a baking tin and cook for 60 minutes to 1½ hours, according to size, with the "Autimo" set at "7". Baste once or twice during this time. ¼ hour before the chicken is cooked, make small bacon rolls from the rashers, place on a skewer, and cook in the baking tin. Serve with clear gravy made from the giblet stock, bread sauce, and the bacon rolls.

41

ROAST VEAL

Mark 6—25 minutes per lb. and 25 minutes over

Loin of veal (2 to 3 lbs.).   *4 ozs. rashers of bacon.*

FORCEMEAT:

Very little grated lemon rind.	*Little marjoram.*	*3 ozs. suet.*
1 teaspoonful lemon thyme.	*6 ozs. breadcrumbs.*	*Beaten egg.*
Few sprigs of parsley.	*1½ ozs. ham.*	*Pepper, salt.*

To make the forcemeat, put all the dry ingredients into a basin, including the chopped rashers, and very finely chopped suet. Make a well in the centre, stir in sufficient beaten egg to enable the mixture to bind. Divide the mixture into two. Shape one portion into balls. Put the remainder of the forcemeat on the veal, cover with greased paper and tie the paper in position with string. Place on a meat stand in a baking tin. Bake in the oven with the "Autimo" set at 6. The time depends on the size of the joint. For stuffed meats, allow 25 minutes for each pound and 25 minutes over. Make a slightly thickened gravy from the meat particles in the tin and a little flour. Serve with red currant jelly.

BAKED STUFFED SHEEP'S HEART

Mark 5—1-1¼ hours

1 sheep's heart.   *1½ ozs. dripping.*

STUFFING:

3 tablespoonfuls breadcrumbs.   *Pepper and salt.*
2 tablespoonfuls finely chopped suet. *½ teaspoonful lemon thyme.*
1 teaspoonful chopped parsley.   *Beaten egg or milk to mix.*
½ teaspoonful marjoram (or 2 teaspoonfuls mixed herbs in place of thyme and marjoram).

Soak the heart in warm salted water and wash it thoroughly. Prepare the stuffing by mixing all the dry ingredients in a basin and stirring in sufficient egg or milk to bind. When the heart is clean, dry, cut off the tube at the top and stuff the heart with the mixture, pressing it in tightly and piling it on top As the stuffing tends to fall off during cooking it is a good plan to cover the top with a small piece of greased paper, tying to keep it in position. Sprinkle the meat with a little pepper and salt, and place small pieces of dripping over the surface. Place in a baking tin and put in the oven with the "Autimo" set at 5 for 1 to 1¼ hours. Any surplus stuffing can be made into balls and baked with the heart in the tin.

BRAISED KIDNEYS WITH TOMATOES

5 *or* 6 *sheep's kidneys.*	1 *tin or bottle English tomatoes.*
1 *oz. dripping.*	1 *carrot, turnip and onion.*
1 *oz. flour.*	*Little celery if available.*
Pepper and salt.	$\frac{1}{2}$ *to* $\frac{3}{4}$ *pint stock or water.*

Melt the dripping and fry the onions slightly. Remove from the pan and fry the well-washed kidneys, which should first be split in halves. When they are fried, remove from the saucepan, add the flour and continue to cook for a few minutes, adding a little extra dripping if necessary to blend the flour. Then add the stock or water, bring to the boil and when boiling, place the carrot, turnip and celery in the bottom of the pan, place the kidneys on top and return the fried onion. Put the tightly fitting lid on the pan and simmer very slowly for half an hour. If a hot oven is available, complete the cooking by putting the saucepan in the oven. Whilst the kidneys are cooking, empty the contents of a tin or bottle of tomatoes into a saucepan, add a small piece of bacon, pepper and salt, and simmer for about 20 minutes. Rub through a sieve and stir the tomato purée into the gravy at the last minute. To serve, place the kidneys on the centre of the dish and strain the gravy over and round.

BAKED MEAT SHAPE

Mark 6—1¾ hours

1½ *lbs. lean beef.*	$\frac{1}{2}$ *pint stock.*	*Pinch of mixed herbs (optional).*
$\frac{1}{2}$ *lb. lean bacon.*	*Beaten egg.*	*Few drops of Worcester sauce.*
6 *ozs. breadcrumbs.*	*Pepper and salt.*	1 *teaspoonful parsley.*

Grease a bread tin, put the minced beef, chopped bacon, breadcrumbs and seasoning into a basin. Mix well, then add a beaten egg, and if necessary, a little milk or water may be added if one egg is not quite enough. Put the mixture into a greased tin, cover with greased paper, and bake in the oven with the "Autimo" set at 6 for 1¾ hours.

BEEF STEAK AND ONIONS IN CASSEROLE

Mark 3—2 hours

1 *lb. beef steak.*	2 *large onions.*	1 *oz. dripping.*
Boiling water.	*Salt and pepper.*	

Melt dripping in saucepan or casserole, when hot, cut up steak into convenient pieces, dredge with a little flour, fry until nicely browned on both sides. Parboil the onions and slice thinly over the meat, add salt and pepper, partly cover with boiling water, put lid on pan or casserole and cook gently.

43

SAVOURY LIVER

Mark 6—¾-1 hour

¾ *lb. liver.* 2 *onions parboiled.* 1 *teaspoonful mixed herbs.*
1 *oz. dripping.* 1 *teaspoonful parsley.*
Little powdered mace. *Seasoned flour.*

Cut up the liver into neat pieces, pass through the seasoned flour; melt the dripping in saucepan or casserole. Fry the pieces of liver until nicely browned on both sides (about 5 minutes). Add onions, sliced thinly, also sprinkling of herbs, chopped finely, and seasonings; add only just sufficient hot water or stock to cover. Put lid or greased paper over the dish and bake in the oven ¾ to 1 hour.

SAVOURY ONIONS

Mark 6—1 hour

4 *onions.* 2 *sheep's kidneys.* *Salt and pepper.*

Peel and boil onions whole for ten minutes; cut the tops off onions, take out a little of the centre, trim kidneys, cut in two; place half a kidney in each onion, season with salt and pepper. Place stuffed onions into a greased dish, with a little water or stock, cover the dish and cook in a moderate oven about 1 hour. The gravy may be thickened with flour and water; dish up the onions, then pour gravy around.

TOAD-IN-THE-HOLE

Mark 6—1-1¼ hours

1 *lb. sausages.* 8 *ozs. flour.* 1 *pint milk.*
2 *eggs.* *Pepper, salt.* 1½ *ozs. dripping.*
1 *level teaspoonful baking powder.*

Remove the skin from the sausages, and divide neatly into four. Prepare the batter thus:—Sieve the flour and baking powder into a basin, make a well in the centre, beat the eggs lightly, and put them into the flour. Mix smoothly, adding the milk gradually to prevent lumps forming. When half the milk has been added, beat well to introduce as much air as possible. Stir in the remainder of the milk. Put the dripping in a meat tin, and allow it to get smoking hot. Place the pieces of sausage in the tin, and pour in the batter whilst the fat is still very hot. Bake in the oven with the "Autimo" set at 6 for an hour or 1 hour and a quarter.

SAUSAGE AND TOMATO PIE (No. 1)

Mark 5—45 minutes

1 *lb. sausages.* 1 *small tin tomatoes.*
Little made mustard. 2 *teaspoonfuls finely chopped parsley.*

Boil the sausages for 10 minutes. Allow to get cold. Remove the skins from the sausages and divide each into four. Roll in a little flour, then fry without any additional fat. When they are golden brown put into a pie dish with alternate layers of tomatoes and sausages, and a sprinkling of parsley, and a little made mustard. Top with mashed potato or shortcrust pastry, whichever is preferred, and bake in the oven with the "Autimo" set at 5 for 45 minutes.

SAUSAGE AND TOMATO PIE (No. 2)

Mark 5—1 hour

½ lb. sausages (raw).   3 or 4 tomatoes, or small jar bottled tomatoes
1 small onion.   1 lb. mashed potatoes.
Pepper and salt.   1 oz. dripping, or margarine.

Lay the skinned sausages in a greased pie dish and spread with the sliced tomatoes and finely chopped onion. Cover with a thick crust of mashed potatoes. Brush over with the melted fat or break it in small pieces over the top. Bake 1 hour on 3rd grid runner from top of oven with "Autimo" set at Mark 5.

SAUSAGE AND ONION PIE

Mark 6—35 to 40 minutes

¾ lb. sausages (raw).   1 medium sized onion.

PASTRY:—

½ lb. plain flour.   2 ozs. fat.   2 teaspoonfuls baking powder.
¼ teaspoonful salt.   Milk and water to mix.

Mix the flour, baking powder and salt together, rub in the fat. Mix fairly stiffly with milk and water. Divide pastry into two pieces and roll each piece to fit a 9in. enamel or tin pie plate. Line the plate with one round of pastry. Place the skinned sausages and finely chopped onion on the pastry, damp the edges and cover with second round of pastry. Bake 35 to 40 minutes on 3rd runner from top of oven with "Autimo" set at Mark 6.

ROAST RABBIT

Mark 6—1¼ hours

1 young rabbit.   Veal stuffing.   Tomato sauce.
Bacon rolls (optional).

Choose a young rabbit for roasting or baking, as old ones would not become tender unless boiled or stewed. Prepare the rabbit in the usual way, and truss for roasting, leaving the head on, if desired. Prepare the veal stuffing in the usual way. If liked, a little chopped, cooked bacon fat can be used instead of suet or melted butter to add to the stuffing. Shape into balls of even size, cover the rabbit with pieces of fat bacon, if available, or, if not, put a little dripping on the back, and cover with greased paper. Bake for 1¼ hours with the "Autimo" set at 6. The Forcemeat balls are cooked in the baking tin with the rabbit, and ¼-hour before the rabbit is cooked, cut some streaky rashers in halves, make into rolls, place on a skewer, and bake in the tin also. Serve with tomato sauce or brown gravy, and red currant jelly.

STUFFED BREAST OF MUTTON

Mark 6—1½ hours

2½ lbs. breast of mutton.

STUFFING:—

4 ozs. breadcrumbs.	1 teaspoonful chopped parsley.
Pepper, salt.	1½ ozs. finely chopped suet.
Beaten egg.	1 teaspoonful mixed herbs.
	2 partly-cooked onions of medium size.

Prepare the forcemeat by putting all the ingredients in a basin, including the finely chopped onions. If liked, the suet can be replaced by finely chopped ham. Make a well in the centre, and stir in sufficient beaten egg to bind. Place the joint of meat on a pastry board, wipe it, and with a sharp knife remove the bone neatly. Spread the stuffing over the meat, roll up, and tie in two or three places with string. Place on a meat stand in a baking tin. Put a little dripping on top of the joint for basting, and bake for 1½ hours with the "Autimo" set at Mark 6. For a larger sized joint allow 25 minutes to the pound and 25 minutes over.

BRAISED NECK OF MUTTON

Mark 6—1½ hours

3 lbs. neck of mutton.	Rasher of bacon.	Pepper and salt.
3 onions.	3 or 4 carrots.	Bunch of herbs.
1 pint of stock.		

Use a saucepan large enough to hold the joint. Fry the rashers slightly and remove from the pan. Leave the carrots and onions whole, and fry them. Then tie up the joint, and brown it also in the saucepan. Place the vegetables in the saucepan to form a bed, placing the joint on top. Add just sufficient stock or water to cover the vegetables, put in a bunch of herbs, pepper and salt. Cover with the lid, and cook in the oven with the "Autimo" set at 6 for about 1½ hours. (If liked, the cooking can be done for ½ hour over a gas ring, and then bake for 1 hour in the oven). To serve, put the mutton on a hot dish, remove the vegetables, and if necessary reduce the gravy in the saucepan. Pour it over the mutton, and serve with new potatoes and peas.

BRAISED CARROTS

1½ lbs. carrots.	¾ pint brown stock.	A little castor sugar.
1½ ozs. butter.	Salt and pepper.	Chopped parsley.

Wash and scrape the carrots, cut into even slices, put into a pan, cover with cold water, bring to the boil and strain off the water. Heat the butter and fry the carrots until golden brown. This is best done in two batches. Add half the stock, sugar, pepper and salt, and cook gently for 40 minutes. Baste the carrots occasionally, and when the carrots are cooked, serve them on a hot dish. Boil the liquor remaining in the pan, hard for 10 minutes, or until it is considerably reduced. Pour over the carrots and sprinkle them with finely chopped parsley.

BAKED ONIONS

Mark 7—1-1½ hours

Choose even-sized onions, fold each onion in greased paper. Place onions in greased dripping tin or with the meat. Bake 1 to 1½ hours. Serve with brown gravy, or white sauce.

STUFFED TOMATOES, BAKED

Mark 6—20 minutes

Six tomatoes, even in size, the tops carefully cut off; remove the inside pulp and put into basin with 2 tablespoonfuls breadcrumbs, 1 tablespoonful chopped suet, 1 teaspoonful chopped parsley, 1 tablespoonful minced ham, salt and pepper.

Mix ingredients together, fill tomatoes with the mixture, place on the tops, put into a well-greased baking tin, sprinkle over with breadcrumbs, bake for 20 minutes, serve on rounds of toast dipped into chopped parsley, or on a bed of mashed potatoes.

GRILLING

G RILLING is cooking food by direct rays of heat, and there is no doubt that cooking under a gas grill is one of the most popular ways of preparing foods. The economy of a gas grill is very great compared with the amount of fuel required when grilling over an open fire. This method is most suitable for cooking small pieces of meat such as chops, steaks, kidneys, and mushrooms, tomatoes, small birds, sausages, fish or ham. With the aid of an efficient and modern cooker, grilling becomes one of the simplest ways of cooking foods. It is only necessary to preheat the grill for 1 to 2 minutes, put the food on the grid in the griller pan and place it in position. When browned on one side the food being grilled must be turned and cooked on the other. Do not pierce the meat when turning. Thick meat such as steak or loin chop should be turned four times, so that when cooking is completed the meat is thoroughly hot through. The gas can be lowered a little once the meat is cooking. One thing to remember in grilling is that whilst it is a very quick method, certain foods such as sausages, kidneys and thick chops require longer cooking than may at first be imagined, ten to fifteen minutes being necessary for cooking chops and steaks.

GET THE BEST OUT OF YOUR GRILLER

The following menus are merely typical of the many appetising dishes that can be cooked to perfection under the grill.

Fish, and cheese recipes for grilling are given in their respective sections.

MIXED GRILL

2 mutton chops.   2 kidneys.   2 rashers of bacon.
2 or 3 tomatoes.   2 sausages.   Mushrooms (if available).

(1) Light the grill and heat up for 1 to 2 minutes before required. (2) Trim the surplus fat from the chops, split the kidneys in halves, brush over with melted butter. (3) Place the food on the grid, already greased, and put under the hot grill. (4) Turn over when brown and cook for a further five minutes. If the chops are thick they will take a few minutes longer. The bacon should not be cooked until after the other food. Serve with gravy which has run out from the meat.

GRILLED CHOPS AND STEAK

(1) Trim the chops to get rid of surplus fat, and remove the spinal cord. (2) Sprinkle with pepper and salt, and pour over a little olive oil or melted butter.

Steak should be well beaten. If nothing else is available, a heavy chopping knife would answer, but a rolling pin is unsuitable, as the wood absorbs meat juices. The object in beating the steak is to break down the fibres and render it more tender. (3) Light the gas grill and allow it to become red hot. (4) Place the chops and steak on the grid in the grill pan. Put under the grill and brown quickly on one side. (5) Then turn the chops and steak and brown the other side. Continue to cook until the meat is sufficiently done. Particular attention should be paid to the bony end, if it be desired to have the chops completely cooked right through. The time allowed for cooking depends on the thickness of the steak and chops. Allow about 8 minutes for neck chops, but as long as 15 minutes for thick chump chops and thick steak.

(6) Serve immediately on a hot plate, garnish with watercress. Ribbon and chipped potatoes are a very usual accompaniment with grills.

GRILLED HAM AND GREEN PEAS

Rashers of ham ¼ in. to ½ in. thick.   Peas.

(1) Heat grill until red. (2) Lay the ham on the grid in pan and place under heated grill, turning the gas down. (3) Turn once allowing four minutes each side. (4) Cook peas and serve hot around the ham on a dish.

GRILLED TOMATOES

1 lb. medium sized tomatoes.   · Butter.

(1) Heat the grill for one to two minutes. (2) Cut tomatoes in halves. (3) Place on grid in pan under grill. Turn down the gas and cook for 8-10 minutes, the time depends on the size of the tomatoes.

GRILLED SAUSAGES AND STEWED APPLE
1 lb. pork sausages. *3 cooking apples.*

(1) Heat grill. (2) Prick the sausages and place on the grid in pan, before placing under the heated grill, turn down the gas, because if the sausages are immediately exposed to a great heat they are liable to split their skins. (3) Turn frequently. They should take 12 minutes to cook. (4) Peel and core the apples, slice in rings, stew until tender. (5) Serve hot with the sausages.

TOASTED TEA-CAKES
Tea-cakes. *Butter.*

(1) Heat the grill until red hot. (2) Split the tea cakes, place on grid in pan under heated grill. (3) Toast the outsides first till brown, turn. (4) Repeat with insides and butter while still hot.

HOW TO MAKE TOAST

A little care is necessary to make good toast. Do not have the bread too new. Use a sharp knife to cut rounds of an even thickness. Heat the grill until the deflector plate is red hot before placing the bread underneath. Toast one side until sufficiently brown before turning over. The pieces of toast should be placed upright in a toast rack as soon as they are taken from the grill pan.

FRYING

FRYING is cooking food in hot fat and is undoubtedly a favourite method with English people, partly because it is very quickly carried out and partly because fried foods are very palatable and crisp. It is not, however, very economical, because as in the case of grilling, only the more tender parts of meat can be fried satisfactorily. Cheap, bony meat will be rendered tough and indigestible if cooked in hot fat.

There are three methods of frying.

1.—Deep. 2.—Shallow, and 3.—Dry Frying.

Dry Frying is a variation of shallow frying, and is so called because no additional fat is required, the food cooked containing sufficient in itself. Bacon and sausages are the two foods which are generally cooked in this way. The sausages are pricked and put into a perfectly dry frying pan. The rashers are freed from rind and also put into a dry pan. Frying is then carried out very slowly until the meat is cooked.

Sausages require from 10 to 15 minutes very slow cooking and they should be turned from time to time so that they are evenly browned.

Shallow Frying is frying in a small quantity of fat in an ordinary frying pan, only sufficient fat is added to prevent the food sticking to the pan and consequently it is necessary to turn the food in order that both sides may cook. This method is only suitable for small pieces of food, such as steak, liver, rashers, fillets of fish, pancakes, onions and potatoes.

The common mistake which must be guarded against when shallow frying is to avoid having the gas too high. Amateurs frequently raise the gas flame so high that the fat burns where the pan comes in close contact with the flame, imparting a scorched flavour to the food. The success of frying depends also on the quality of the pan. Thin metal pans are most unsuitable.

Whether lard, dripping or oil is used, it should be free from moisture. For this reason, care should be taken when using dripping to see that it does not contain gravy, as the presence of moisture in the fat causes considerable spluttering and splashing.

Deep Frying

Deep or French frying is cooking in a deep pan containing sufficient fat to cover completely the food being cooked. Any ordinary strong saucepan can be used, or special round and oval deep fry pans. With the exception of fritters, the food to be fried is put into a frying basket and then lowered into the fat. The success of this method of cooking depends entirely on the temperature at which the food is cooked. If the fat is too cool it penetrates the food, making it sodden and greasy, and if too hot the outside is scorched and browned before the food has an opportunity of cooking. The rough and ready method of judging the temperature is to note the amount of blue smoke that is rising from it. For frying the majority of food, only a faint blue smoke should be observed. The *thicker the food* to be cooked, the *cooler should be the fat.*

The following are the temperatures for frying the more common foods.

Fillets of Fish	370° F. to 380° F. for two to three minutes, according to thickness.
Chipped potatoes ..	370° F. for 3-5 minutes.
Rissoles, Fish Cakes, etc.	350° F. for 3-5 minutes.
Doughnuts	310° F. for 10 minutes.
Fritters	380° F. to 400° F.

Special thermometers are available for reading the temperature of fat. They should be immersed in the pan when it is put on to heat, and watched from time to time to see when it is nearing the required temperature, in order to avoid over-heating and burning the fat. The unpleasant smell often associated with frying can be largely avoided if care be taken not to over-heat the fat.

Suitable fats to be used when deep frying, are lard, clarified fat or dripping, special cooking oil; olive oil is particularly good, but is too expensive for general use—butter or margarine is not suitable, owing to the amount of moisture they contain.

For reasons of economy, the fat should always be strained after use. This prevents tiny particles of food, breadcrumbs, batter, etc., remaining in the fat and burning the next time it is heated. Other points to remember in connection with deep frying are:

(a) Care should be taken to prevent water or moisture coming in contact with the hot fat, as this causes considerable spluttering.

(b) It is very important to re-heat the fat after each batch of food has been fried.

(c) The fat should only reach half way up the pan in order to obviate any risk of boiling over when the food is immersed. Should a pan of deep fat at any time "boil" over and ignite, sand should be thrown on the flames immediately, or pan completely covered with a flat cake tray to smother the flame.

(d) After frying is completed, any surplus fat should be drained off. Raise the basket containing the food above the fat, and hold it for a few seconds, allowing the fat to drip back into the pan. With care, the same batch of fat can be used for numerous fryings, but if used extravagantly, largely by taking up a quantity of fat with each basket of food, this method of cooking does not prove economical, as the fat has to be added to too frequently.

(e) In order to improve both the appearance and palatability of food cooked in deep fat, the food should be placed on kitchen paper as soon as it is taken from the pan to absorb all surplus grease. It should then be served on a dish paper.

(f) All fried food should be eaten as soon as possible after cooking, otherwise the moisture in the food is liable to penetrate the crust or outer coating and make it sodden.

SCOTCH EGGS

4 *sausages.*   *White breadcrumbs and beaten egg for coating.*
Tomato sauce.   4 *hard boiled eggs.*

Remove the shells from the eggs and the skins from the sausages. Coat each egg with the sausage meat as evenly as possible, making them a good shape by pressing with the hand. Brush over with beaten egg, coat with breadcrumbs, place in a frying basket and fry in a pan of deep fat from which a faint blue smoke is rising, until they are well browned and the sausage meat is cooked. Drain on kitchen paper. Cut each egg in halves, place on croûtons of fried bread, cut side uppermost, and serve with tomato sauce.

SAVOURY OMELET

4 *eggs.*   2 *teaspoonfuls finely chopped parsley.*
1 *oz. butter.*   *Pepper and salt.*
½ *teaspoonful finely chopped herbs including if possible a little*
tarragon.

Have ready an omelet pan previously well cleaned by scouring with salt, break the eggs into a basin, add pepper and salt and beat them lightly with a fork.   Long beating is not necessary.   Put the butter in a pan over sharp heat, when it starts to smoke and change colour, pour in the beaten eggs containing the herbs and seasonings, and cook quickly moving the pan backwards and forwards sharply stirring the contents of the pan at the same time.   As the mixture begins to set tilt the pan away from you, fold the top and bottom edges together to form an oval shape.   Have a warm dish ready in the left hand, and holding the omelet pan in the right turn it upside down, so that the omelet drops on to the dish.   As the success of the omelet depends on quick cooking, the butter should be very hot and the cooking should take only 1 to 2 minutes.

PANCAKES

4 *ozs. plain flour.*   ½ *pint milk, or milk and water.*
Pinch salt.   1 *egg.*

Mix flour and salt in a mixing bowl, make a well in the centre.   Add egg (unbeaten), and the milk, gradually drawing in the flour, until a smooth batter is formed.   Beat well and set aside half an hour, or longer, before using.   Melt a small piece of lard in a suitably sized frying pan.   When quite hot and the pan greased all over, pour in almost half teacupful of the batter.   Cook until the underneath is slightly brown.   Turn and cook on the other side.   Turn on to a sugared dish.   Roll up and serve with lemon (when available) or jam.

SAVOURY PANCAKES

4 *ozs. plain flour.*   ½ *teaspoonful chopped parsley.*
1 *dried egg.*   ½ *pint milk and water.*
4 *ozs. cold meat or corned beef, minced or chopped finely.*
1 *or* 2 *tablespoonfuls thick gravy.*   1 *tomato (optional).*

Mix flour, dried egg and parsley together.   Make a well in the centre, pour in milk and water to mix to a coating batter consistency.   Stand for ½ hour, or longer, if possible.   Heat the meat in a little thickened gravy with sliced tomato, if used.   Season with pepper and salt.   Melt a little dripping in a small frying pan, pour in sufficient batter to cover the pan thinly.   Brown the pancakes on both sides, put a spoonful of the heated meat on each pancake.   Roll up and serve with gravy.

FRIED STEAK AND ONIONS

¾ *to* 1 *lb. steak.*   3 *or* 4 *large onions.*

Remove the skin from the onions, and slice evenly. Melt 1 oz. of dripping in a shallow frying pan, and fry the onions until golden brown. The secret of success is not to overcrowd the frying pan, otherwise the onions tend to stew instead of to fry. When the onions are crisp and cooked, remove from the frying pan and put on to a dish to keep hot. Add a little more dripping to the pan, sprinkle the steak with pepper and salt, and, if liked, a little flour. When the fat is smoking hot, put the steak in, and cook quickly for the first minute or two to seal the albumen, or pores, then turn the meat over and seal the other side. Turn again, and complete the cooking. Personal taste must decide exactly the extent of the cooking. To serve, place the fried steak on a dish, with the onions either on top of the steak or at both ends of the dish.

GLAZED ONIONS

Six onions, even in size. Peel and fry them whole in a stewpan, containing 1 oz. dripping, until well browned, then add 1 oz. brown sugar, and fry a little longer, add ½ pint stock, season with salt and pepper, simmer gently about 1 hour; take out the onions. The gravy may be thickened with 1 teaspoonful of flour blended with water.

POTATO CHIPS

Wash, peel and cut potatoes into long pieces or into scallops. Dry potatoes in a clean cloth, fry in deep hot fat, from which blue vapour is rising, until golden brown. Drain on crumpled paper. Sprinkle with salt and pepper. Serve in hot tureen.

DUCHESS POTATOES

½ *lb. mashed potatoes.*   *Yolk of* 1 *egg.*   *Salt and pepper.*

Mix well together, form into rolls on a floured board, coat with egg, toss in breadcrumbs. Fry in hot fat until a golden brown; drain, serve garnished with parsley.

POTATO SURPRISES

1 *lb. mashed potatoes.*   ½ *lb. sausage meat.*
Egg and breadcrumbs for coating.   *Salt and pepper.*

Divide mashed potatoes into 8 parts, slightly flatten out on a floured board, put a piece of sausage meat on the centre of each, work potato over; form into rolls, brush over with egg, toss in breadcrumbs, fry in hot fat.

CASSEROLE COOKERY

WHILST the use of casseroles has always been popular, during the last few years they have come into more general use, probably due to the attractive glass and china cooking-ware which is now obtainable in a wide variety of different shapes and sizes.

"Casseroles" when referred to in a general sense, include soufflé cases, ramekins, au gratin dishes and baking pans, in fact, any utensil of fireproof china or glass designed for oven use.

Points which make casserole cooking popular are (1) Very gradual heat is required, as slow cooking softens the fibres of meat. Consequently cheaper cuts and bony parts of meat can be cooked satisfactorily "en casserole". (2) Food does not readily burn in a casserole, and (3) Washing-up is easy.

Dishes that are suitable for cooking en casserole are stews of meat, fish and game, such as Irish Stew, Stewed Veal, Jugged Hare, Baked Fish, Vegetarian Dishes, Baked Beans with Bacon, Lentil Stew and Vegetable Hot Pots. They are also very suitable for cooking vegetables conservatively, that is, cooking them in a very small quantity of liquid, which is allowed almost to evaporate during cooking, and thus none of the goodness and mineral salts is lost.

HOT POT

Mark 2—2-2½ hours

1 *lb. lean beef or stewing steak.* 4 *large onions.* 1 *pint water.*
Small tablespoonful flour. 2 *lbs. potatoes.* ½ *oz. dripping.*
Little mushroom ketchup or Worcester sauce, if available.
Pepper and salt.

Cut the meat into neat pieces, and pass through seasoned flour made by mixing pepper, salt and flour together. Slice the onions, and sprinkle them with a little of the seasoned flour. Cut each potato into four or eight, according to size. Put the dripping into the bottom of the casserole, with a good layer of onion at the bottom, then a layer of potato and meat, continue until the vegetables and meat are used up but reserve plenty of potato to go on top. Add the water, place the lid on the casserole or cover with a piece of greased paper. Place Hot Pot in centre of oven. Commence with boiling water, or heat at Mark 7 until water is boiling. About 20 minutes before the meat is cooked, take off the lid or greased paper and brown the potatoes, and add a little more water or stock if necessary.

LANCASHIRE HOT POT

Mark 2—2-2½ hours

1 *lb. middle neck of mutton.*	1 *oz. dripping.*	2 *lbs. potatoes.*
Boiling water to cover.	2 *onions*	*Salt and pepper.*

Cut up meat into neat pieces. Put into an earthenware casserole with 1 oz. dripping. Allow to cook until slightly browned on both sides. Remove from the casserole, arrange potatoes, thinly sliced, and onions chopped finely, with the meat in layers, leaving a layer of potatoes for the top. Add seasonings. Almost cover with boiling water. Put the lid on. Cook for 2 to 2½ hours. Remove the lid half an hour before the end, to allow the potatoes to brown on the top.

RABBIT EN CASSEROLE

Mark 2—1½ hours

1 *rabbit.*	2 *onions*	2 *carrots.*
Bunch of herbs.	3 *cloves*	*Pepper and salt.*
1 *oz. butter.*	1 *oz. flour.*	*Milk to cover.*

The rabbit should be cut into neat joints, slice the vegetables and tie the herbs and cloves in a piece of muslin. Put the joints into a fireproof casserole, add the vegetables and cover with milk. For reasons of economy a little water can be added if liked. Put the lid on the casserole, or cover with greased paper and bake in a very moderate oven for 1½ hours, or until the rabbit is tender. Strain off the milk, melt the butter in a small saucepan, stir in the flour and add the strained milk. Bring to the boil and simmer for 8 minutes to cook the flour, adding a little pepper and salt if necessary. Pour the sauce over the rabbit, return the casserole to the oven for a few minutes, and serve.

CASSEROLE OF VEGETABLES

Mark 2—1-1½ hours

1 *lb. potatoes.*	2 *onions.*	6 *tablespoonfuls lentils.*
2 *carrots.*	2 *leeks.*	*Stock or water to cover.*
¼ *lb. mushrooms.*	*Pepper and salt.*	1 *or 2 rashers of bacon.*

Cut the rashers into small pieces. Prepare the vegetables in the usual way by cutting the potatoes into four and slicing the onion. Stew the stalks of the mushrooms in the stock or water for about an hour, then strain. Wash the lentils well and arrange the vegetables and bacon in the layers. Cover with the stock, add pepper and salt to season, and a very little chopped parsley and thyme; place on the lid, or cover with greased paper, and stew very slowly in the oven until the vegetables are tender and cooked. If the gravy has evaporated a little more can be added immediately before serving.

SAVOURY MINCE
Mark 5—40 minutes

1 *gill haricot beans.*	2 *medium carrots.*	2 *sticks celery.*
1 *teaspoonful chopped parsley.*	2 *small onions.*	2 *tomatoes.*
½ *lb. minced meat (optional)*	*Salt and pepper.*	2 *ozs. dripping.*

1½ *gills vegetable stock, gravy, or milk and water.*

Soak the beans for 24 hours, then boil until tender. Cut the onions into rings, fry in smoking hot dripping until golden brown. Place all in a casserole, add the sliced carrots and celery, stirring until all the dripping is absorbed. Add the liquid, then the sliced tomatoes, meat if any, chopped parsley, and lastly the beans. Season each layer, cover and stew gently for 40 minutes, or cook in the oven for 40 minutes with the "Autimo" set at 5.

Recipes for Fish cooked en casserole will be found on pages 14 and 15.

SAVOURY HARICOT BEANS
Mark 1

½ *lb. beans.*	1 *oz. dripping.*	1 *teaspoonful brown sugar.*
Salt and pepper.	*Stock or water.*	

Soak the beans overnight with boiling water with a small piece of soda; wash beans well, put into a pan, cover with cold water. Bring to the boil, simmer gently 1 hour, drain off water; place beans in a stew jar, add the dripping, brown sugar, salt and pepper, cover with stock or water. Cook gently in the oven for a few hours until beans are soft and most of the liquid taken up, a little pork or ham cut into small pieces greatly improves the dish.

RÉCHAUFFÉ COOKING

HOWEVER carefully a housewife caters, it is extremely difficult, and well nigh impossible, to avoid "left-overs". It is therefore important to know a few rules as to the best way of utilising such food. The chief thing to remember is that when food has been once cooked it only requires to be reheated. It is, however, necessary to add flavourings, vegetables and condiments, to make up for the lack of flavour of cooked meat, fish, etc.

Not only is there loss of flavour, but loss of food value occurs if the food is subjected to a high temperature for any length of time. Therefore, when making mince or hash, the thickened gravy or sauce, carefully seasoned and flavoured with vegetables, only requires thorough cooking, and the meat should be added to it just a sufficient length of time to enable it to be heated thoroughly.

When making Shepherd's Pie it is advisable, if onions are to be added, to cook them first, as both the potatoes and meat are cooked, and only require thoroughly heating and browning on the top. If, therefore, the onion is not to be served raw it should be cooked before it is added.

As previously mentioned, careful seasoning and flavouring is important, but as highly spiced food and herbs are unpopular with many palates such culinary aids must be used judiciously, otherwise the dishes themselves become unwelcome, merely through dislike of the flavourings used.

Twice cooked or reheated food generally looks more attractive if served in small portions, such as Croquettes, Rissoles, Fish Cakes, Meat Patties, small Entrées, with minced meat and vegetables.

The palatability or otherwise, of réchauffé dishes depends largely on the care exercised in their preparation. For example, skin, gristle and fat should be removed from cold meat, all bones and skin from fish, etc. Meat should be minced finely or sliced thinly, and fish finely flaked.

A DELICIOUS HASH

1 *lb. cold meat, mutton or beef or a mixture of both.*   1 *onion.*
Small bunch of herbs.   1 *pint stock   Small carrot.*   ½ *turnip.*
4 *mushrooms.*   1¼ *ozs. dripping.*   1½ *ozs. flour.*   1 *shallot.*

Chop up the onion and shallot finely; melt the dripping in a saucepan, and fry the onion and shallot golden brown. Then remove from the saucepan and fry the mushrooms slightly. Take out, and fry the sliced carrot and turnip, remove and stir the flour into the fat remaining in the pan, lower the gas and cook very slowly until evenly browned, stirring all the time to prevent the flour from burning. Add one pint stock or gravy, bring to the boil, stirring meanwhile to prevent lumps forming. Return the onion, shallot, sliced carrot, turnip and mushrooms, and simmer gently for 40 minutes over a very low heat, keeping the lid on the saucepan. Meanwhile, cut the meat into thin slices, removing all fat, gristle and skin. When the sauce has been cooking for 40 minutes, place the thin slices of meat in the gravy and allow it to become thoroughly hot through. Serve the hash on a dish garnished with the mushrooms.

The appearance of the dish is improved if sippets of toast or fried bread are placed on the edge of the dish.

N.B. If a joint of meat with a bone such as a shoulder or leg is being reheated, the meat should be cut off, and the bone used for making the stock. To do this, chop the bone into one or two pieces, put into a saucepan, cover with cold water, add half a teaspoonful of salt and half a carrot and onion and simmer very gently for one hour. Strain and use for making the sauce.

SHEPHERD'S PIE

Mark 5—If cooked in an oven

¾ lb. cooked meat, beef, mutton or veal.   *Pepper and Salt.*
1 teaspoonful finely chopped parsley.   *Good pinch mixed herbs*
2 to 3 tablespoonfuls milk   1 onion.   *½ oz. butter.*
1½ lbs. mashed potatoes.   *Stock to moisten.*

Put the onion on to cook, when cooked, strain and chop. Boil the potatoes in the usual way, when quite soft, strain off the water, stir in the butter, milk, salt and pepper, and beat hard to make them creamy. Grease a pie-dish and line with mashed potatoes, reserving plenty for the top crust. Mince the meat finely, after removing gristle and fat, mix it with the chopped cooked onion, parsley and herbs, and moisten with stock. Place inside the potato lined pie-dish and pile up the rest of the potato rockily on top. Decorate with a fork or whisk, put into a very moderate oven to heat the meat, then brown, either in a hot part of the oven or under the gas grill.

Economical Shepherd's Pie can be made by altering the above recipe slightly; use 2 lbs. mashed potatoes instead of 1½ lbs., and mix bulk of the potato with the meat and other ingredients. Place in the pie-dish and use the remainder of the potato for the top crust.

RABBIT CROQUETTES

6 ozs. finely minced rabbit.   *2 streaky rashers, chopped finely.*
Pinch of powdered mace.   *½ a small onion   ½ oz. dripping.*
1 or 2 mushrooms if available.   *Pinch of dried herbs.   ½ oz. flour.*
1 teaspoonful chopped parsley.   *Pepper and salt.   ¼ pint stock.*

Melt the dripping in a saucepan, stir in the chopped onion and fry until golden brown. Then remove from the saucepan, stir in the flour, lower the gas and cook very slowly until the flour is evenly browned. It is necessary to stir all the time the flour is browning to prevent burning. Add the stock, stir whilst it is coming to the boil, add the finely chopped onion, mushrooms, herbs and mace. Then add the meat and finely chopped rashers, beat well to blend the ingredients, and stir in sufficient egg to bind. Turn on to a plate, spread evenly and allow to cool. Divide into eight or ten pieces of even size, flour a board and shape each portion into a flat cake or ball, brush over with beaten egg, coat with fine breadcrumbs; place in a frying basket, lower into a pan of deep fat from which a faint blue smoke is rising, and fry until golden brown. Drain on kitchen paper, serve on a dish paper garnished with parsley.

BEEF OR MUTTON CROQUETTES

These are made in exactly the same way as the Rabbit Croquettes, except that Mutton or Beef is used instead of rabbit, and the rashers can be omitted if wished, although their use improves the flavour.

SAUSAGE CROQUETTES

½ *lb. sausage meat.*   ¼ *lb. mashed potatoes.*
Salt and pepper.   *Egg and breadcrumbs for coating.*

Mix potatoes and sausage well together, add seasonings, turn mixture on a floured board, form into balls, coat with egg, toss in breadcrumbs. Fry in hot fat, drain, serve garnished with parsley.

CURRY OF COLD MEAT

1 *small onion*	*Cold meat.*	1 *oz. dripping, or margarine.*
½ *pint stock.*	¼ *lb. boiled rice.*	1 *tablespoonful chopped apple.*
1 *dessertspoonful curry powder.*		*A little lemon juice.*
1 *dessertspoonful flour.*		1 *level teaspoonful salt.*

(1) Chop the onion and apple finely; cut the meat into small squares. (2) Melt the fat in a saucepan, and fry the onion; add the flour and curry powder; mix well, gradually adding the liquid. (3) Stir until it boils. (4) Add the apple and seasoning. (5) Put the lid on the saucepan, and simmer for 20 minutes. (6) Add the lemon juice. Allow to cool a little, and then stir in the meat. (7) Reheat and serve, placing boiled rice around the edge of the dish.

Curry Powder.

A combination of Eastern Spices used for flavouring meat, poultry, fish, cereals and vegetables.

MUTTON OR BEEF RISSOLES

8 *ozs. minced or finely chopped beef or mutton.*   *Pinch of herbs.*
Few drops Worcester sauce or mushroom ketchup.   1 *egg.*
1 *level teaspoonful finely chopped parsley.*   ½ *oz. flour.*
Small pinch powdered mace.   1 *fairly small onion.*   ¾ *gill stock.*
Short Crust or Flaky Pastry.   *Pepper and salt.*   ½ *oz. dripping.*

Melt the dripping in a saucepan, fry the chopped onion until golden brown. Then remove from the pan and brown the flour, add the stock, bring to the boil and simmer for 6 minutes. Stir in all the other ingredients with the exception of the egg, beat thoroughly well to amalgamate the mixture, add a little egg—about half should be sufficient—and stir into the other ingredients. Turn the mixture on to a plate and divide into equal pieces. Have ready some shortcrust or flaky pastry, trimmings will do quite well for this purpose. Roll it out very thinly, cut into rounds with a cutter, place about two teaspoonfuls or more according to the size of the pastry rounds, in the centre of each; moisten the edges, fold over the pastry, tap up the edges and decorate with the back of a knife. Brush over the top with the remainder of the beaten egg, sprinkle with a little crushed vermicelli, place in a frying basket and lower into a pan of deep fat from which a faint blue smoke is rising. When golden brown, remove from the pan, drain on kitchen paper, serve on a paper d'oyley garnished with parsley.

MINCE AND MACARONI

12 *ozs. cooked beef or mutton.*	1 *oz. dripping.*	1 *oz. flour.*
¾ *pint gravy or stock.*	*Small carrot.*	1 *onion.*
3 *ozs. stale grated cheese.*	3 *ozs. macaroni.*	
Mushroom ketchup.	*Pepper and salt.*	

Chop the onion finely and slice the carrot. Melt the dripping in a saucepan, fry the onion until golden brown, remove from the pan and fry the thinly sliced carrot. Remove the carrot from the pan, stir the flour into the fat remaining in the pan (if necessary a little more may be added, but only sufficient to absorb the flour is required). Cook over a very low gas until the flour is evenly browned, add the stock or gravy, stir whilst it is coming to the boil. When simmering, add the carrot, turnip, pepper, salt, mushroom ketchup, and simmer very gently for 40 minutes. Meanwhile, break the macaroni into pieces of even lengths, or if preferred, cut macaroni can be used, and plunge into a saucepan of fast boiling salted water. Allow it to boil fast until thoroughly tender; then strain away the water, stir in the finely grated cheese, and blend well. When the gravy is made, stir in the minced beef or mutton and allow it to reheat for a few minutes.

To serve, place the mince in the middle of a dish and a border of macaroni and cheese around it.

HAZEL EGGS

Mark 7—15 minutes

½ *pint bread sauce.*	1 *oz. butter*	3 *eggs.*
Salt and pepper.	1 *tablespoonful grated cheese.*	

Pour bread sauce into a buttered pie dish. Carefully break eggs into the sauce. Sprinkle over cheese and salt and pepper. Put on a few pats of butter. Bake in a hot oven for 15 minutes, with mark 7 as the "Autimo" setting.

CHEESE DISHES

In comparison with other foods cheese stands very high, when real food-values are considered. Rich in bone forming materials, cheese is particularly beneficial for growing children. It is one of our finest foods for maintaining good health, as well as for building good physique.

Cheese contains elements needed for:—

Group I   Food to build the body.
Group II   Food to give energy to do daily work.
Group III Food to protect the body, and to keep it healthy.

CHEESE AND POTATO PIE

Mark 8—10-15 minutes

1 *lb. potatoes, boiled and mashed.*	½ *lb. grated cheese.*
1 *oz. margarine.*	1 *egg.*
Salt and pepper.	1 *cupful warm milk.*

(1) Mash the potatoes with milk and margarine, add grated cheese, beaten egg and seasonings. (2) Beat well, put into buttered pie dish, rough surface with a fork. (3) Brown under the grill, or in the oven. NOTE. Sliced tomatoes placed around the edge of the dish before browning greatly improves the flavour and appearance of the dish.

CHEESE PUDDING (1)

Mark 5—40 minutes

| 4 *to* 6 *ozs. cheese* | 6 *to* 8 *slices bread and butter.* | 2 *eggs.* |
| 1 *pint milk.* | *Pepper, salt and a little mustard.* | |

(1) Sprinkle the bread and butter with pepper and salt, and spread it with a little made mustard. (2) Cut it in neat pieces, and arrange in a well-buttered pie dish. Sprinkle the grated cheese on to the bread. (3) Beat the eggs in a basin, with a little pepper and salt. (4) Stir in the milk, and strain over the bread and butter. (5) Allow to stand about ¼ hour before baking. (6) Bake slowly for about 40 minutes with the "Autimo" set at 5. If cooked as part of an unattended dinner, the "Autimo" may be set at 6.

CHEESE PUDDING (2)

Mark 6—15 minutes

| 4 *tablespoonfuls breadcrumbs.* | ½ *pint milk.* | 1 *egg.* |
| 3 *ozs. grated cheese.* | *Salt and pepper.* | |

(1) Butter a pie dish, and put in the breadcrumbs; boil milk and pour it over the breadcrumbs. (2) Add cheese, yolk of egg and seasoning, whip white to a stiff froth. (3) Fold in the mixture, bake for 15 minutes at Mark 6.

CHEESE AND ONION PIE

Mark 7—25 minutes

| 2 *large onions.* | 3 *ozs. grated cheese.* | *Salt and pepper.* |
| 1 *oz. margarine.* | *Short pastry.* | |

(1) Boil the onions until soft, drain and chop finely, add the cheese, margarine, and salt and pepper. (2) Line a pie dish with Short Pastry, put in cheese mixture, and cover with pastry. (3) Bake about 25 minutes at Mark 7.

MACARONI CHEESE

Mark 6—20 minutes

3 *ozs. macaroni.*   3 *ozs. cheese.*   1½ *ozs. butter.*
1½ *ozs. flour.*   1 *pint milk.*

(1) Break the macaroni into pieces of equal length, boil in salted water for about 20 minutes until tender. Strain off the water. (2) Whilst the macaroni is cooking, prepare the sauce. Melt the butter, stir in the flour, blend, add the milk, bring to the boil, stirring meanwhile. (3) Simmer for 10 minutes. Add seasonings, including a little mustard. Stir in the cheese and add the cooked macaroni. (4) Mix all the ingredients together, put into greased pie dish. (5) Insert in the oven with the "Autimo" set at 6 for 20 minutes, or if desired it can be browned under a grill.

MACARONI CHEESE WITH TOMATOES

Mark 8—10-15 minutes

2 *ozs. macaroni.*   ½ *pint White sauce.*   2 *ozs. grated cheese.*
A *little mustard.*   1 *tomato or 2 tablespoonfuls tinned tomatoes.*

(1) Break the macaroni into small pieces, cook in boiling salted water about 20 minutes until tender. (2) Make White Sauce (see recipe, page 131) add macaroni, cheese, mustard and tomato, season well. (3) Pour the mixture into a buttered pie dish. (4) Place in a hot oven at Mark 8 or under the grill to brown.

CHEESE SOUFFLÉ

Mark 7—20 minutes

½ *oz. butter.*   ½ *oz. flour.*   ¼ *pint milk.*
2 *eggs.*   2 *ozs. cheese.*   Salt and Pepper.

(1) Melt the butter in a saucepan. When boiling add the flour and cook for a minute. (2) Add the milk, and cook till the sauce thickens, stirring all the time. (3) Add the grated cheese, seasonings, and beaten yolks of eggs. (4) Whip the whites very stiffly and fold in to the mixture. (5) Pour into a greased soufflé mould and bake in a hot oven with the "Autimo" at Mark 7 for 20 minutes. Serve immediately. This recipe may be made using Fish in place of the Cheese.

CHEESE AND TOMATO ON TOAST

1 *tomato.*   Small *piece margarine.*   Salt and Pepper.
1 *tablespoonful milk.*   2 *ozs. grated cheese.*

(1) Remove skin from the tomato, by putting in boiling water for a few minutes, put a small piece of margarine in saucepan and melt. (2) Slice in tomato, cook for a few minutes; add the grated cheese, milk and the salt and pepper. (3) Heat thoroughly, pour over buttered toast.

CHEESE OMELET
(See Frying Section page 49).

1 *oz. grated cheese.*	*¾ oz. butter.*	2 *eggs.*
1 *tablespoonful cold water.*	*Salt and pepper.*	

(1) Mix together the eggs, cheese, water and seasonings. (2) Heat the butter on the omelet pan, pour in the egg mixture, and stir until it begins to set. (3) Roll up and serve hot.

CHEESE SCONES
(The Art of Cake Making on page 68).

Mark 8—10-15 minutes

8 *ozs. flour.*	2 *ozs. grated cheese.*
2 *ozs. butter.*	4 *rounded teaspoonfuls baking powder.*
Salt and pepper.	*¼ pint sour milk or butter milk.*

(1) Sieve together the flour, baking powder, salt and pepper. (2) Rub in the fat, add the grated cheese, mix to a dough with milk. (3) Roll out to ½ in. thick, and cut into rounds. (4) Brush over with egg or milk. (5) Place on greased baking tin, and bake in a hot oven with "Autimo" set at Mark 8 for 10-15 minutes.

CHEESE STRAWS
(For Pastry Making, please see pages 89-90).

Mark 8—8-12 minutes

4 *ozs. flour.*	1 *egg.*	*¼ teaspoonful baking powder.*
¼ teaspoonful salt.		2 *ozs. butter or margarine.*
2 *ozs. cheese, finely shredded.*		*Pinch of cayenne pepper.*
¼ teaspoonful dry mustard and pepper mixed.		

(1) Mix the flour, salt and baking powder together. (2) Rub in the fat lightly, and add the shredded cheese. Mix to a stiff paste with egg. (3) Roll out thinly. Cut into rings and straws. (4) Place on a greased baking sheet, bake on the 2nd runner from top of oven for 8-12 minutes with the "Autimo" at Mark 8.

SANDWICH FILLINGS

LUNCH SANDWICH FILLING

2 *ozs. cheese.*	1 *large carrot (raw).*
¼ teaspoonful Marmite (optional).	

(1) Grate the cheese and carrot finely. (2) Mix thoroughly together, adding a little Marmite, if liked. (3) Use for spreading thickly in bread sandwiches, or small rolls.

SWEET SANDWICH FILLING

½ *lb. chestnuts.*   ¼ *lb. dates.*   *Milk.*

(1) Cut the ends off the chestnuts, put into a saucepan with cold water, bring to boiling point and boil about 10 minutes. (2) Remove outer and inner skins from the nuts. (3) Replace nuts in the saucepan with barely enough milk to cover. (4) Cook carefully until the nuts are quite soft. (5) Mash well with a fork, add dates, chopped finely. (6) When cold, spread between thin bread and butter, or small bridge rolls.

BREAD MAKING

WHITE BREAD

Mark 7—60 minutes

3½ *lbs. flour.*   1 *oz. yeast.*   ½ *oz. salt.*
1¾ *pints tepid water.*   1 *teaspoonful castor sugar.*

Sieve the flour and salt into a warm mixing bowl. Put the yeast and sugar into a small basin and work them together. When they are creamy add a little of the warmed water. Make a well in the centre of the flour, add the yeast mixture and the remainder of the water, this should be at blood heat to encourage the yeast to work. If too hot, the yeast plant is killed. Put aside in a warm place to set the sponge for about 20 minutes. Then mix, preferably with the hand, turn on to a floured board and knead for a few minutes. Return to the basin, cover with a cloth, and stand in a warm place; on the plate shelf of the cooker grill unit would be a suitable spot, or on the hotplate, or in the storage drawer if the oven is in use. The cloth protects the dough from cold draughts and dust. Allow to rise for 1 hour, then turn on to a floured board, knead thoroughly and mould. Moulding is shaping into cottage loaves, coburgs or rolls, whichever is required. If tin loaves are wanted, the bread pans should be greased lightly and floured. Set the "Autimo" to mark 9 and pre-heat the oven for 20 minutes. During this time "prove" the dough in a warm place. When ready insert the dough, re-set the "Autimo" at Mark 7, and bake 1 lb. loaves 40-45 minutes, and 2 lb. loaves 55-60 minutes. When two tiers of loaves are baked simultaneously, their positions should be changed after 35 minutes' baking, the top right hand loaf being moved to bottom left hand and so on. This should be done quickly.

BREAD ROLLS, COBURG LOAVES, ETC.

When the dough has risen, divide into suitable pieces, mould to the shape required, place on greased baking trays, "prove" for about 20 minutes and bake for the following times:—

1 oz. Rolls—20 minutes.
1 lb. Coburg Loaves—30 minutes.
2 lb. Coburg Loaves—45 minutes.

WHOLEMEAL BREAD
Mark 7—60-75 minutes

3½ lbs. wholemeal flour.	1 oz. yeast.
1½ ozs. lard or dripping.	3 teaspoonfuls salt.
1¾ pints to 1 quart water.	1 teaspoonful sugar.

Add the salt to the wholemeal, rub in the lard or dripping and put into a warmed basin. Put the yeast and sugar in a small basin and work together with a wooden spoon until creamy, then add a little of the tepid water, make a well in the centre of the flour, pour in the yeast mixture, and the remainder of the tepid water. Mix to a soft dough. Care must be taken in doing this to prevent adding too much water, but it will be found that wholemeal absorbs more than white flour, and if mixed too dry the bread is not satisfactory. After mixing, knead thoroughly, return to the basin and put in a warm place to rise. When it has doubled its size, shape or mould into tins, which should be greased and floured. Prove in a warm place, until the bread rises to top of tins. Pre-heat at Mark 9 for 20 minutes, then re-set the "Autimo" to Mark 7 and insert loaves. The length of time depends on the size of the loaf, but large ones will require about 1¼ hours. See notes, page 64, on White Bread.

WHOLEMEAL FRUIT LOAVES
Mark 7—35 minutes

14 ozs. wholemeal flour.	2 ozs. white flour. 3 ozs. sugar.
6 ozs. fruit (dates or sultanas).	¼ pint milk (about). 1 oz. yeast.
1 tablespoonful syrup or treacle.	¼ teaspoonful salt. 3 ozs. fat.

Place flour, salt, and most of the sugar in a mixing bowl. Rub in the fat and add the fruit. Cream yeast with 1 or 2 teaspoonfuls of the sugar in a small basin until it liquifies, and pour on to it about ¼ tea-cup tepid milk. Make a well in centre of flour, pour into it the yeast mixture, sprinkling a little of the flour on top. Cover the bowl with a cloth, stand in a warm place, away from draught, about 20 minutes, or until the yeast mixture appears frothy. Add the warmed syrup and enough tepid milk to mix to a soft dough. Turn on to a floured board and knead for 2 to 3 minutes. Divide the dough into 3 pieces and put each piece into a greased and warmed 1 lb. bread or cake tin. Leave to rise in a warm place about 1½ hours, or until the dough has almost doubled in size. Bake the loaves on 3rd runner from top of oven for 35 minutes, with "Autimo" set at Mark 7.

IRISH SODA BREAD
Mark 8—15 minutes

½ lb. flour.	1 teaspoonful baking soda.
¼ teaspoonful salt.	Buttermilk to mix.

Sieve the flour and the carbonate of soda and salt together. Make a well in the centre, and stir in sufficient buttermilk to make a soft dough. Turn on to a floured board, and shape the dough into rounds about ½ in. thick. Mark each into four triangular pieces. Cook on a well greased girdle until brown on one side. Then turn and brown on the other side. Alternatively, bake in a hot oven for about 15 minutes with the "Autimo" set to 8, on the second and fourth runners from the top.

DOUGH CAKE

Mark 7—30-50 minutes

2 ozs. butter or margarine.	1 lb. bread dough.	1 egg.
3 ozs. sultanas.	1 oz. currants.	2 ozs. sugar.
Little mixed spice, if liked.	½ oz. peel.	

Take 1 lb. bread dough which has been allowed to rise for 1 hour. Beat in the egg, cleaned fruit, warmed fat, and chopped peel, sugar and spice and beat hard with the hand to amalgamate all the ingredients. If necessary, more milk may be added, as the mixture is required to be slightly softer than for bread. Put into one or two well greased and floured bread pans or cake tins, prove for about ¼ hour, until the cake is well risen, and bake with the "Autimo" set at 7, for about 30 to 50 minutes, on the 3rd or 4th runners from top, according to whether two or one cake is made from the mixture.

YORKSHIRE TEA CAKES

Mark 8—10 minutes

1 lb. flour.	1 oz. lard or butter.	1 oz. yeast.
1 oz. currants.	1 oz. sultanas.	1 oz. sugar.
½ pint milk.	Small teaspoonful salt.	

Warm the flour and sieve it with the salt. Rub in lard or butter, add sugar. Cream the yeast with tepid milk and a little water. Make a well in the centre of the flour and pour in the yeast and milk. Beat well, put in a warm place and allow to rise for about an hour. Flour a pastry board, turn the dough on to it, knead lightly, divide into eight cakes, form into small balls, allow to stand a few minutes to rise, then roll out, put on two baking sheets, and allow to stand in a warm place for about 15 to 20 minutes, then bake on the 2nd and 4th runners from top, with the "Autimo" set at 8 for about 10 minutes.

SALLY LUNNS

Mark 6—20-25 minutes

8 ozs. flour.	¼ pint tepid milk.	½ oz. yeast.
1 oz. butter.	1 egg.	Pinch of salt.

Warm the flour and sieve it with the salt. Cream the yeast with a pinch of sugar, and add the tepid milk. Make a well in the centre of the flour and pour in the yeast and milk. Put in a warm place, cover with a cloth and leave for 20 minutes. (This is called "setting the sponge"). Then add the beaten egg, melted butter and mix to a softish dough. Beat well, put in a warm place and allow it to rise for about an hour. Flour a pastry board well, turn the dough on to it, knead lightly, divide into two and put into two well greased tins of equal size. Put to rise in a warm place for 20 to 25 minutes, brush over with beaten egg and bake on the 3rd runner from top of the oven, with the "Autimo" set at 6.

HOT CROSS BUNS

Mark 6—15-20 minutes according to size

1 *lb. flour.*	1 *oz. yeast.*	$\frac{1}{4}$ *teaspoonful salt.*
4 *ozs. currants or sultanas.*	2 *oz. butter.*	2 *ozs. sugar.*
$\frac{1}{4}$ *teaspoonful cinnamon.*	1 *oz. chopped peel.*	1 *egg.*
$\frac{1}{4}$ *teaspoonful grated nutmeg.*		
Tepid milk and water—approx. 1$\frac{1}{2}$ *gills.*		

Sieve the flour and salt into a basin. Rub the butter into the flour, and make a well in the centre of the flour. Put the yeast in a small basin, and work it with a teaspoonful of sugar until it is moist and creamy. Add the tepid milk to the yeast, and put it in the centre of the flour. Cover the basin and put in a warm place for 20 minutes for the mixture to sponge. Then mix in the remaining ingredients —currants, sugar, peel and mixed spices—and mix to a fairly slack dough, adding a little more tepid liquid, if necessary. Beat thoroughly, and put to rise until the dough doubles its bulk. The time required is usually about 1$\frac{1}{2}$ hours. Flour a board and turn the mixture on to it, divide into 12 or 14 pieces of even size, shape each piece into a bun, put on a floured and greased baking tin, mark with a cross, put to prove in a warm place for from 15-20 minutes. Bake on the 2nd and 4th runners from top of the oven with "Autimo" set at 6. When the buns are almost cooked, brush over with a little milk containing sugar in solution. Return the buns to the oven for a few minutes. Cool on a wire tray.

BATH BUNS

Mark 6—20 minutes

$\frac{1}{2}$ *lb. flour.*	3 *ozs. castor sugar.*	1$\frac{1}{2}$ *ozs. crushed loaf sugar.*
$\frac{1}{2}$ *oz. yeast.*	1 *oz. orange peel.*	2$\frac{1}{2}$ *ozs. butter or margarine.*
1 *egg.*	2 *ozs. sultanas.*	$\frac{1}{8}$ *teaspoonful salt.*
$\frac{1}{2}$ *gill milk.*		

Warm the flour and salt together in a mixing bowl, rub in the fat and add castor sugar. Break up the yeast in a small basin, add to it the tepid milk, make a well in centre of flour, pour in the yeast and milk, also beaten egg. Mix to a soft dough, cover the bowl with a cloth, put to rise in a warm place for about 1 hour. Shape the mixture into buns with floured hands, place on a well greased baking tin. Stand in a warm place, about 20 minutes. Brush buns with beaten egg and sprinkle coarse sugar on top. Place on 2nd and 4th runners from top, and bake for 20 minutes with "Autimo" set at Mark 6.

DOUGHNUTS

½ *pint milk (warmed)*.	2 *ozs. margarine*.
½ *oz. yeast*.	14-16 *ozs. plain flour*.
1 *egg.* *Pinch of salt*.	2 *ozs. sugar.* *Jam*.

(1) Cream the yeast with a little sugar. (2) Add the warmed milk and stir in about 4 ozs. of flour to make a thin batter. (3) Cover and put into a warm place until risen and dropped. (4) Add cool melted margarine, salt and beaten egg, beat well, then lastly add the rest of the sifted flour to make a dough. (5) Leave to prove 45-60 minutes. (6) Knead dough and divide into 20 pieces. (7) Roll each piece into a ball, flatten slightly. (8) Put jam into centre. Moisten the edges of the dough and seal edges together. (9) Place on a lightly floured cloth to prove. (10) Fry in hot deep fat 5-7 minutes. Turn over and cook other side. (11) Drain on kitchen paper, and roll in a mixture of Cinnamon and castor sugar.

THE ART OF CAKE MAKING

CAKE making is a distinct branch of cooking, and it is not uncommon to find that a person who is a successful cook in other respects fails to achieve success in cake making. There is certainly a good deal to learn, for not only must the mixing be carefully carried out, but the oven must be thoroughly well understood, and one should be conversant with the correct temperatures at which to cook different varieties of cakes. Scones for example, would be close and heavy if cooked in a cool oven, whilst gingerbread requires a very low temperature and would be scorched and burnt if baked in an oven suitable for scones. A good rule to remember is—the larger the quantity of sugar in a recipe, the cooler the oven required.

In the space available, an endeavour will be made to give information on both the theory and practice of cake making. There are actually four different methods of making cakes.

1. By rubbing the fat into the flour. This is the simplest and quickest, and is used for plain cakes, buns and scones.

2. Creaming the fat and sugar together. All cakes such as Madeira, Cherry, Sultana, Pound mixtures and rich fruit cakes are made by this method.

3. Beating the eggs and sugar together. This is the method employed for making cakes which do not contain fat, or only a small proportion. Sponge cakes, sponge rolls and sponge sandwiches are examples of cakes prepared by this slower method.

4. When the fat and sugar are melted together. Ginger-bread and Parkin are examples of cakes prepared in this way.

General Rules for Cake Making

1. Attend to the oven. If it has not been used previously, light the gas at least 15-20 minutes before it is required, setting the "Autimo" at the number given on the chart.

2. Irrespective of the method of mixing to be employed, the first step in cake making is to prepare the tins. If one large tin is used it should be greased and floured, or lined with paper. If small fancy tins are to be used they should be brushed over with melted butter or unsalted fat, and dredged with flour. For making rock cakes or scones a flat baking sheet or tray is required, and this should be warmed for a few minutes on the stove and then rubbed over with a small piece of dripping or suet, and dredged with flour.

3. All ingredients should be carefully weighed, using good quality flour if best results are desired. It is largely a matter of personal taste whether self-raising or plain flour is used. In the recipes which follow plain flour is used entirely. If self-raising flour is substituted in any of the recipes, the baking powder must, of course, be omitted, otherwise there will be too much chemical raising agent in the ingredients, resulting in a very open texture. The cake is also very likely to rise rapidly at first and later to sink, taking the fruit to the bottom.

A Foundation Mixture

Many people who are inexperienced in cake making imagine that it is necessary to know a very large number of recipes in order to obtain variety. This is not so, but it is necessary to know a "foundation recipe" that is the proportion of sugar, butter and flour which can be used, and the extent to which it can be varied. Then a large number of cakes can be evolved by introducing raisins, sultanas, currants, or a mixture of these, cherries, walnuts, little grated lemon rind, seeds, spice, etc.

Foundation for a plain cake consists of 8 ozs. flour, 4 to 6 ozs. fat, butter or margarine or a mixture of both, or dripping, 4 to 6 ozs. sugar, 1 egg and 1 level teaspoonful baking powder. (Dripping can be used to replace a portion of the fat when spice and/or treacle are included in the recipe, masking the flavour). For a richer cake the foundation is slightly varied, thus, 8 ozs. flour, 6 to 8 ozs. fat, butter or margarine—butter should always be used when a good cake is required—6 to 8 ozs. sugar, 3 to 4 eggs.

Further variations in the above ingredients for both plain and richer cakes, can, of course, be made; for example, the flour can be varied, some cornflour or potato flour can be introduced, and an equal quantity of ordinary flour eliminated.

A close study of any of the recipes that follow will show that the above proportions are adhered to, although additional ingredients are introduced such as ground almonds, semolina, ground rice, currants, chopped almonds, peel, coffee, chocolate and fruit of all kinds.

The Baking of Cakes

The use of gas for baking proves very economical, for when once the oven has been thoroughly heated a very low flame is sufficient to maintain a baking temperature. The most usual mistake made by novices, often resulting in burning the bottom of cakes, is to put them in when the oven has only been alight for 10 minutes, and keep the gas full on or moderately full on during baking. This is quite the wrong method. With the aid of the "Autimo" no user need make this mistake, for the correct positions at which the indicator should be set are given on the chart.

Another important point which should be borne in mind is that the baking **sheet or tray** on which rock buns, scones and small cakes are put to bake **should not be greater than the baking tray supplied with the cooker,** in order to ensure the circulation of hot air round the oven and that the cakes do not come in very close contact with the sides of the oven.

Although it is possible to test when large cakes are cooked by inserting a warmed skewer, it is better to learn how to judge when cooking is completed by the appearance, smell and feel. A large cake should be golden brown and smooth on the outside, and the centre of the top when pressed gently with the finger should spring back.

Cake recipes are usually of particular interest. Various recipes are known by other names in different parts of the country. This applies particularly to various types of sponges.

Many housewives find the ready mixed packet cake and sponge powders a useful addition to their store cupboard. Usually these proprietary mixtures require a somewhat hotter oven than is used for household recipes.

Large fruit cakes should be baked on the fourth or fifth runner from top. Particular care should be taken to ensure that the oven is sufficiently heated before inserting the cake. If an extra large cake is being baked, the "Autimo" mark may be lowered during the final $1\frac{1}{2}$ to 2 hours' baking time.

Plain cake mixtures containing a small quantity of fat, sugar and eggs should be baked at mark 4, but a *rich* cake at mark 2, or for a longer period at mark 1.

PLAIN CAKES, BUNS AND SCONES

RICE BUNS

Mark 6—15-20 minutes

3 ozs. flour.   2 ozs. ground rice or fine semolina.
Pinch of salt.   ½ teaspoonful baking powder.   2½ ozs. sugar.
1 egg.   3 ozs. butter or margarine.   1½ tablespoonfuls milk

(1) Sieve the flour, ground rice, baking powder, and salt, into a basin.
(2) Rub in the butter with the tips of the fingers, stir in the sugar. (3)
Make a well in the centre, stir in the beaten egg and sufficient milk to
make the mixture moderately stiff.   (4) Three parts fill greased patty
pans, or paper cases with the mixture, and put on a baking sheet. (5)
Put on 2nd and 4th runners from top of oven with the "Autimo" set
at 6, and bake for 15-20 minutes, according to the size of the buns.

ROCK CAKES

Mark 6—15-20 minutes

6 ozs. flour.   1 oz. light weight candied peel.   3 ozs. sugar.
Pinch of salt.   1 level teaspoon baking powder.   3 ozs. currants.
1 egg.   1 or 2 tablespoonfuls milk.   3 ozs. margarine.
¼ teaspoonful nutmeg, spice and ginger mixed.

(1) Grease and flour a baking sheet.   (2) Sieve the flour, spices, salt
and baking powder into a basin.   (3) Rub in the margarine with the
tips of the fingers, add the currants and sugar, mixing all the dry
ingredients together.   (4) Make a well in the centre, stir in the beaten
egg and just sufficient milk to make a very stiff mixture.   (5) With
the aid of two forks put rocky heaps of equal size on the baking tray.
(6) Place on the 2nd and 4th runners from top of the oven and bake
for 15-20 minutes, according to the size.   NOTE: the successful
appearance of rock cakes depends entirely on a stiff mixture, the
addition of too much milk causes the cakes to flatten.

SULTANA SCONES

Mark 7—10-15 minutes

8 ozs. flour.   2 ozs. butter or margarine.   ¼ teaspoonful salt.
1½ ozs. sugar. 1 level teaspoonful cream of tartar   2 ozs. sultanas
½ level teaspoonful bicarbonate of soda   1 gill milk to mix.

(1) Sieve the flour, bicarbonate of soda, cream of tartar and salt into
a basin.   (2) Rub in the butter.   (3) Add the sugar and cleaned
sultanas.   (4) Make a well in the centre and mix thoroughly to a
fairly firm dough, adding the milk gradually.   (5) Turn the dough
out on to a floured board, handle as lightly as possible, and avoid
over-kneading.   (6) Roll out to a thickness of ½ an inch, using as
little flour as possible.   (7) Cut into rounds with a cutter, and place
on a greased and floured baking sheet.   (8) Put in oven and bake for
10-15 minutes, according to size, on the 2nd and 4th runners from
top.   NOTE: Two level teaspoonfuls of baking powder can be substituted if bicarbonate of soda and cream of tartar are not available.

71

TREACLE SCONES

8 ozs. plain flour.   1 tablespoonful golden syrup or treacle.
Pinch of salt.   ¼ teaspoonful ground cinnamon (optional).
Milk to mix.   ½ teaspoonful bicarbonate soda.   1 oz. fat.
(Sufficient for 12 to 14 scones.   2½ in. diameter).

(1) Mix dry ingredients together, rub in fat.   (2) Warm syrup slightly and pour into flour, carefully adding enough milk to make a fairly soft dough.   (3) Roll out rather less than ½ in. in thickness.   Cut into rounds with a plain cutter.   (4) Evenly heat a thick frying pan (not enamel)—or iron girdle, on the largest boiling burner.   (5) Rub over with a piece of greased paper.   Turn the gas down very low. (6) Place the scones at intervals round the pan and cook 4 or 5 minutes on each side.   Lay on a cloth to cool.
N.B.   Treacle Scones can also be baked at Mark 7 for about 15 minutes.

WHOLEMEAL SCONES
Mark 7—15-20 minutes

8 ozs. wholemeal or brown flour.1 teaspoonful salt.   1 oz. sugar.
4 teaspoonfuls baking powder.   3 ozs. margarine.   ½ pint milk.
8 ozs. plain white flour.   2 ozs. sultanas.

(1) Add salt and baking powder to the flour, then rub the fat in lightly.   (2) Add sugar and sultanas, mix to a fairly soft dough with milk.   (3) Roll out on a floured board to half an inch in thickness, cut into rounds.   (4) Place on a greased baking tin, and brush over with egg.   (5) Bake for 15 to 20 minutes at Mark 7, on the 2nd and 4th runners.

POTATO SCONES
Mark 7—15-20 minutes

6 ozs. cooked mashed potato.   5 ozs. flour.
½ teaspoonful salt.   2 ozs. butter.
2 rounded teaspoonfuls baking powder. About ½ cupful milk.

(1) Sieve together flour, salt and baking powder.   (2) Rub in the butter and mix in the potatoes.   (3) Add sufficient milk to make a soft dough.   (4) Turn on to a floured board and roll out about ½ in. thick.   (5) Cut into rounds, and place on greased baking tin.   (6) Put in oven, on 2nd and 4th runners, and bake at Mark 7 for 15 to 20 minutes, according to size.   (7) Serve hot with butter.

SHORTBREAD
Mark 3— 25-30 minutes

8 ozs. flour.   2 ozs. sugar.   4 ozs. butter.   A little yolk of egg.

(1) Sieve the flour into a basin.   (2) Rub in the butter until it is finely divided.   (3) Add sugar and blend all ingredients together.   (4) Mix with very little yolk of egg.   (5) Flour a board, turn the paste on to it,

knead it well. (6) Roll out to about ¼ in. in thickness and cut into oval shapes or rounds with a fancy cutter, (7) Put on to greaseproofed paper on the baking tray (to avoid too much browning beneath). Decorate with a small piece of cherry or angelica on each biscuit. (8) Place on the 2nd and 4th runners from top of oven and bake until golden brown and firm, 25-30 minutes. (9) Allow to cool before removing from the tray.

CURRANT CAKE

Mark 4—1 hour

8 *ozs. flour.*	4 *ozs. margarine.*	2 *teaspoonfuls baking powder.*
4 *ozs. sugar.*	4 *ozs. currants.*	2 *tablespoonfuls milk.*
2 *eggs.*	*Pinch of salt.*	

(1) Grease and flour a moderately small cake tin (6½″ dia.). (2) Sieve the flour with the baking powder and salt into a basin. (3) Rub the butter in with the tips of the fingers. (4) Stir in the cleaned currants and sugar. (5) Make a well in the centre, stir in the beaten egg, adding just sufficient milk to make the mixture moist enough to drop from the spoon when jerked slightly. (6) Put the mixture into the prepared tin, place in the oven on the fourth runner from top, for 1 hour.

RASPBERRY BUNS

Mark 6—15-20 minutes

8 *ozs. flour.*	1 *level teaspoonful baking powder.*	*Pinch of salt.*
1 *egg.*	3 *ozs. castor sugar.*	*Milk to mix.*
Raspberry jam.	4 *ozs. margarine.*	

(1) Grease and flour a baking tray. (2) Sieve the flour, salt and baking powder into a basin. (3) Rub in the fat. (4) Add the sugar and mix to a soft dough with egg and milk. (5) Flour a pastry board, turn the dough on to it, knead up lightly then roll out until it is about ⅜ in. thick. (6) Cut into rounds with a floured cutter; put a good teaspoonful of raspberry jam into the centre of each, gather up the pastry, pinch together and place on a baking tray with the smooth side uppermost. (7) Mark lightly on the top with a cross, brush over with a little milk containing dissolved sugar. (8) Place on the 2nd and 4th runners from top of the oven and bake for 15 to 20 minutes according to the size of the buns.

SEED CAKE

Mark 4—1-1¼ hours

8 *ozs. flour.*	4 *ozs. margarine.*	1 *teaspoonful carraway seeds.*
4 *ozs. sugar.*	2 *eggs.*	2 *tablespoonfuls milk.*
½ *oz. finely chopped candied peel.*		2 *teaspoonfuls baking powder.*
Pinch of salt.		

Use the same method as given above for Currant Cake, substituting the seeds and peel for the currants. Bake on the 4th runner from top.

RAISIN CAKE

Mark 4—1-1¼ hours

8 *ozs. flour.*	4 *ozs. butter.*	2 *level teaspoonfuls baking powder.*
2 *eggs.*	4 *ozs. sugar.*	2 *tablespoonfuls milk.*
3 *ozs. raisins.*	*Pinch of salt.*	*Pinch mixed spice.*

(1) Sieve the flour, baking powder, spice and salt into a basin. (2) Rub the butter in with the finger tips until it resembles fine bread-crumbs. (3) Add the sugar and the raisins, stoned and cut in halves. (4) Mix fairly stiffly with the beaten egg, adding milk lastly. (Care must be taken not to mix the cake too moistly, otherwise the raisins, being heavy, will all sink to the bottom). (5) Put into a well greased and floured cake tin (6½″ dia.), place in the oven on the fourth runner from top, and bake for 1-1¼ hours.

DATE AND WALNUT ROLL

Mark 5—40-50 minutes

16 *ozs. flour.*	4 *ozs. sugar.*	2 *level teaspoonfuls baking powder.*
1 *egg.*	8 *ozs. milk.*	2 *ozs. margarine.*
1 *cupful chopped dates.*		1 *cupful chopped walnuts.*
Pinch of salt.		

(1) Rub the fat into sifted flour, baking powder and salt. (2) Add dates and walnuts, and mix to stiff consistency with beaten egg and milk. (3) Drop in equal quantities into two greased 1 lb. cocoa tins and cover with greased lids. (4) Bake on fourth runner, standing upright. (5) To serve, cut very thin slices and spread with butter.

PARKIN

Mark 2—1¼-1½ hours.

8 *ozs. lard.*	6 *ozs. sugar.*	1 *level teaspoonful mixed spice.*
3 *eggs.*	7 *ozs. syrup.*	1 *level teaspoonful ground ginger.*
1½ *ozs. plain flour.*		1 *level teaspoonful baking powder.*
14 *ozs. fine oatmeal.*		

(1) Heat the fat, sugar and syrup over a gentle flame, just sufficient to disperse the fat. (2) Add beaten egg. (3) Sift flour, oatmeal and spices and baking powder, and add to syrup, etc., mixing well. Bake in a greased meat tin.

YORKSHIRE SPICE CAKE

Mark 4—1¼ hours

1 *lb. flour.*	½ *teaspoonful salt.*	1 *teaspoonful mixed spice.*
3 *eggs.*	6 *ozs. mixed fruits.*	1 *teaspoonful baking powder.*
6 *ozs. sugar.*	1 *oz. milk.*	6 *ozs. butter or margarine.*
2 *teaspoonfuls treacle.*		

(1) Sieve flour, salt and spice into a basin. (2) Rub in the butter, add sugar and fruits. (3) Add the beaten eggs and melted treacle

and milk. (4) Lastly add the baking powder. Mix well. (5) Put mixture into a greased cake tin (7¾″ dia. or 8″ square). (6) Place in oven on 3rd runner from top, and bake for 1¼ hours.

BURY SIMNEL CAKE

Mark 4—1 hour

8 *ozs. plain flour.*	½ *teaspoonful salt.*	½ *teaspoonful spice.*
2 *eggs.*	4 *ozs. brown sugar.*	1 *oz. candied peel.*
4 *ozs. currants.*	4 *ozs. sultanas.*	4 *ozs. butter*
½ *teaspoonful baking powder.*		*or margarine.*
2 *ozs. almonds, blanched and chopped.*		

(1) Rub the butter into the flour. (2) Add all the dry ingredients. (3) Mix to a stiff paste with eggs (add a little milk if necessary). (4) Roll out ½ in. in thickness, make into round cakes and cover with chopped almonds. (5) Place on two greased baking sheets, put in oven and bake one hour.

FIG SQUARES

Mark 7—15-20 minutes

8 *ozs. plain flour.*	1 *oz. sugar.*	½ *teaspoonful baking powder.*
5 *ozs. margarine.*	1 *egg.*	½ *teaspoonful salt.*
4 *ozs. chopped figs, stewed for about* 10 *mins. with a little water.*		
A little milk.		

(1) Add salt and baking powder to the flour. Cut up, and rub the fat in. Melt sugar in the milk. (2) Mix to a stiff pastry with egg and milk. (3) Divide the pastry, roll out each piece thinly. (4) Place one piece of pastry on a greased baking tin, spread the fig mixture over pastry, cover with second piece of pastry, press edges together. (5) Square across, and across the top with a knife. On 3rd runner from top, bake 15-20 minutes at Mark 7. Jam, or lemon curd may be used in place of figs.

CAKE MAKING BY THE CREAMING METHOD

Beginners should make a special point of reading this method very carefully.

The following are recipes for cakes made by creaming the butter and sugar together. General rules given at the commencement of this lesson all apply, but a few hints regarding the actual creaming process and the mixing will be of help to those who find difficulty in making the richer kind of cakes. It is advisable to assemble all ingredients on the work table, allowing all to reach the room temperature, i.e., about 70°F. The butter and sugar must be worked together in a basin until they form a mixture resembling whipped cream. A wooden spoon is the best kind to use. Ingredients should be pressed against the side of the basin with the back of the spoon until they are well mixed. A basin of moderate size is most convenient, for if too small it is impossible to work the butter and sugar together conveniently without spilling, and if a large basin is used one finds a difficulty in keeping the two ingredients sufficiently together to get them well blended. In cold weather when the fat is rather hard the process takes longer, though matters are facilitated by warming the fat slightly. It should not, however, be allowed to oil or melt. Having attained the appearance of whipped cream, the eggs may be added. Lightly beat the eggs and add at six intervals, beating well between each addition. Should signs of curdling appear, a little of the dry flour should be folded in between each egg. All the dry ingredients may be introduced alternately with the milk.

To test if the cake mixture is of the right consistency a spoonful should be lifted out and held above the basin. If it just drops with the merest shake or jarring of the spoon the consistency is correct for fruitless cakes. Cakes containing fruit require to be slightly stiffer and a slight jerk should be necessary to make it drop from the spoon.

MADEIRA CAKE

Mark 4—1-1¼ hours

6 *ozs. flour.* 1 *teaspoonful baking powder.* 4 *ozs. castor sugar.*
2 *eggs.* 4 *ozs. butter or margarine.* *Slice citron (optional)*
2 *ozs. milk.* *Little grated lemon rind.* *Pinch of salt.*

(1) Grease and flour a cake tin of about 5½ in. diameter. (2) Sieve the flour, baking powder, and salt, into a basin, add the grated lemon rind. (3) Cream the butter and sugar together. (4) Beat in the egg a little at a time, and add milk. (5) Fold in the dry ingredients as lightly as possible. (6) Put mixture into cake tin and place in the oven on the fourth runner from top and bake for about 1 to 1¼ hours. (7) When the cake has been baking for about ¾ hour, carefully place on the top a piece of citron which has been previously warmed. NOTE.—If liked, 2 ozs. currants, and an extra ½ teaspoonful baking powder may be added to the above recipe.

ROYAL ICING

3 *whites of eggs.* *Juice of* 1 *medium size lemon.*
2 *lbs. icing sugar (about).*

(1) Mix the strained lemon juice and whites of eggs together in a large bowl. (2) Gradually stir in the sieved icing sugar, beating thoroughly all the time, until a very thick icing is formed. (3) Spread over the cake, using a long knife, dipped in cold water to obtain a smooth surface.

N.B.—Suitable for one large birthday, or Christmas cake, etc.

CHOCOLATE FILLING

2 *ozs. butter.*   2 *ozs. plain chocolate.*   2 *ozs. icing sugar.*

(1) Grate the chocolate and work it over a very gentle heat. (2) As soon as it is soft, beat it into the creamed butter and sugar.

BUTTER CREAM ICING

2 *ozs. butter.*   3 *ozs. sieved icing sugar.*
Few drops vanilla essence.

(1) Put the butter into a basin and work it with a wooden spoon. (2) Add the icing sugar and beat until smooth and creamy. (3) Stir in the flavouring and a few drops of colouring if this be required. Butter cream icing is used for piping on to cakes iced with Glacé Icing, and also as a cake filling.

COFFEE BUTTER ICING

4 *ozs. fresh butter.*   5 *or* 6 *ozs. sieved icing sugar.*
A little coffee extract.

Made in exactly the same way as Butter Cream Icing, adding coffee essence in place of the vanilla essence.

GLACE ICING

8 *ozs. sieved icing sugar.*   *Few drops of flavouring essence.*
A little colouring.   3 *tablespoonfuls warm water.*

(1) Put the icing sugar and flavouring in a small saucepan and stand in another containing hot water. (2) Add the water very gradually to the icing sugar, stir whilst it is warming, but do not allow it to get hot or the icing will be spoilt. (3) When thick enough to coat the back of a spoon, pour it over the cakes to be iced. N.B. If it is too thin, more icing sugar can be added, to make it of the right consistency. Any flavouring or colouring can be used.

CHOCOLATE ICING

3 *ozs. powdered chocolate.*   6 *ozs. icing sugar.*
2 *tablespoonfuls water.*   *Small piece of lard or margarine.*

(1) Place all the ingredients into a bowl, put the bowl in a warm place until the mixture becomes soft. (2) Do not allow it to get too hot, then beat well and spread over the cakes.

WATER ICING

8 *ozs. icing sugar.*   1 *teaspoonful lemon juice.*
3 *tablespoonfuls cold water.*

Beat well together, any colouring desired may be added.

CHRISTMAS CAKE

Mark 1—3-3½ hours

3 *ozs. lard.*	8 *ozs. plain flour.*	3 *ozs. candied peel.*
3 *ozs. margarine.*	8 *ozs. sultanas.*	2 *ozs. shelled almonds.*
6 *ozs. castor or*	8 *ozs. currants.*	¼ *teaspoonful mixed spice.*
brown sugar.	2 *ozs. raisins.*	1½ *ozs. dark treacle.*
3 *eggs.*	1 *oz. cherries.*	*A pinch of salt.*

(1) Cream the fats and sugar. (2) Beat in egg a little at a time. (3) Sift in flour, salt and spice. (4) Then sift in the cleaned fruit and nuts, last of all, treacle. Put into a 7½ in. diameter cake tin lined with greaseproof paper and a collar of brown paper tied round the outside of tin. Smooth the mixture to avoid a peak forming in the centre. Bake on the fourth or fifth runner at Mark 1 for 3-3½ hours. Double this quantity can be baked in a 9 in. tin for approx. 4 hours.

SIMNEL CAKE

Mark 2—2-2½ hours

6 *ozs. butter.*	6 *ozs. sugar.*	1 *oz. candied peel, chopped finely.*
6 *ozs. currants.*	8 *ozs. flour.*	½ *teaspoonful mixed spice.*
6 *ozs. sultanas.*	3 *eggs.*	½ *teaspoonful baking powder.*

(1) Beat the butter and sugar to a cream. (2) Beat in the eggs and add the dry ingredients, fruit and spice, and mix well together. (3) Put the mixture into a greased and paper lined tin. (4) Place in the oven on the 4th runner and bake for 2-2½ hours. (5) Take out the cake, and egg-wash round the edge. (6) Roll out the almond paste in a long roll and put round the cake; mark with a fork, egg-wash and put back into the oven to brown. (7) When cake is cold, decorate the centre with crystallized fruits, Easter eggs, etc.

Almond Paste for Top of Cake

½ *lb. ground almonds.*	½ *lb. castor sugar.*
1 *tablespoonful rum (if desired).*	1 *egg.*

Mix ingredients together, work well with hands until smooth but not oily.

VICTORIA SPONGE SANDWICH

Mark 5—20-25 minutes

3 *ozs. butter.*	4 *ozs. castor sugar.*
5 *ozs. flour.*	*Pinch of salt.*
2 *eggs.*	*Level teaspoonful baking powder.*

(1) Cream butter and sugar together. (2) Add beaten eggs gradually. (3) Fold in lightly, flour sifted with baking powder and salt. (4) Put into a greased tin, 7¾ inches wide. (5) Place in oven on 3rd runner and bake for 30 minutes. (6) When cold, split and sandwich together with jam, or butter icing.

LUNCH BUNS

Mark 6—15-20 minutes

6 *ozs. flour.*	5 *ozs. sugar.*	4 *ozs. butter or margarine.*
3 *ozs. currants.*	2 *eggs.*	1 *teaspoonful baking powder.*
Little milk.	*Pinch of salt.*	½ *oz. candied peel.*
		¼ *teaspoonful spice.*

(1) Beat the butter and sugar to a cream. (2) Beat in the egg a little at a time, if curdling should appear, add a little flour. (3) Stir in the flour and baking powder, add spice, peel and currants. Blend well together, adding a little milk, if necessary. (4) Grease bun tins, and fill to three parts full with the mixture. (5) Put tins on baking tray; place in oven and bake on 2nd and 4th runners for 15-20 minutes.

TRI-COLOURED SANDWICH

Mark 5—25-30 minutes

5 *ozs. butter or margarine.*	6 *ozs. sugar.*	7 *ozs. flour.*
1 *teaspoonful baking powder.*	2 *eggs.*	*Carmine.*

(1) Grease and flour two sandwich tins 7 in. diameter. (2) Cream fat and sugar. (3) Add beaten eggs gradually. (4) Fold in lightly the flour sieved with the baking powder. (5) Divide the mixture into two equal parts, colour one half with carmine or cochineal, spread the mixture into the tins. (6) Place in oven on the 2nd and 4th runners and bake for 25-30 minutes. (7) When cold split and spread with chocolate filling, place the coloured half on the plain half, cut up and sprinkle with castor sugar.

POUND CAKE

Mark 2—2-2½ hours

6 *ozs. flour.*	6 *ozs. butter.*	6 *ozs. eggs* (3 *of average size*).
6 *ozs. sugar.*	2 *ozs. mixed peel.*	½ *oz. ground almonds.*
6 *ozs. currants.*	6 *ozs. sultanas.*	2 *ozs. glace cherries.*
Grated rind of ½ *lemon.*		¼ *teaspoonful baking powder.*

(1) Grease and line a cake tin 7 in. to 7½ in. diameter with paper. (2) Sieve the flour, salt and baking powder into a basin. (3) Add the ground almonds, cherries cut into four, also the cleaned and picked sultanas and currants. (4) Cream the butter and sugar together, beat in egg a little at a time. (5) Fold in the dry ingredients as lightly as possible. (6) Put into the lined cake tin, and place on the 4th runner in the oven, and bake for 2-2½ hours.

WALNUT CAKE

Mark 4—1½ hours

8 *ozs. flour.*	6 *ozs. butter or margarine.*
6 *ozs. sugar.*	3 *eggs.*
3 *ozs. chopped walnuts.*	¼ *teaspoonful baking powder.*
Little milk if necessary.	½ *teaspoonful vanilla essence.*
Pinch of salt.	

(1) Grease and line a cake tin with paper. (2) Sieve together the

79

flour, salt and baking powder, add the walnuts, reserving a few for decoration when cake is iced. (3) Cream the butter and sugar together. (4) Beat in egg a little at a time. (5) Fold in the dry ingredients as lightly as possible, adding a little milk if necessary. (6) Put into the prepared cake tin, and place in the oven on the 4th runner from top, and bake for 1½ hours. (7) When cold, coat with soft white icing, and decorate with a few halved walnuts. For decoration, cherries may be used instead of walnuts.

ORANGE LAYER CAKE
Mark 5—About 20 minutes

5 *ozs. flour.*	1 *oz. cornflour.*	½ *teaspoonful baking powder.*
Pinch of salt.	5 *ozs. butter.*	*Rind of* 1 *orange.*
5 *ozs. sugar.*	2 *eggs.*	*Little milk if necessary.*

(1) Grease and line two 7 in. diameter tins or one *deep* sandwich tin. (2) Sieve the flour, cornflour, baking powder and salt on to a piece of kitchen paper. (3) Mix in the finely grated orange rind. (4) Cream the butter and sugar in a basin, beat in egg a little at a time. (5) Fold in the dry ingredients, adding a little milk as required. (6) Put the mixture into two cake tins, place in the oven and bake for about 20 minutes, with the "Autimo" set at Mark 5. NOTE.—If one cake is required, set the "Autimo" to Mark 4 for 45 minutes. (7) When cold, split and spread with butter icing and coat with orange icing.

QUEEN CAKES
Mark 5—17-20 minutes

8 *ozs. sugar.*	10 *ozs. flour.*	8 *ozs. margarine.*
Pinch of salt.	4 *eggs.*	1½ *teaspoonfuls baking powder.*

(1) Beat butter and sugar to a cream, add eggs gradually and beat thoroughly. (2) Stir in flour, baking powder and salt. (3) Put into small paper cases or greased Queen Cake tins. (4) Bake about 17-20 minutes on 2nd and 4th runners from top of oven, with "Autimo" set at No. 5. Sufficient for 32 cakes. 2 ozs. fruit can be added if desired.

BANBURY CAKES
Mark 7—15-20 minutes

1 *oz. cake crumbs.*	8 *ozs. flaky pastry (see recipe on page 95).*
2 *ozs. sugar.*	2 *ozs. butter or margarine.*
2 *ozs. currants.*	1 *oz. candied peel.*
2 *ozs. raisins.*	½ *teaspoonful mixed spice.*

(1) Cream the fat and sugar. (2) Add the rest of the ingredients. (3) Roll out pastry thinly, cut out with oval-shaped cutter. (4) Put a spoonful of mixture on half the pastry, moisten edges and fold over. (5) Roll slightly, brush over with egg, and, on the 2nd and 4th runners, bake in a hot oven for 15-20 minutes. Sufficient for 10 cakes.

COCONUT CAKE

Mark 4—1¼ hours

| 7 ozs. flour. | 6 ozs. sugar. | 5 ozs. butter or margarine. |
| 3 eggs. | 3 ozs. coconut. | 1 teaspoonful baking powder. |

(1) Beat the fat and sugar to a cream. (2) Beat in egg a little at a time. (3) Mix in the flour and baking powder then the coconut. Add a little milk if necessary. (4) Put the mixture in a greased cake tin, place in oven and bake on the 4th runner for about 1¼ hours.

HONEYSUCKLE CAKE

Mark 4—50-60 minutes

| 3 eggs. | 6 ozs. castor sugar. | 4 ozs. butter. |
| 6 ozs. flour. | ½ teaspoonful baking powder. | |

(1) Sieve together flour and baking powder. (2) Beat together eggs and sugar for about 15 minutes, or until they begin to thicken and go pale. (3) Fold in the flour using a metal spoon, then stir in the melted but cool butter. (4) Pour into a 7 in. tin which is already greased and dusted with flour. (5) Place in the oven on the third runner from top, with the "Autimo" set at Mark 4 for 50-60 minutes.

VELVET CAKE

Mark 4—1 hour

4 ozs. butter or margarine.	2 eggs.
3 tablespoonfuls cold water.	½ teaspoonful cream of tartar.
8 ozs. castor sugar.	8 ozs. flour.
Pinch of salt.	¼ teaspoonful bicarbonate of soda.
A spot of each—vanilla, almond and lemon essence.	

(1) Beat the butter and sugar to a cream. (2) Beat in egg a little at a time, then add cold water with flavouring. (3) Sieve together cream of tartar, bicarbonate of soda and flour and stir into the mixture. (4) Put into a greased deep sandwich tin (7 in.). (5) Place in oven and bake on the 4th runner for about 1 hour at Mark 4.

CHOCOLATE LAYER CAKE

Mark 4—Approx. 40 minutes

2 ozs. cooking fat.	5 ozs. flour.
7½ ozs. sugar.	2 ozs. margarine.
1¼ ozs. cocoa.	4¾ ozs. milk.
2 large eggs.	1 level teaspoonful baking powder.
Pinch of salt.	1 level teaspoonful bicarbonate soda.
Vanilla essence.	

(1) Cream fats and sugar. (2) Blend in the flour, cocoa, baking powder, salt and 3¾ ozs. milk. Do not beat. (3) Add balance of milk (1 oz.) and egg to form a light batter. (4) Pour into greased or paper lined tin (7½ in. diameter). (5) Bake on the 4th runner at Mark 4. (6) When cold, split and spread with butter cream icing, and if liked, can be coated with chocolate icing and decorated with shelled walnuts.

81

CHERRY CAKE

Mark 4—1 hour

4 *ozs. sugar.* 4 *ozs. margarine.* 1 *teaspoonful baking powder.*
2 *eggs.* 8 *ozs. plain flour.* 4 *ozs. cherries (cut in halves).*
2 *ozs. milk.* *Pinch of salt.*

(1) Cream the margarine and sugar, add beaten eggs slowly. (2) Mix together flour and baking powder, add to the mixture. (3) Add cherries, mix lightly, finally adding milk. The mixture must not be beaten too much or cherries will sink to the bottom of the cake. (4) Put into a greased tin (6½ in. diameter). Bake 1 hour on 4th runner at Mark 4.

GENOA CAKE

Mark 2—2½ hours

3 *ozs. margarine.* 3 *ozs. lard.* 1 *level teaspoonful baking powder.*
3 *ozs. cherries.* 6 *ozs. sugar.* 1 *tablespoonful milk.*
5 *ozs. currants.* 3 *eggs.* 4 *ozs. sultanas.*
3 *ozs. almonds.* 4 *ozs. peel.* *Lemon rind.* 8 *ozs. plain flour.*

(1) Cream fats and sugar until light. (2) Add beaten egg a little at a time to avoid curdling. (3) Mix in sifted flour and baking powder very gently, then the milk and any flavouring. (4) Finally add the prepared fruit and place it into a paper lined tin (7½ in. diameter). Arrange almonds on the smoothed top. Bake on 4th or 5th runner.

THE MAKING OF SPONGE MIXTURES

The chief difference between this variety of cake and those made by the creaming method is that sponge cakes do not contain fat, and depend for their lightness on the air bubbles incorporated by the beating and whisking of the eggs. As sponge cakes are so useful and popular a little trouble should be taken to master the method of making them. They can be used for Jam Sandwiches, Jam Rolls, Sponge Loaves and Fingers, and for Tipsy Cake and Trifle.

Tins in which sponge cakes are to be cooked must be well greased with cooking fat and dusted with a mixture of flour and castor sugar. To obtain a crisp surface on a cake, the top may also be dusted before baking with a mixture of flour and sugar.

As eggs form the principal ingredient of sponge cakes and their lightness depends on them, it is important that they should be new laid; the slightest mustiness of a single egg is sufficient to spoil the flavour of the cake. It is therefore better to use new laid eggs, but preserved eggs, provided they are in good condition, are satisfactory, but each must be broken into a small basin to test for freshness before adding to the cake mixture.

SWISS ROLL

Mark 6—About 10 minutes

2 *large eggs.*	2 *ozs. flour.*	4 *ozs. granulated sugar.*
Pinch of salt.	1 *oz. warm water.*	

(1) Line Swiss Roll tin (12 in. by 9½ in.) with greaseproof paper.
(2) Break the eggs into a large basin. (3) Add granulated sugar and whisk, preferably with rotary beater, until thick enough to retain the impression of the whisk, i.e., about 15 minutes. (4) Fold in the sifted flour and salt, very gently and slowly. (Speed at this stage would knock out all the air you have just beaten into the batter). (5) Add warm water to help the batter to pour and settle evenly. (6) Pour into prepared tin and bake on 2nd or 3rd runner at Mark 6. Top surface should spring back when lightly pressed.

(7) Have ready some warmed raspberry or apricot jam. (8) Turn the cake on to a perfectly clean tea cloth wrung very tightly out of warm water and dredge liberally with castor sugar. (9) Peel off paper very gently, allowing to cool slightly before spreading with jam, and with the aid of the cloth roll up the sponge fairly tightly. Trim off the edges of the roll. (10) Put on a cake tray to cool.

SPONGE SANDWICH

Mark 5—15-20 minutes

4 *eggs.*	5 *ozs. sugar.*	5 *ozs. flour.*

(1) Well grease and flour two sandwich tins of the same size, about 7 in. diameter. (2) Whisk the eggs and sugar together until they are light in colour and firm enough to show the mark of the whisk. (3) Fold in the sieved flour as lightly as possible. If only 3 eggs are used, add 3 tablespoonfuls of warm water after flour is added. (4) Blend all ingredients well. This process should be carried out as lightly as possible, to prevent breaking down the air bubbles. (5) Pour equal quantities of the mixture into the two tins. (6) Place in oven on the 2nd and 4th runners and bake for 15 to 20 minutes. The sandwich on the 2nd runner will be baked a few minutes earlier than that on the 4th. (7) Cool on a wire cake tray—When cold, sandwich together with jam, or butter icing. (8) Dredge with castor sugar.

SPONGE BORDER MOULD

Mark 4—25 minutes

3 *ozs. flour.*	3 *ozs. granulated sugar.*
3 *eggs.*	1 *level teaspoonful baking powder.*

(1) Grease a 9 in. dia. ring mould and dust with a teaspoonful of sugar and one of flour. (2) Beat the eggs and sugar, for about 20 minutes, to a thick creamy batter. (3) Fold in the sifted flour and baking powder. (4) Pour into prepared tin. Place on 4th runner and bake for approximately 25 minutes.

SPONGE CREAM BUNS

Mark 5—20 minutes

6 *ozs. sugar*	2 *eggs.*
3 *ozs. butter or margarine.*	½ *lb. flour.*
1 *teaspoonful cream of tartar.*	*A little buttermilk or sour milk.*
¼ *teaspoonful bicarbonate of soda.*	

(1) Beat sugar and eggs together, add melted fat, sifted flour, and milk. (2) Mix together bicarbonate of soda and cream of tartar, and stir in the mixture which must be of a soft consistency. (3) Three parts fill greased bun tins or cake cases, bake on 2nd and 4th runners from top, about 20 minutes at Mark 5. (4) Allow to cool. (5) Then cut off the top; put in a little jam, and whipped cream; place tops on again, dredge with icing sugar.

CHOCOLATE SWISS ROLL

Mark 6—10-12 minutes

2 *eggs.*	4 *ozs. sugar.*	1 *tablespoonful warm water.*
3 *ozs. flour.*	*Pinch of salt.*	¼ *teaspoonful vanilla essence.*

½ *oz. cocoa, or 1 oz. chocolate powder.*

BUTTER CREAM (*see page 77 for filling*).

(1) Beat the eggs and sugar together over warm water for 10 minutes, until the mixture thickens. (2) Add the water and vanilla essence. (3) Fold in the sifted flour and chocolate powder, using a metal spoon. (4) Pour the mixture into paper lined tin, place in oven on second or third runner from top, and bake for 10-12 minutes. (5) Turn out on to sugared tea cloth, then spread with butter cream, roll up evenly and finally trim edges.

ORANGE AND CREAM LAYER CAKE—
A PARTY CAKE

Mark 6—About 20 minutes

4 *ozs. sugar*	4 *ozs. flour.*	2 *eggs.*

BUTTER CREAM ICING. GLACE ICING.

See Recipes page 77 using orange juice for flavouring.

(1) Make the cake by beating the eggs and sieved sugar together until thick and creamy. (2) Sieve the flour and fold into the beaten eggs as lightly as possible. (3) Pour into a greased sandwich tin and bake in a moderate oven with the "Autimo" set at 6 until cooked and lightly browned. (4) When cooked, cool on a cake tray. (5) Split and spread with butter icing made by blending the butter and sugar together and adding a few drops of orange juice. (6) Put together and pour over glacé icing made as follows:—

(1) Sieve the sugar, put into a saucepan and stir in sufficient strained orange juice to make the icing of such a consistency that it will just coat the back of the spoon. (2) Add a few drops of orange colouring and stir well.

MERINGUES

Mark ¼—Time 2-3 hours

4 *whites of eggs.*   8 *ozs. castor sugar.*

(1) Whip whites of egg till very stiff.   (2) Beat in two dessertspoonfuls of sugar.   (3) Fold in the remainder of sugar, very lightly, using a metal spoon.   (4) Put the mixture into a forcing bag and squeeze into egg shapes on to a tin previously greased and dusted with flour. (If preferred, the mixture can be put on to the tin with a tablespoon previously dipped in cold water).   (5) Place in the oven and leave till quite dry and crisp.   (6) To serve, stick two together with whipped cream.   N.B.   It is necessary for the "Autimo"to be set at Mark ¼ whilst pre-heating the oven.

BISCUIT MAKING

"**B**ISCUIT" comes from French, "bis"—two, and "cuit" from cuire—to cook, meaning twice-cooked, and the derivation is not hard to understand, for biscuits are essentially well baked and crisp, and many recipes taken from old cookery books describe how they were cooked a second time.

In discussing Biscuits, it is well to point out that the housewife must not expect to obtain the same results or to make all the same variety as biscuit manufacturers, who provide themselves with specialised and elaborate equipment, including ovens of varying temperatures, through which the biscuits travel, so that they can be subjected to any degree of temperature required.

There are, however, a number of very attractive and popular biscuits which can be made at home with little trouble.   The following recipes are examples of "easy-to-make" biscuits.

BRANDY SNAPS

Mark 3—15 minutes

4 *ozs. flour.*   4 *ozs. butter or margarine.*
4 *ozs. golden syrup.*   4 *ozs. castor sugar.*
1 *teaspoonful ground ginger. Squeeze of lemon juice.*

(1) Sieve the flour and ginger together.   (2) Put the butter, sugar and syrup into a saucepan, and melt gently.   (3) Stir in the flour gradually, mixing thoroughly.   (4) Have ready a well greased baking tin, and put the mixture on to this in spoonfuls, bearing in mind that the mixture spreads and runs during the cooking.   (5) Put on the 2nd and 4th runner of the cooker with the "Autimo" set at 3 and bake for 15 minutes.

DIGESTIVE BISCUITS

Mark 4—20-25 minutes

4 *ozs. plain flour.*	4 *ozs. medium oatmeal.*
¼ *teaspoonful salt.*	¼ *teaspoonful bicarbonate soda.*
1 *tablespoonful milk (about).*	1 *tablespoonful sugar.*
3 *ozs. fat (dripping, margarine or cooking fat).*	

(1) Mix all dry ingredients together, rub in the fat. (2) Mix to a stiff dough with a very little milk. (3) Roll out thinly, stamp into rounds with 2½ in. plain cutter. (4) Bake on greased cake trays on 2nd and 4th runners from top of oven for 20-25 minutes, with "Autimo" set at Mark 4.

This mixing will make 24 to 26 biscuits of above size.

SHORTBREAD BISCUITS

Mark 4—15-20 minutes

6 *ozs. flour.*	*Pinch of salt.*	*Few glacé cherries.*
4 *ozs. butter.*	2 *ozs. sugar.*	*Little candied peel.*
Yolk of egg.		

(1) Grease and flour a baking tray. (2) Sieve the flour and salt into a basin, rub in the butter with the tips of the fingers. (3) Stir in the sugar and mix with the yolk of egg. If necessary, a very little water may be added. (4) Flour a pastry board lightly and roll out the dough. Cut into rounds or ovals with a crinkled cutter. (5) Place a small cherry or piece of peel on top of each biscuit. (6) Put on a greaseproof papered tray, and bake on the 2nd and 4th runners with the "Autimo" set at 4, for 15 to 20 minutes.

SPICED BISCUITS

Mark 4—15 minutes

8 *ozs. flour.*	4 *ozs. butter.*	2 *ozs. sweet almonds.*
3 *ozs. sugar.*	*Beaten egg.*	*Grated rind of half an orange.*
1 *level teaspoonful ground cinnamon, or mixed spice.*		

(1) Sieve the flour into a basin with the cinnamon. Add the grated orange rind. (2) Rub the butter into the flour, and mix stiffly with the beaten egg. (3) Roll out and cut into rounds with a crinkled cutter. (4) Brush over the top with a little beaten egg, mix the remainder of the sugar and chopped almonds together, and sprinkle over the top of the biscuits. (5) Bake in the oven on 2nd and 4th runners, with the "Autimo" set at 4 for 15 minutes.

CHOCOLATE RING BISCUITS

Mark 4—About 15 minutes

4 *ozs. flour.*	2 *ozs. butter.*	2 *ozs. sugar.*
Yolk of egg.	*A little water.*	*Chocolate icing.*

(1) Rub the butter into the flour with the tips of the fingers. Add the sugar. (2) Mix to a stiff dough with the yolk of egg and a little

water. (3) Put on to a pastry board and knead until smooth. Cut into rounds; place on a greased baking sheet. (4) With two cutters, cut out some rings to fit the biscuits. (5) Bake in an oven on 2nd and 4th runners, with the "Autimo" set at 4 until golden brown. (6) When cold, coat the biscuits with the chocolate icing, place the ring in position immediately, and decorate the tops with a little red currant jelly.

COCONUT BISCUITS

Mark 4—15 minutes

4 *ozs. flour.*	4 *ozs. butter.*	*Beaten egg to mix.*
4 *ozs. sugar.*	4 *ozs. coconut.*	$\frac{1}{4}$ *teaspoonful baking powder.*

(1) Sieve the flour and baking powder into a basin, with a pinch of salt. (2) Rub in the butter with the tips of the fingers, add the sugar and coconut. (3) Mix all the dry ingredients well, then stir in just sufficient egg to make it into a stiff dough. (4) Flour a board, roll out, cut into rounds or squares, and put on a greased tray. (5) Bake on 2nd and 4th runners with the "Autimo" set at 4 for 15 minutes.

EASTER BISCUITS

Mark 4—15-20 minutes

6 *ozs. flour.*	3 *ozs. butter or margarine.*	$\frac{1}{2}$ *oz. chopped peel.*
1 *egg.*	$\frac{1}{4}$ *teaspoonful cinnamon.*	1 *oz. currants.*
3 *ozs. sugar.*		

(1) Sieve the flour, salt and cinnamon. (2) Put the butter and sugar into a basin and work it together until it resembles whipped cream. (3) Beat in the egg, and fold in the flour, fruit and peel. Mix stiffly. (4) Flour a board, turn the biscuit dough on to it, knead up smoothly. (5) Roll out until it is about $\frac{1}{4}$ in. thick, cut into rounds, put on a greased tray. (6) On the 2nd and 4th runners, bake in the oven with the "Autimo" set at 4 until golden brown.

ORANGE BISCUITS

Mark 4—10-15 minutes

8 *ozs. flour.*	4 *ozs. butter.*	*Grated rind of* 1 *orange.*
4 *ozs. sugar.*	1 *egg.*	

(1) Grease a baking sheet, grate the rind of the orange, and add to the flour. (2) Cream the butter and sugar together, and beat in the egg. (3) Fold in the sieved flour and orange peel, mix to a stiff dough, turn on to a floured pastry board. (4) Roll out until it is $\frac{1}{4}$ in. thick, cut into rounds or ovals with a fancy cutter, and put on a greased baking tray. (5) Bake on 2nd and 4th runners, in a moderate oven with the "Autimo" set at 4 for 10 to 15 minutes.

FLAP JACKS

Mark 4—25-30 minutes

8 *ozs. Quaker oats.*   5 *ozs. butter.*   3 *ozs. Demerara sugar.*
2 *ozs. golden syrup.*   *Pinch of salt.*   *Squeeze lemon juice.*

(1) Melt the butter, sugar and syrup in a saucepan. (2) Stir in the lemon juice and oats. (3) Spread the mixture in a well greased Yorkshire Pudding tin, pressing it well down. (4) Place on the fourth runner with the "Autimo" set at Mark 4 for 25 to 30 minutes. (5) Remove from oven, and cut into fingers whilst still warm.

ALMOND BISCUITS

Mark 4—15-20 minutes

4 *ozs. flour.*   3 *ozs. sugar.*   1 *oz. sweet almonds.*
1 *egg.*   2 *ozs. butter.*   *Little almond or ratafia flavouring.*
About 1½ *tablespoonfuls milk.*

(1) Blanch and chop the almonds coarsely. (2) Cream butter and sugar together, add the beaten egg, chopped almonds, flour and flavouring. (3) Add sufficient milk to mix to a stiff cake batter. (4) Put small teaspoonfuls of the mixture on to greased cake trays, leaving room for the biscuits to spread. (5) Bake on 3rd and 5th runners with the "Autimo" set at Mark 4 for 15-20 minutes.

GINGER SNAPS

Mark 6—12-15 minutes.

1 *lb. flour.*   4 *ozs. cooking fat.*   ¼ *oz. bicarbonate of soda.*
5½ *ozs. syrup.*   ½ *oz. ginger.*   3 *ozs. water.*
7 *ozs. sugar.*
     (This quantity makes approximately 5 dozen).

(1) Rub fat into sieved flour, bicarbonate of soda, ginger and sugar. (2) Dough up with slightly warmed syrup and water. (3) Roll out ¼ in. thick and cut with 1¾ in. cutter. (4) Sprinkle with cold water and place on lightly greased tins.

ANZAC BISCUITS

Mark 4—15 minutes

1 *cupful flour.*   1 *cupful coconut.*
4 *ozs. butter or margarine.*   2 *tablespoonfuls golden syrup.*
1 *cupful brown sugar.*   1 *teaspoonful bicarbonate of soda.*
1 *cupful Quaker oats.*   1 *tablespoonful hot water.*

(1) Mix together all dry ingredients (except the soda). (2) Warm syrup and butter together, do not make hot, merely melt. (3) Pour hot water over bicarbonate of soda and mix all ingredients well together. (4) Roll into balls, put on greased tin, well apart to allow to spread. (5) Bake on 2nd and 4th runners, 15 minutes at Mark 4.

SHREWSBURY BISCUITS

Mark 4—20-30 minutes

4 *ozs. butter or margarine.*	4 *ozs. sugar.*	1 *egg.*
A little lemon rind, or a few seeds.	½ *lb. flour.*	

(1) Cream fat and sugar. (2) Add the egg, beat well, mix in the flour until it can be handled easily. (3) Turn out on floured board. Roll out thinly, cut into rounds, put on greased tin. (4) Bake on 2nd and 4th runners for 20-30 minutes with "Autimo" set at Mark 4.

GRASMERE SHORTBREAD

Mark 4—15 minutes

5 *ozs. butter.*	6 *ozs. white or brown flour.*
2 *ozs. castor sugar.*	1 *oz. ground or finely chopped almonds.*
¼ *teaspoonful salt.*	1 *teaspoonful ground ginger.*

(1) Beat butter and sugar to a cream. (2) Add dry ingredients, mix well until pastry is formed. (3) Roll out ¼ in. thickness, cut into rounds or fingers. (4) Bake in a moderate oven on 2nd and 4th runners for 15 minutes with the "Autimo" set at Mark 4.

OATEN BISCUITS

Mark 4—25 minutes

6 *ozs. rolled oats.*	3 *ozs. margarine.*
3 *ozs. flour.*	½ *teaspoonful baking powder.*
3 *ozs. sugar.*	¼ *teaspoonful salt.* *A little milk.*

(1) Mix the oats, flour, salt, baking powder and sugar together. (2) Rub in the fat and mix to stiff dough with milk. (3) Roll out to ¼ in. thickness and cut into 2 in. rounds. (4) Bake on greased trays.

A LESSON IN PASTRY MAKING

THE success of pastry making depends almost equally on correct manipulation and baking. Carefully made pastry can be ruined by incorrect baking, and correct baking cannot alone produce good results if poor methods have been used in making it. When baking pastry alone without any filling a really hot oven is required, but when pastry is used to cover or enclose uncooked meat or fruit, it is obvious that a slower oven must be used, otherwise the pastry will be overcooked before the filling is done.

General Rules for Pastry Making

Here are four methods of making pastry—shortcrust, flaky, rough puff and puff—but the general rules apply to all.

1. Keep everything as cool as possible. 2. Sieve the flour before use.
3. See that the oven is of the correct temperature before putting the

pastry in. 4. When rolling out avoid working in any unnecessary flour. 5. Roll in one direction only and handle the pastry lightly. 6. Always allow pastry to recover for 15-30 minutes before baking.

Shortcrust Pastry

Shortcrust pastry is the simplest to make and it forms the basis of many sweet dishes, such as tartlets, fruit pies, and some savoury dishes, such as Cornish Pasties. The necessary ingredients are:

> 8 *ozs. flour.*   3-5 *ozs. fat, lard, margarine, butter or dripping.*
> *Good pinch of salt.* ½ *teaspoonful baking powder.*
> *Cold water to mix.*

When a less economical pastry is required the proportion of fat can be increased to 6 ozs. or three-quarters by weight of fat to flour.

The Method

Sieve the flour, salt and baking powder into a basin. Put the butter into the flour and cut into five or six pieces, then proceed to rub into the flour until it resembles fine breadcrumbs. Make a well in the centre and with the aid of a knife mix to a stiff dough, adding the water gradually. The definite quantity of water cannot be stated, being dependent on the moistness of the flour, and whether the fat contains much water, approximately ¼ pint water will be found necessary to mix 8 ozs. flour. Flour the pastry board, turn the dough on to it; flouring the fingers, knead it up very lightly to work out the creases. Should pastry seem too moist do not add more flour, but put on one side and allow to stand five minutes. Then roll out in one direction, keeping the pastry into an oblong. This can easily be done if, between each rolling, the pastry is pulled into shape with the hands. The pastry is then ready to be used for a variety of purposes, such as cranberry and apple pie, custard tart, strawberry flan and syrup tart.

Heat resisting glass does not produce the best results for baking Plate Pies if very good under-browning is required. Greater satisfaction will be obtained by using enamelled or tin pie plates. If good browning is required on the base, pre-heat a cake tray, then place the pie or tart plate on to this hot surface.

When baking two pies, place them on 2nd and 4th runners from top of oven, reversing the position of pies after about 25 minutes' baking. If only one pie is being baked use the 3rd runner from top of oven. The first runner position from top of oven is not intended as a baking position, but can be used for hanging joints, poultry, etc., with the meat tin placed on a lower runner to catch fat, etc.

CRANBERRY AND APPLE PIE

Mark 7—About 40 minutes

> 1 *lb. apples.* ¼ *lb. cranberries.* 2 *tablespoonfuls golden syrup.*
> *Cold water.* *Shortcrust pastry.*

(1) Peel, core and slice the apples, put them into a pie-dish in alternate layers, with the cranberries. (2) Put the golden syrup on top of

the fruit, and add sufficient water to fill three-parts of the dish. (3) Roll out the pastry until it is rather more than ¼ in. thick, cut off a strip about ½ in. wide from the pastry, moisten the edge of the pie-dish, put the strip in position. Cover the top of the dish with the pastry, trim off the surplus, tap up the edges and decorate. (4) Bake in the oven with the "Autimo" set at 7 until golden brown. Time required about 40 minutes.

PLATE CUSTARD TART

Mark 6—30-35 minutes

| 1 egg. | 1 oz. sugar. | *A little grated nutmeg.* |
| ½ pint milk. | Shortcrust pastry. | |

(1) Roll out the pastry and line an enamel or tin plate. Be sure that all the air is pressed out from between the pastry and the plate. (This is important). (2) Cut off the surplus pastry and mark the edge with a fork or knife. (3) Beat the egg and sugar together. (4) Heat the milk almost to boiling point. (5) Pour on to the egg and whisk for a few minutes. (6) When cold pour the custard on to the pastry and grate over it a little nutmeg. (7) Put into oven at once on a pre-heated baking tray on the third runner from top with the "Autimo" set at Mark 6.

CUSTARD TART

Mark 6—35-40 minutes

| 1 egg. | 1 oz. sugar. | *Little grated nutmeg.* |
| ¾ pint milk. | Short pastry. | *Pinch of salt.* |

(1) Roll out the pastry and line a pie-dish. Trim off edges of pastry. (2) Warm the milk in a saucepan, add sugar. Pour over well beaten egg. Mix well. (3) Allow to go cold and fill pastry lined dish. Sprinkle with nutmeg. (4) Place in the oven at once on a pre-heated baking tray on third runner from top and bake with the "Autimo" set at Mark 6.

TREACLE OR SYRUP TART

Mark 6—About 30 minutes

Shortcrust pastry, about 6 ozs.   *6 or 7 tablespoonfuls golden syrup.*
4 tablespoonfuls breadcrumbs.   *Very little grated lemon rind.*
Juice of ½ a lemon.

(1) Mix the lemon rind and breadcrumbs together. (2) Roll the pastry out until it is rather less than ¼ in. thick, and line a round tin with it. (3) Put the syrup in the tart, add the lemon juice and sprinkle in the breadcrumbs and lemon rind. (4) Bake on third runner in an oven with the "Autimo" set at Mark 6 for about ½ hour until golden brown and evenly baked.

APPLE SLICES

Mark 6—About 20 minutes

6 *ozs. short pastry.*   *Sugar to taste.*   1 *lb. cooked apples.*
A little water.   2 *tablespoonfuls lemon cheese.*

(1) Roll the pastry out and line a Swiss Roll tin with it.   (2) Spread on a little lemon cheese.   (3) Peel and core apples, stew with a little water, add sugar, spread apple pulp over the lemon cheese.   (4) On the 3rd runner bake in the oven with the "Autimo" set at Mark 6 for about 20 minutes.   (5) White of egg meringue may be put on top if desired.

PLATE APPLE TART

Mark 7—35-40 minutes

8 *ozs. shortcrust pastry (for recipe see page* 90).   1 *lb. apples.*
A little cold water.   4 *ozs. sugar.*

(1) Line the plate with shortcrust pastry rolled thinly.   (2) Peel apples, slice thinly on pastry, cover with sugar, moisten edge of pastry with water.   (3) Cover with pastry, being careful not to stretch pastry, press the edges together and bake on the 3rd runner with the "Autimo" set at Mark 7.

APPLE PIE

Mark 7—35-40 minutes

8 *ozs. shortcrust pastry.*   2 *lbs. apples.*   3 *cloves, if liked.*
Sugar to sweeten (about 4 *ozs.).*   *Water.*

(1) Peel, core and slice the apples. Place in the pie-dish with the sugar, and sprinkle with water.   (2) Roll out the pastry a little larger than the pie-dish, cut off a strip about ½ in. wide.   (3) Damp the edges of the dish and cover with the strip, damp this pastry and cover with the remainder, being most careful not to stretch the pastry. (4) Bake on 3rd runner for 25 minutes, then transfer, if necessary, to lower runner, to ensure thorough cooking of the apples.
When cooked with a whole dinner, place below meat on the 5th runner and bake 50-60 minutes.
See page (xxii) for further details.

JAM TARTLETS

Mark 7—15-20 minutes

Shortcrust pastry.   *Jam.*

(1) Roll out the pastry thinly.   (2) Stamp into rounds which will fit easily into the ungreased Tartlet tins without stretching, allow to rest 15 to 30 minutes to avoid shrinkage.   (3) Place a small teaspoonful of jam into each Tartlet. Jam, to spread evenly, should be diluted.   (4) Bake 20 minutes at Mark 7 on 2nd and 4th runners

from top of oven if two trays are being baked, or on 3rd runner if one tray only is being used.

Lemon Cheese can be substituted for jam in LEMON CHEESE TARTLETS.

SHORT PASTRY FLAN

Mark 7—15 minutes

6 ozs. flour. $\frac{1}{2}$ teaspoonful salt. $\frac{1}{2}$ teaspoonful baking powder.
3 ozs. butter and lard mixed.   Cold water for mixing.

(1) Add the salt and baking powder to flour, rub in the fat.   (2) Mix to a stiff paste with cold water.   Roll out fairly thinly.   (3) Turn a sandwich tin upside down—place pastry over, to cover tin completely.   Trim off the edges.   (This method dispenses with putting rice, etc., inside the flan pastry).   (4) Bake on 3rd runner on a baking tray for 15 minutes with the "Autimo" set at Mark 7.

This pastry is suitable for vegetable flan.   Sweet pastry may be used if required for Fruit Flan.

VEGETABLE FLAN

Mark 7—20 minutes

One baked short pastry flan.   Cooked vegetables cut into dice:
1 hard boiled egg.   carrots, peas, onion, etc.
Salt and pepper. $\frac{1}{2}$ pint White Sauce.

(1) Fill flan with vegetables.   (2) Pour over white sauce, decorate with hard boiled egg—cut up, and chopped parsley.   (3) Place in oven on 2nd runner for about 20 minutes to brown.

FRUIT FLAN

Any variety of fruit can be used for filling the special pastry cases, such as sections of oranges, uncooked raw grapes, tinned pineapple, tinned peaches, or apricots, fresh strawberries, fresh raspberries, in fact any fruit that is in season, or if preferred, a combination of two fruits can be used.   The method of making is always the same.

FLAN OR SWEET PASTRY

Mark 6

8 ozs. flour.   4 ozs. butter. $\frac{1}{8}$ teaspoonful salt.
1 egg yolk.   A little water.   2 teaspoonfuls sugar.

(1) Sieve the flour and salt into a basin (no baking powder or raising agent is required).   (2) Rub the butter into the flour until it resembles fine breadcrumbs.   (3) Add the sugar, mix the egg yolk with a little cold water, and mix the pastry to a stiff dough with the egg and water.   A little more water may be added if needed.   (4) Flour a pastry board lightly, turn the pastry on to it, knead up to remove creases, roll out until it is about $\frac{1}{4}$ inch thick.   (5) Line sandwich tins or flan rings with the pastry.   (6) Avoid stretching the pastry,

trim off the surplus with a sharp knife, and prick the bottom lightly to prevent it rising and forming a bubble. (7) Butter a piece of greaseproof paper, place it inside the pastry-lined sandwich tin or flan ring. Cover with rice or dry beans. Pastry may be baked on the outside of flan tin, thus avoiding covering the bottom of pastry with rice or beans. (8) Bake until golden brown with the "Autimo" set at 6, and remove the paper and rice. N.B. Use 3rd runner for baking one flan, use 2nd and 4th for two flans. (9) Return to the oven for a few minutes to dry the bottom of the pastry. (10) When cold, fill the case neatly with fruit. The whole appearance of the dish depends largely on the neatness and arrangement of the fruit. (11) Cover with glaze.

There are several different glazes, and the most attractive is obtained by warming a little home-made red currant jelly and pouring it over the fruit. A less expensive glaze can be obtained by melting a packet of jelly to which some fresh fruit juice has been added. Needless to say when adding fresh fruit juice less water must be used for making the jelly, and it should not be poured over the fruit until it is on the point of setting. If put on hot it would make the pastry sodden.

FRENCH PASTRY

The same ingredients can be used as for Short Crust Pastry (see page 90), with 2 ozs. of sugar added, and a similar method employed, except that egg and milk should be used for mixing to a stiff paste.

COCONUT FINGERS

Mark 6—20 minutes

8 *ozs. French pastry* (*see previous recipe*).   2 *ozs. sugar.*
A little raspberry jam.   *A little egg.*
4 *ozs. coconut.*

(1) Roll out the pastry into strips about 3 inches wide, lay on a greased baking tin, spread with the raspberry jam. (2) Mix together the coconut, and sugar, with a little egg; spread unevenly on the jam, to produce a marbled effect. (3) Bake on 3rd runner in a moderately hot oven for 20 minutes. (4) Cut into fingers, sprinkle with sugar.

MAIDS OF HONOUR

Mark 6—20-25 minutes

1 *egg.*   1 *oz. sugar.*
1 *oz. melted butter.*   2 *ozs. ground almonds.*
4 *ozs. desiccated coconut.*   ½ *teaspoonful vanilla essence.*
Shortcrust pastry.

(1) Roll out the pastry thinly and line patty tins. (2) Whisk the eggs and sugar together in a basin till they are light and frothy. (3) Stir

in melted butter, ground almonds, coconut and vanilla essence. (4) Half fill the lined patty tins with this mixture and bake on the third shelf with the "Autimo" set at 6 for 20-25 minutes. (5) When cold sprinkle with castor sugar.

FLAKY PASTRY

Flaky Pastry is so called because the fat is introduced in small flakes, and the pastry when cooked is not short, but is in very thin layers and flakes when broken. The following is the method of making this type of pastry.

FLAKY PASTRY

8 ozs. flour.	4-6 ozs. fat, butter, lard or margarine.
Pinch of salt.	Squeeze of lemon juice if liked.
	About ¼ pint cold water.

(1) Sieve the flour and salt into a basin, divide the fat into four, rub one quarter into the flour with the tips of the fingers. (2) Make a well in the centre, mix to a soft dough with about ¼ pint of cold water and squeeze of lemon juice. (3) Flour a board, roll out into a strip about 6 in. wide. (4) Spread one-fourth of the fat over the middle third of the pastry, fold into three by placing the bottom edge two-thirds up the strip of pastry and bringing the top edge over so that it lies along the folded edge, then turn the pastry to the left so that the open side is towards the right hand. (5) Press the edges together with the floured rolling pin, dredge the board, allow to rest 10-15 minutes between each rolling process to permit recovery of resilience, and roll out again into a strip as before. (6) Repeat the process twice more, rolling in a quarter of the fat each time.

SAUSAGE ROLLS

Mark 7—15-20 minutes

1 lb. sausages.	Flaky pastry.

(1) Remove the skins and divide each sausage into two or three, according to the size of rolls required. (2) Roll out the flaky pastry and divide into an equal number of squares. (3) Place a piece of sausage in the centre of each, fold over, moisten the edges, press together and mark the centre and both ends with the back of a knife. (4) Brush over with beaten egg and bake on 2nd and 4th runners in the oven with the "Autimo" set at 7.

CORNISH PASTIES

Mark 6—45-55 minutes

Short or flaky pastry.	6 ozs. raw mutton or beef.
1 onion.	2-3 potatoes of medium size.
Salt and pepper.	Cold water.
Chopped parsley.	

(1) Cut the meat into small pieces or mince it coarsely, similarly

treating the onion and potato. (2) Mix all together on a plate with the salt, pepper and parsley. (3) Roll out the pastry until rather more than ¼ in. thick, cut into rounds with a plain cutter. (4) Put equal quantities of the mixture on to the pastry, moisten the edges, bring together across the top and flute the fold with the fingers. (5) Brush over with beaten egg and bake on a baking sheet on 3rd runner with the "Autimo" set at 6. N.B.—Less time is required for cooking if the meat used be already cooked.

ECCLES CAKES

Mark 7—15-20 minutes

8 *ozs. flaky pastry.*	4 *ozs. currants.*
1 *oz. chopped candied peel.*	1 *tablespoonful castor or*
A little grated lemon rind.	*brown sugar.*
A little mixed spice.	1 *oz. butter.*

(1) Mix all the ingredients together on a plate. (2) Prepare the flaky pastry according to the directions given on page 95. (3) Roll out until it is about ⅛ in. thick. (4) Cut into rounds with a large saucer or pastry cutter. (5) Put equal quantities of the currant mixture in the centre of each round, moisten the edges of the pastry with a little water; gather them up fairly tightly, turn over so that the smooth side is uppermost, and roll out with a rolling pin until the fruit just shows through the pastry. (6) Place on a baking sheet, and bake in the oven on 2nd and 4th runners with the "Autimo" set at 7 until golden brown.

ROUGH PUFF PASTRY

8 *ozs. flour.*	6 *ozs. mixed fats.*	*Pinch of salt.*
Lemon juice.	*Cold water (about ¼ pint).*	

(1) Sift flour and salt. (2) Cut up fats into pieces about the size of a walnut and add to the flour. (3) Mix into a dough with water and a squeeze of lemon juice. (4) Turn out on to board, knead lightly and roll out into a strip about 7 in. wide. (5) Fold pastry into three, press edges together to seal in air. (6) Turn the pastry to the right and roll out again. (7) Repeat this turning and folding process three times, but allow to rest 20-30 minutes between each double rolling, and again up to 1 hour before baking, to allow pastry to recover its elasticity, and avoid shrinkage when in the oven.

STEAK AND KIDNEY PIE

Mark 4—1¾ hours

Rough puff pastry.	1 *lb. steak.*	1 *tablespoonful flour.*
4 *ozs. kidney.*	*Cold water.*	¼ *teaspoonful pepper.*
1 *teaspoonful salt.*		

(1) Cut the meat very thinly into strips, and pass through seasoned flour, made by mixing the flour, salt and pepper together. (2) Cut

the kidney into small pieces and mix this also with the seasoned flour. (3) Roll up the strips of meat, placing a small piece of kidney inside each. Arrange neatly in a pie-dish. (4) Three-parts fill the dish with cold water and sprinkle in any seasoned flour that may have been left over. (5) Cut a narrow strip of pastry ½ in. wide. (6) Moisten the rim of the dish and place the strip in position, pressing it on firmly; then place the pastry over the pie, trim off the surplus, tap up the edges and decorate with the back of the knife. Use the trimmings to cut out pastry leaves and either a rose or tassel. (7) Make a hole in the top of the pie into which the rose should be placed with the leaves around it. (8) Brush over with beaten egg and bake in an oven with the "Autimo" set at 4 and cook for 1¾ hours. (9) When the meat is tender and cooked, remove the rose, fill up with stock or water.

N.B.—It is preferable for the meat to be stewed before being placed in the dish. Allow the meat to cool. Cover with pastry, and bake on 3rd runner at Mark 6 for half an hour.

PUFF PASTRY

Puff Pastry is used for rich dishes such as Mince Pies, Chicken Patties, Jam Puffs, and Fancy Sweet Pastry and Gateau. It is most important when preparing it, owing to the large proportion of butter to flour, to keep everything cool, and when possible to roll out on a marble slab or enamelled iron table, and in order to prevent the fat working through the pastry it should be put aside in a cool place at least two or three times between the seven rollings.

PUFF PASTRY

1 *lb. flour.*   1 *lb. butter or lard.*   1 *teaspoonful salt.*
Cold water to mix, about ½ pint.   1 *teaspoonful lemon juice.*

Sieve the flour and salt into a basin, make a well in the centre, add the lemon juice and mix to a soft dough with the cold water. Turn on to a floured board, knead with the fingers until smooth and free from creases. Then roll out into a strip about 7 in. wide. Shape the butter or lard into a neat cake, place in the middle of the pastry. Bring the top end of the pastry over to enclose the fat and the bottom end up so that it lies against the folded edge, then turn a half-turn to the left, press the edges together with the rolling pin and roll out in exactly the same way as described for rough puff pastry. Repeat seven times, putting the pastry aside for at least ½ hour between the second and third rolling, and fifth and sixth rolling. If time will permit it is better to wait between each rolling to give the pastry an opportunity of becoming firm. If a refrigerator is available, put the pastry in it between the rollings.

JAM PUFFS

Mark 7—15-20 minutes

Puff pastry.   *Jam.*

(1) Roll the pastry out until it is rather less than ¼ in. thick.   (2) Cut into circles with a fairly large cutter, place the jam in the middle. (3) Moisten the edges, fold a third of the pastry to the centre and the same with the remaining two-thirds, pressing the edges together. (4) Put on a floured baking sheet, and bake on 2nd and 4th runners in the oven with the "Autimo" set at 7 for 15-20 minutes.   (5) Cool on a wire cake tray and dredge with castor sugar, or if preferred, the puffs can be brushed over with a little beaten white of egg.   (6) Dredge with castor sugar and return to the oven for a few minutes.

MINCE PIES

Mark 7—15-20 minutes

Mincemeat as prepared below.   *Puff pastry or flaky, about ½ lb.*

(1) Roll out the pastry until it is about ¼ in. thick.   It can be a little thicker if wished.   (2) Cut out the required number of rounds, reserving the first rolling out for the tops.   (3) Line patty pans with the pastry; pile up an equal quantity of mincemeat in the centre of each lined tin.   (4) Put the tops into position, tap up the edges and decorate.   (5) Place in the oven on 2nd and 4th runners with the "Autimo" set at 7.   Cook until the pastry is golden brown and well risen.   The time will depend on the size of the pies.   (6) When cold, dredge the tops with icing sugar.

MINCEMEAT

½ *lb. raisins.*	½ *lb. sultanas.*	½ *lb. currants.*
½ *lb. dates.*	1 *lb. cooking apples.*	¼ *lb. candied peel.*
1 *orange.*	¼ *lb. sugar.*	¼ *lb. walnuts or almonds.*
6 *to* 8 *ozs. suet.*	*Salt, spice.*	2 *tablespoonfuls marmalade*

2 *or* 3 *tablespoonfuls sherry or rum* (*optional*).

(1) Chop the raisins, sultanas, and dates, or mince them.   (2) Chop suet and nuts finely.   (3) Bake the apples and remove pulp.   (4) Place all ingredients, currants, chopped raisins, sultanas, dates, apples, nuts, suet and sugar in a mixing bowl.   Add a little salt and spice to taste, also grated rind and juice of orange, if used, and the marmalade.   Mix well together, adding the sherry or rum, if used. Cover the bowl with a cloth and leave for about 12 hours.   (5) Stir the mincemeat again, thoroughly, and put into dry jars.   Cover closely with jam pot covers, and store in a cool dry place.

OYSTER PATTIES

Mark 8—12-15 minutes

8 ozs. puff or flaky pastry (see recipe page 95).

(1) Roll out thinly, cut into rounds for number of patties required, again cut smaller ones for covers. (2) Put on a baking sheet, brush over with egg. (3) Bake on 2nd and 4th runners in a hot oven about 15 minutes.

OYSTER MIXTURE

½ *oz. flour.*	½ *oz. butter or margarine.*
¼ *pint milk.*	1 *tablespoonful evaporated milk.*
6 *oysters.*	*A little lemon juice.* *Seasonings.*

(1) Make above ingredients into a sauce. (2) Add oysters, cut up, and evaporated milk lastly. (3) Put one teaspoonful oyster mixture in pastry shells, place on cover. LOBSTER may be used instead of oyster.

VEAL AND HAM PATTIES

Mark 7—40 minutes

8 ozs. veal.	*8 ozs. puff or flaky pastry.*
¼ *pint thick white sauce.*	2 *ozs. ham, or streaky bacon.*
Pepper and salt.	*Very little chopped lemon.*
Thyme.	1 *teaspoonful finely chopped parsley.*

(1) Roll the pastry out until it is rather less than ¼ in. thick. (2) Cut out fourteen rounds to fit patty pans. (3) Gather up the trimmings, roll out again, cut out and use these for lining the patty pans. (4) Mince the veal and ham, or cut into small pieces. (5) Blend with the sauce, pepper, salt, parsley and lemon thyme. (6) Put an equal quantity of this mixture into the patty pans, moisten the edges. (7) Place on the pastry tops from the first rolling out, brush over with beaten egg. (8) Put on to a baking sheet and bake on the 2nd and 4th runners in an oven with the "Autimo" set at 7 for about 40 minutes, according to the size of the patty and meat to be cooked.

CHOUX PASTRY

½ *pint water.*	4 *ozs. flour.*	2 *ozs. butter or margarine.*
½ *teaspoonful salt.*	3 *eggs.*	2 *teaspoonfuls sugar.*
Vanilla essence.		

(1) Put water, fat, and salt in a pan. (2) Bring to the boil, draw off the light, add flour. (3) Mix well, cook a few minutes, when cool add the sugar and beaten eggs, beat well until mixture is quite smooth.

ECLAIRS

Mark 6—30 minutes

(1) Put Choux pastry into a forcing bag, press out into finger lengths, on to a greased tin. (2) Bake in a hot oven on 2nd and 4th runners for about 30 minutes, or until dry. (3) Allow to cool, fill with whipped cream, and ice with chocolate or coffee icing.

CREAM BUNS

Mark 6—30-45 minutes

(1) Using the same recipe, (2) pipe out or drop Choux pastry in balls on a wet tray. (3) Cover with a meat tin to retain steam under the tin. Place on 2nd and 4th runners. (4) Do not lift the covering tin before 30 minutes. Allow to cool, fill with cream, and dredge with icing sugar.

JAM MAKING

WITH the aid of a modern gas cooker, jam making becomes a very simple task, for the burners can be so regulated that a large preserving pan can be kept at simmering point, or, when required the contents of the pan can boil intensely. It is very important not to allow the jam to stick to the bottom of the pan and burn.

The Theory of Jam Making

Although it is not possible in this book to discuss the theory of jam making in detail, some information regarding the behaviour of fruit and sugar when boiled together will be given, as the whole success of jam making depends on these facts.

Wholesome home-made jams generally consist of equal parts of fresh fruit and sugar boiled together. When cooked, it consists of the fruit itself and a form of jelly, produced by the boiling of the juice with the sugar. The setting or "jelling" of the preserve depends on the presence of pectin—a natural gum-like substance contained in the fruit—and acid. Without an adequate amount of both, the jam or jelly will not set, but provided the sugar, pectin and acid are present in the right proportion, a well set preserve is obtained which will keep satisfactorily almost indefinitely.

The making of jam would indeed be a very simple matter if all fruit contained the same quantity of this natural gum and acid, but this is not so, some fruits containing very much more than others. Moreover, the amount of pectin and acid present in any fruit varies according to its degree of ripeness, the acid decreasing as the fruit ripens, and the natural sugar increasing.

The amount of pectin is greatest when the fruit is just ripe. As it becomes over-ripe, changes take place in the fruit and the pectin breaks down, and this explains why jam should only be made from freshly gathered fruit which is in perfect condition. It is true that poor quality and over-ripe fruit is sometimes used for jam making, but the results will be disappointing unless other ingredients are introduced.

It is common knowledge that green gooseberries, slightly under-ripe plums and green apples when boiled with sugar set without difficulty, whereas strawberry jam, and jam made from fully ripe blackberries will often produce a poor set.

Fruit which is rich in acid and pectin is often combined with that which lacks these ingredients to make a good preserve. For example, red currants are combined with raspberries, and red currant juice is often added to strawberry jam. If suitable acid fruit is not available, tartaric acid or lemon juice can be added instead; the acid acts on the cell walls of the fruit, breaking them down and bringing the pectin into solution.

There is also another reason why acid is added—to prevent crystallization, for when cane sugar is boiled in the presence of acid, part of it is changed to invert, or a non-crystalline sugar, and so crystallization of the jam which is often present in the home-made variety is obviated.

As the ideal to be aimed at by the amateur jam maker should be a preserve of bright colour and fresh fruit flavour, attention should be paid to the methods advocated in the following recipes.

It will be noticed in every case that the fruit should be completely cooked before the sugar is introduced, so that the actual time of cooking with the sugar is about 10 to 20 minutes. In this way the temperature of the jam is not raised above 220° F. and there is then little risk of the jam losing its natural colour and flavour of the fruit. When ready, the fruit will sink in the syrup and the scum will stop rising. To disperse the scum, add a small piece of butter or margarine.

Although these few notes on the theory of jam making are very brief, it is hoped that they will be sufficient to enable the housewife to achieve success when jam making, and provided the instructions are followed carefully, perfect jam of good-keeping quality will be produced.

Sealing the Pots

Before passing on to the recipes, reference should be made to the sealing of the pots. After carrying out numerous experiments it has been proved fairly conclusively that the most satisfactory method to adopt is to cover the jam immediately it is potted and whilst still hot, with a circle of waxed paper. The heat from the jam is sufficient to melt the wax and to make a perfect seal. As a further precaution against the entry of mould spores, the top covers, whether of parchment paper, parchment, cellophane or screw caps, should be placed in position at once.

If cork linings are used to the screw tops, or if cardboard discs are used it is advisable either to dip them in a little alcohol or brush them over with vinegar. Both these liquids have the power of killing mould spores. Needless to say, the jars should be washed and rinsed in very hot water, and dried, preferably in the oven, before being used. This renders them sterile. After labelling, store in a cool dark place.

The first recipe to be given will be for STRAWBERRY JAM as this is the one which most housewives find difficult.

STRAWBERRY JAM

4 *lbs. strawberries.*   *Juice of* 4 *lemons, or*
3½ *lbs. sugar.*   1 *teaspoonful tartaric acid.*

(1) Hull the strawberries, put them into a preserving pan with the lemon juice or tartaric acid.   (2) Simmer until the fruit is cooked, and reduced somewhat.   (It is difficult to say exactly how long this will take, as it depends on the size of the gas flame, and the shape of the pan, but usually 35-40 minutes hard boiling is sufficient).   (3) Add the sugar, bring to the boil, and boil hard for 10-15 minutes, or until the jam sets when tested on a cold saucer.   (4) Pot and seal immediately. (See note on page 101).

STRAWBERRY AND GOOSEBERRY JAM

3 *lbs. strawberries.*   1½ *lbs. gooseberries.*   4 *lbs. sugar.*

(1) Hull the strawberries, wash and top and tail the gooseberries. (2) Put the strawberries and gooseberries in a preserving pan over a very low heat at first.   (3) Bring to simmering point, and allow them to simmer gently for about half an hour.   (4) Add the sugar, bring to the boil and boil briskly for about 10 minutes.   (5) Test for jelling. As soon as it sets, pour immediately into hot sterilized jars and seal with waxed circles.

CHERRY JAM

5 *lbs. stoned cherries, Morello or May Dukes are most suitable.*
3½ *lbs. sugar.   Juice of* 5 *lemons, or* ½ *oz. tartaric acid.*

(1) Put the stoned cherries into a preserving pan with the lemon juice or tartaric acid.   (2) Cook slowly until the fruit is tender and the contents of the pan have been reduced considerably.   Stir frequently in order to break up some of the cherries.   (3) Add the sugar, bring to the boil, and boil fast for 10-20 minutes.   (4) Test for jelling. When the preserve sets on a cold plate, turn out the gas, cool slightly (this is in order that the cherries may be suspended and not rise to the top).   (5) Pot and seal as directed.

BLACK CURRANT JAM

Owing to the tough skins of black currants, it is advisable to add water to the fruit in order that boiling may be prolonged until the skins are thoroughly tender. The excess of water must, of course, be evaporated before the sugar is added. If the sugar is added before the currants are cooked, it causes the skins to become tough and hard.

BLACK CURRANT JAM

2 *lbs. black currants.*   1½ *pints water.*   3¼ *lbs. sugar.*

(1) Pick the black currants, put them into a preserving pan with the water and simmer gently until the fruit is tender, the contents of the pan reduced, and the fruit thickened. (2) Add the sugar, bring to the boil, and boil for 5 minutes. (3) Test for jelling, pot and seal immediately.

RASPBERRY JAM

4 *lbs. raspberries.*   4 *lbs. sugar.*

(1) Put the raspberries into a preserving pan, and place over a low heat. (2) Cook gently at first, then simmer for about 20 minutes, the fruit should then be thoroughly tender, and the contents reduced. (3) Add the sugar, and boil for 5 minutes, or until the fruit stiffens when dropped on a cold saucer. (4) Pot and seal immediately.

RASPBERRY AND RED CURRANT JAM

2 *lbs. raspberries.*   2 *lbs. red currants.*   4 *lbs. sugar.*

(1) Wash and pick the currants and put into a preserving pan with the raspberries. (2) Cook gently at first, then simmer for about 20 minutes, or until the fruit is thoroughly tender and the contents of the pan are reduced. (3) Add the sugar, boil for 5 minutes. (4) Test for jelling, and if it sets, pot and seal immediately.

LOGANBERRY JAM

The same quantities and method as for Raspberry Jam.

GOOSEBERRY JAM

6 *lbs. gooseberries.*   7½ *lbs. sugar.*   2 *pints water.*

(1) Wash, and top and tail the gooseberries. (2) Put them, with the water, into a preserving pan over a very low heat at first. (3) Bring to simmering point, allowing to simmer gently for about half an hour. (4) Add the sugar, stir until dissolved, bring to the boil and boil rapidly for about 10 minutes. (5) Test for jelling, and as soon as it sets, pour immediately into hot sterilized jars, and seal with waxed circles.

PLUM JAM

4 *lbs. plums.*   4 *lbs. sugar.*

(1) Stone the plums, obtain the kernels from about an eighth, blanch them and put into a preserving pan with the plums.   (2) Cook very gently at first, simmer until the fruit is thoroughly cooked.   (3) Add the sugar, bring to the boil, and continue fast boiling for about 10 minutes.   (4) Test for jelling.   As soon as the preserve sets when placed on a cold plate, pot in sterilized jars, and seal with waxed circles.

PLUM AND APPLE JAM

2 *lbs. plums.*   3 *lbs. windfall apples.*   4 *lbs. sugar.*

(1) Peel, core and slice the apples and cook to a pulp over a very low gas, with just sufficient water to prevent burning.   (2) Add the plums which may be stoned, with some of the kernels, if desired.   (3) Simmer until the plums are cooked.   (4) Add sugar, stir until dissolved.   (5) Boil quickly about 10 minutes, or until the jam sets when a little is placed on a cold plate.   (6) Pot in sterilized jars, and seal with waxed circles.

BLACKBERRY AND APPLE JAM

4 *lbs. cooking apples.*   2 *lbs. blackberries.*   4 *lbs. sugar.*

(1) Peel, core and slice the apples and cook to a pulp over a very low gas, with just sufficient water to prevent burning.   (2) Add the blackberries and simmer until the fruit is cooked.   (3) Add sugar, stir until dissolved.   (4) Boil quickly about 10 minutes, or until the jam sets when a little is placed on a cold plate.   (5) Pot in sterilized jars, and seal with waxed circles.

DAMSON JAM

4 *lbs. damsons.*   ½ *pint water.*   4 *lbs. sugar.*

(1) Wipe the fruit, remove all stalks, and place in a preserving pan with the water.   (2) Simmer gently until the damsons are tender.   (3) Add the sugar, stir until it dissolves, bring to the boil and continue to boil rapidly for about 15 minutes.   (4) Test for jelling, if it sets, pot and seal immediately.

DRIED APRICOT JAM

1 *lb. dried apricots.*   3 *pints water.*   *Juice of two lemons.*
2 *or 3 ozs. almonds.*   3 *lbs. sugar.*

(1) Well wash the apricots.   Bring the water to the boil and pour on to the washed apricots.   (2) Cover and allow to soak overnight, or for several hours.   (3) Put them in a saucepan with the water in which they have been soaked, together with the lemon juice and the blanched almonds.   (4) Cook slowly until the apricots are thoroughly tender.   (5) Add the sugar, bring to the boil and boil rapidly for 10 minutes.   (6) As soon as it sets pour into sterilized jars, and cover with waxed circles.

FRESH APRICOT JAM

3 *lbs. sugar.*   3 *lbs. apricots.*   *Juice of half a lemon*

(1) Remove the stones from a quarter of the apricots, take out the kernels and blanch them.   (2) Put the lemon juice and apricots and kernels into a saucepan and cook slowly.   (3) Add the sugar, bring to the boil and boil for 5 minutes.   (4) Test for jelling.   As soon as it sets pour into hot sterilized jars and cover with waxed circles.

GREENGAGE JAM

4 *lbs. greengages.*   3 *lbs. sugar.*   1 *cupful water.*
Juice of 4 lemons, or 1 teaspoonful tartaric acid.

(1) Wash and wipe the fruit; stone about ½ lb., blanch, and put into a preserving pan with the rest of the fruit and the water, and lemon juice or tartaric acid.   (2) On a low heat, cook very gently at first. (3) Simmer until the greengages are thoroughly cooked.   (4) Put the sugar in, bring to the boil, and keep contents boiling quickly for about 10 minutes.   (5) Test for setting, if ready pot and seal immediately.

RHUBARB JAM

6 *lbs. rhubarb.*   6 *lbs. sugar.*   2-3 *ozs. bruised ginger.*
Rind and juice of 2 lemons.

(1) Wash the rhubarb, and cut the sticks in 2 in. lengths.   (2) Put into the preserving pan with the lemon juice, and with the ginger and lemon rind tied in muslin.   (3) Bring slowly to the boil, continue boiling until rhubarb is tender, stir as necessary.   (4) Add the sugar, and boil briskly for about 10 minutes.   (5) Test for setting.   If right, pot and seal at once.

MARROW JAM

1½ *lbs. vegetable marrow (weighed when peeled and seeds removed).*
1½ *lbs. sugar.*   1 *oz. root ginger.*
½ *gill water.*   1 *teaspoonful citric or tartaric acid.*

(1) Peel the marrow, remove seeds and cut into small cubes.   (2) Place the marrow in a mixing bowl with the sugar and water.   Cover the bowl and leave for 24 hours.   (3) Place marrow, sugar, citric acid, and bruised ginger tied in muslin, into a preserving pan.   (4) Bring to boil and boil gently in a covered pan from 1½ to 2 hours, or until marrow is clear and syrup thickens.   (5) Remove ginger, pour into clean warm jars and seal with waxed covers.

LEMON CHEESE

8 *ozs. sugar.*   4 *ozs. butter or margarine.*
2 *or* 3 *eggs.*   2 *lemons, rind and juice.*

(1) Put ingredients into a jar, place jar in pan of boiling water. (2) Cook until mixture thickens, stirring frequently.

MARMALADE

4 lemons, or 3 lemons and 1 large orange,   *2 lbs. sugar.*
   or 2 lemons and 2 large oranges.   *3 breakfast cupfuls water.*

(1) Wash and dry the fruit and cut each orange and lemon into 4 or 8 pieces. (2) Shred finely, removing pips. (3) Cover the shredded fruit with 2½ breakfast cupfuls of cold water, and the pips in a separate basin with half-cupful water. (4) Stand for 24 hours. (5) Strain water from pips and put with fruit and water in a covered saucepan. (6) Boil steadily 30 minutes. (7) When cool add the sugar. (8) Stir until boiling, again boil about 45 minutes, or until a little poured out on to a cold plate sets. (9) Pour into hot sterilized jars, and cover with waxed pot covers.

ORANGE MARMALADE

9 Seville oranges.   *2 lemons.*   *2 sweet oranges.*
8 lbs. loaf sugar.   *9 pints cold water.*

(1) Cut the fruit in halves and squeeze out the juice, removing the pips. Shred the peel as thinly as possible. (2) Put the peel, juice and cold water into a preserving pan and allow to remain for 24 hours. (3) Bring slowly to boiling point, and boil until the contents of the pan have been reduced by half. (4) Add the sugar, bring to the boil, boil briskly for 10 minutes. (5) Test for jelling, pour into sterilized jars, seal with waxed circles immediately.

LEMON MARMALADE

6 lemons.   *Sugar, 1½ lbs. to each pint of pulp.*
6 pints cold water.

(1) Wipe the lemons, cut in halves, squeeze out the juice. Shred the rind thinly. (2) Put the lemon juice, the shredded rind and water into a preserving pan and allow to stand for 24 hours. (3) Bring to the boil, simmer until the rind is tender, and until the contents of the pan are reduced by half. (4) Add the sugar, allowing 1½ lbs. to each pint of pulp. Bring to the boil, and boil fairly briskly for ½ hour. (5) Test for jelling. As soon as it jells, put into hot sterilized jars. Cover with waxed circles.

GRAPEFRUIT MARMALADE

4 grapefruit.   *5 lemons.*   *9 lbs. sugar.*   *6 quarts water.*

(1) Wipe the fruit, or wash it, cut it in halves, and squeeze out the juice. Reject the pips, and the centre core of the grapefruit. (2) Shred the rind of the grapefruit and lemons thinly. (3) Put the pith, peel, juice and water into a large preserving pan and allow to remain for 24 hours. (4) Simmer slowly until the contents of the pan have been reduced by half. (5) Add the sugar, bring to the boil, and stir to prevent the sugar sticking to the pan. (6) Boil briskly until it jells when tested on a cold saucer. The time required is generally from 15 minutes to half an hour. (7) Pour at once into hot sterilized jars and seal with waxed circles.

JELLY MAKING

ALL the important facts relating to jam-making (given on pages 100-102) apply equally to jelly-making. To quote one or two, successful jellies cannot be made unless the fruit contains sufficient pectin or natural fruit gum and acid. If either of these is absent, other fruit juice containing them must be combined, or prepared pectin, either in a liquid or powdered form, can be added, and acid, such as lemon juice, gooseberry juice or tartaric acid can be used. Another fact which applies equally to jellies as to jams is that long boiling after the sugar has been added spoils both the flavour and appearance. This is due to the fact that when the sugar is boiled, the temperature rises about 212° F. (that of boiling water) slowly and gradually, until its whole character is changed, and if the boiling is continued long enough the sugar changes to caramel—a brown substance with a very definite and marked flavour, so pronounced that it would ruin the jelly. It is, therefore, important to complete practically all the cooking before the sugar is added.

Jelly-making is a slower process than jam-making, and is not as economical a way of utilising fruit as jam, because only the juice is used, all the fleshy part and skin being discarded. For this reason it is regarded as a greater delicacy. Skilful jelly-makers produce a clear and transparent product of bright colour, having the flavour of the fresh fruit.

The success of jelly-making depends very much on the quality of the fruit, and unless it is thoroughly ripe and juicy, a very poor yield is obtained, and although in dry seasons, it is often necessary to add a good deal of water to the fruit in order to get a reasonable yield, the flavour is not as good as when very little water is added. For hard fruits such as gooseberries, and woody ones like raspberries, the addition of some water is essential in order to bring the pectin into solution, but it must be added with discretion. Practically all English fruits, both soft and stone, can be made into jelly without any difficulty, with the exception of strawberries and cherries.

TWO PROCESSES IN JELLY-MAKING

1. Extracting the juice.
2. Setting it by boiling the extracted juice with sugar.

The first process is a slow one and must not be hurried.

A very good way of getting the juice from the fruit is to place it in a large covered container; an aluminium basin or large saucepan would do, or glass or earthenware casserole; and leaving it in the oven with the "Autimo" set at ½ for an hour or two. If the fruit is not very ripe, "Autimo" setting No. 1 could be used. A quicker way of extracting the juice is to cook it in a large preserving pan over a very low gas flame, with the necessary amount of water added, but no sugar.

107

APPLE JELLY

8 *lbs. sharp cooking apples* (*windfalls*).   4 *lemons.*
Sugar, equal weight to liquid jelly.   3 *quarts water.*

(1) Wash the apples well, remove the stalks, but do not peel or remove the core.   Cut into thick slices or chunks, removing all maggoty parts.   (2) Put into a large preserving pan with the lemon juice, cover with water and bring slowly to the boil, allow to simmer until the apples are soft.   (3) Strain through a jelly cloth or scalded linen tea towel.   (4) Weigh the extract, that is the jelly which has dripped through the cloth, put into a preserving pan with an equal weight of sugar, bring to the boil.   (5) Boil briskly for 5 minutes.   (6) Test for jelling.   If liked, a few drops of red colouring can be added. As soon as it jells, put into small sterilized pots, cover with waxed circles.

MINT JELLY

Prepare this in exactly the same way as Apple Jelly, but towards the end of the time the apple and water are boiling together, put in a handful of clean fresh young mint, and allow it to simmer for about 5 minutes.   Later, when the sugar is boiling in the extract, the handful of mint can again be held in the jelly for about 5 minutes until sufficient flavour has been extracted to give the jelly a good flavour of mint.   Add a few drops of green colouring.   As soon as the liquid jells when tested on a cold plate, put it in sterilized jars and cover with waxed circles.

RED CURRANT JELLY

6 *lbs. red currants.*   1 *pint water.*   *Sugar.*

Gather the fruit when it is quite ripe.   If unripe, a good deal is wasted, as the juice is not easily extracted from it.   (1) Wash the fruit very carefully, but it is not necessary to stalk it.   Pick over to remove any leaves.   (2) Put the currants and the water into a preserving pan, heat slowly at first, and then simmer gently until the fruit is cooked.   It is permissible to break it with a fruit masher, or a wooden spoon.   (3) When no more whole fruit can be seen, strain through a jelly cloth or scalded tea cloth, and allow to drip slowly. (4) When all the juice has drained away, measure the extract, and put it into a preserving pan with an equal weight of sugar, bring to the boil and boil briskly for about 8 minutes.   (5) Test for jelling.   As soon as it sets, pour into small sterilized jars, and cover at once with waxed circles.

GOOSEBERRY JELLY

6 *lbs. gooseberries.*   2 *lbs. sugar, approximately.*   *Cold water.*

(1) Wash the gooseberries, there is no need to top and tail them.   (2) Put into the preserving pan, cover liberally with cold water, and bring

to the boil, and boil until the fruit is thoroughly mashed, stirring frequently. If too much water boils away, a little more may be added. (3) Strain through a jelly cloth, leave overnight. (4) Remove the pulp that is in the cloth, reboil with another 1½ pints of water, and strain as before. (5) Combine the two extracts, weigh, and to each pound allow 1 lb. sugar. Put the juice and sugar into a preserving pan, bring to the boil, boil hard for 5 minutes. (6) Test for jelling. Pot and seal as directed.

DAMSON AND APPLE JELLY

3 *lbs. damsons.*	6 *lbs. apples.*
2 *quarts water.*	*Sugar.*

(1) Wash the apples, remove any damaged parts, slice without peeling or coring, put them with the damsons in the pan. (2) Add the water and simmer gently until the fruit is mashed. (3) Strain through a jelly cloth. (4) When all the juice has dripped through, weigh it, put it into a preserving pan or saucepan, bring to the boil. (5) Add an equal weight of sugar, and boil briskly for eight to ten minutes. (6) As soon as the jelly sets when tested on a cold plate, put it into hot sterilized pots. Cover with waxed circles and tie down when cold.

PEAR JELLY

4 *lbs. pears.*	3 *pints water.*	4 *lemons.*
5 *or 6 cloves.*	*Sugar.*	*Small piece of cinnamon.*

(1) Wash the pears, and slice without peeling or coring. Cover immediately with cold water to prevent the fruit discolouring. (2) Add the cloves, cinnamon and lemon juice and the thinly peeled rind of 1 lemon. (3) Cook very slowly for 2 hours, or until the pears are tender and mashed. (4) Strain through a cloth, weigh the strained juice, put into a saucepan with an equal weight of sugar. (5) Stir until it comes to the boil, then simmer for 10 minutes. (6) Test for jelling. As soon as it sets when put on to a cold plate, pot, cover with waxed circles and tie down when cold.

PICKLES AND CHUTNEYS

PICKLED PEARS

7 *lbs. pears.*	4 *lbs. sugar.*
1 *stick cinnamon, about 4 in.*	½ *oz. cloves.*
3 *pints vinegar.*	*Rind and juice of 1 orange.*
Rind of half a lemon.	1 *piece of root ginger.*
¼ *teaspoonful allspice.*	

(1) Peel the pears and cut them into equal sized pieces, either eighths or quarters, according to the size of the pears. (2) Crush the root

ginger and put it with the other spices in a piece of muslin, and tie it up. (3) Put the sugar on to boil with the spices, orange and lemon if available, with the prepared pears, and simmer very slowly until they are quite tender. The time required is about 1½ hours. (4) Put the pears neatly into pickle or jam jars. (5) Boil the vinegar until it becomes slightly syrupy and pour over the fruit, and cover entirely. (6) Tie the jars down and keep for several months before using.

PICKLED ONIONS

4 *lbs. onions.*   *Spiced vinegar.*   *Brine.*

(1) Peel the onions, and put to soak in sufficient brine to cover. The strength of the brine should be 1 tablespoonful of salt to every pint of water. (2) Soak for 24 hours. (3) Drain the onions, pack them neatly into jars, and pour cold spiced vinegar over.

PICKLED CABBAGE

1 *red pickling cabbage.*   1 *dessertspoonful pepper.*
1 *tablespoonful allspice.*   1 *quart vinegar.*

(1) Cut the cabbage into quarters or eighths, according to its size. (2) Discard the outer leaves and hard centre core; then shred each section evenly. (3) Place the cabbage out on a dish, sprinkle each layer with salt, and leave until next day. (4) Put the cabbage in a colander, and allow to drain thoroughly. This must not be over-looked, otherwise the pickle will be too salt. (5) Put the cabbage in a large jar, pour on the spiced vinegar made by boiling the vinegar for 20 minutes, with the spices. (6) Tie down when cold, and use within a month. It is not advisable to keep Pickled Cabbage too long as it loses its crispness.
N.B.   If preferred, spiced vinegar prepared according to directions given on page 111 can be used.

MARROW PICKLE

1½ *lbs. vegetable marrow.*   4 *ozs. onions.*
6 *ozs. sultanas (or dates).*   ½ *lb. cooking apples.*
6 *peppercorns.*   4 *ozs. sugar.*
¾ *pint vinegar.*   ½ *teaspoonful cinnamon.*
1 *teaspoonful ginger.*   *Salt.*

(1) Cut marrow into cubes, sprinkle with salt and stand for 12 hours. (2) Strain off the liquor and put marrow into a saucepan, with chopped apples, onions, sugar, vinegar, dried fruit and spices. (3) Stir over a low gas until sugar dissolves. and ingredients reach boiling point. (4) Cover the pan, cook for about 45 minutes, or until mixture is quite thick. (5) Stir frequently to prevent pickle sticking to saucepan. (6) Pour into hot sterilized jars, and cover with waxed pot covers.

SPICED VINEGAR

1 *quart vinegar.*	2 *ozs. peppercorns.*
2 *ozs. bruised ginger.*	1 *clove of garlic.*
Small stick of horse-radish, if available.	8 *cloves.*
1½ *ozs. mustard seed.*	4 *blades of mace.*

(1) Put all the spices into a saucepan with the vinegar. (2) Allow to simmer very slowly for 20 minutes. The horse-radish can be omitted if a hot pickle is not preferred. If used, however, the horse-radish should be scraped.

DAMSON PICKLE

4 *lbs. damsons.*	1 *lb. onions.*	2 *small cups vinegar.*
2 *lbs. sugar.*	1 *cupful water.*	

The following spices tied in a muslin bag:—

3 *small pieces root ginger.*	1 *tablespoonful peppercorns.*
8 *cloves.*	1 *teaspoonful ground cinnamon.*
½ *teaspoonful ground mace.*	¼ *teaspoonful cayenne pepper.*
¼ *teaspoonful paprika (optional)*	½ *teaspoonful allspice.*
2 *sprigs fresh thyme.*	1 *sprig marjoram.*

(1) Wash the damsons, and chop the onions. (2) Place in a saucepan with the water, vinegar and bag of spices. (3) Bring to boil, press the damsons gently with a wooden spoon, removing as many stones as possible as they boil up, simmer for about 30 minutes. (4) Add 2 lbs. sugar (or more if liked). Stir frequently and boil until very thick, usually 40 to 60 minutes. (5) Pour into hot sterilized jars, and cover closely.

TOMATO SAUCE

6 *lbs. tomatoes.*	¾ *oz. salt.*
½ *lb. sugar.*	¼ *oz. paprika pepper.*
½ *pt. spiced vinegar.*	

(1 & 2) Prepare the spiced vinegar according to directions given above. (3) Wash the tomatoes, cut them in halves, put them into a saucepan, heating slowly at first. (4) Boil until much of the moisture is given off. (5) Rub the tomatoes through a sieve, and put the tomato puree in a saucepan with the sugar, vinegar, pepper and salt. (6) Bring to the boil, carefully stirring to prevent contents from sticking to the pan, continue to boil until the sauce is of the right consistency. It must not be too thick or too liquid, but should be rather like rich cream. (7) Pour into hot sterilized sauce bottles and seal when cold.

APPLE CHUTNEY

2 *lbs. apples.*   1 *lb. sultanas.*
$\frac{1}{4}$ *oz. mustard seed.* $\frac{1}{4}$ *oz. salt.*
$\frac{1}{8}$ *teaspoonful cayenne pepper.* $\frac{1}{2}$ *lb. onions.*
2 *lbs. brown sugar.*   1 *banana.*
Juice of half a lemon and $\frac{1}{2}$ *oz. whole ginger.*
    very little grated rind. $1\frac{1}{2}$ *pints vinegar.*

(1) Peel, slice and chop apples, onions and banana. (2) Put into a saucepan with the lemon juice and rind, vinegar, sultanas, and the condiments. (3) Tie the ginger and mustard seed in a small piece of muslin, and cook with the other ingredients. (4) Boil very slowly until all ingredients are tender, and until the vinegar has evaporated sufficiently to make the mixture of a chutney consistency. (5) Throw away the ginger, and mustard seed. (6) Put the chutney into sterilized jars, and when cold, tie down.

FRUIT BOTTLING

THE bottling of fruit can be carried out satisfactorily by an amateur if a good gas cooker is available, and it is a matter of choice whether the oven or hotplate is used. The hotplate method is, however, to be recommended unless a large fish kettle, saucepan or similar flat bottomed vessel is not available. Directions will be given for both methods.

Before proceeding it will be helpful if an explanation is given of the process of "bottling" and how it keeps fruit and vegetables in a wholesome condition.

Decay in fruit and vegetables is due to the presence of micro-organisms, all of which must be destroyed if the preserves are to be satisfactory. Moreover, it is also essential to prevent the entry of any other micro-organisms into the containers when once the contents have been rendered sterile, or bacterial life destroyed. In fruit bottling this is done by heat, and the bottles are then made airtight either by the use of special vacuum bottles or by sealing with mutton fat and covering with parchment paper or bladder.

Undoubtedly the most satisfactory method is to use the proper bottles, as there is then little risk of a faulty seal, resulting in the spoilage of the contents. Vacuum bottles are obtainable in several sizes and glass or metal lids can be used. Rubber bands have to be used in conjunction with the bottles to make an airtight seal between the lids and rims, and the lids are kept in position by screw bands or clips during the sterilizing process.

Preparing the Fruit

Wash the fruit in the ordinary way, rejecting any that is over-ripe. Grade it, putting all of the same size into one bottle. A clean, smooth piece of wood or a bone spoon should be used for packing the bottles.

Tough skins from nectarines and peaches should be removed before bottling; this is quickly done by dropping the fruit into boiling water for a minute or two when the skins will peel off easily. It is advisable to wash blackberries and loganberries in water containing a little salt in order to draw out the grubs often found in them. Fill the bottles to within half an inch of the top, then prepare a syrup by dissolving one to one and a half pounds of sugar to two pints of water, according to the sweetness of the fruit. Put the sugar on to boil with the water, remove any scum that rises, allow the syrup to cool and then pour it over the fruit.

In order to prevent the bottles coming in close contact with the bottom of the sterilizer, possibly causing them to crack, some non-conducting material such as a piece of thick felt, slats of wood or several thicknesses of brown paper should be then put in the bottom of the sterilizer.

Place the bottles, which should be of even size, in a large fish kettle or sterilizer, having previously placed the lids in position and fastened them with the screw bands or clips. The bands should be screwed on tightly and then unscrewed a half-turn. Place sufficient water in the sterilizer to cover the bottles completely, place over a low gas and bring very slowly to a temperature of 165° F. taking 1½ hours to do so, and maintain this temperature for 30 minutes. For some soft fruits which cook very quickly, such as raspberries and currants, the length of time they remain in the sterilizer at a temperature of 165° F. can be shortened to 15 to 20 minutes. Lift the bottles out of the sterilizer, place on a wooden table, or if on to a metal surface, it should be covered with several thicknesses of paper. Screw the bands down tightly. Next day unscrew the bands and test the seal by ascertaining whether the lid is absolutely firm. If the seal is perfect and the bottles airtight it should be possible to lift and hold the bottles by the lid.

If a thermometer is not available, the water should be raised to simmering point, that is, when small bubbles can be seen rising from the bottom of the sterilizer and bursting on the surface of the water.

If special vacuum bottles are not being used, but jam jars or pickle jars instead, a slightly different procedure must be followed. The bottles must be packed in exactly the same way and the fruit covered with syrup.

They should then be placed in the fish kettle on some good non-conducting material, cold water should then be poured in so that it just comes to the neck of the bottle. It is therefore important to use bottles of the same size and height. Put over a low gas and bring very slowly to the same temperature, namely 180° F. or simmering point, and allow it to remain at this temperature for 20 to 30 minutes, according to the fruit being cooked. Plums should show a cracked skin and gooseberries should change their colour, becoming pale, and the skins of a few should also have cracked. The bottles should then be lifted on to a wooden table and about half an inch of melted mutton fat poured on to each, tied down with bladder or strong parchment paper.

When tying down, use damp string and take great care to make a firm knot. When the string dries, it shrinks and tightens.

The Oven Method of Fruit Bottling

The method of preparing fruit and packing the bottles is the same, but the syrup is not put into the jars until the fruit is cooked. After filling the jars with fruit they should be stood on a baking sheet or tray and placed in a very slow oven, and allowed to cook slowly until the fruit begins to crack, change colour, and have the appearance of being cooked.

It must also show signs of shrinkage, but must not be allowed to get too dry. Remove one bottle at a time from the oven, fill up with boiling syrup, place the rubber bands, glass lids and screw bands or clips, whichever are used, in position. As it is important to maintain a steady temperature in the oven—and that only a cool one—the "Autimo" should be set at Mark ½.

Some non-conducting material such as asbestos board, sand or wood should be placed underneath the bottles to obviate cracking.

Times to be allowed for sterilizing in the oven:—

Apricots ..	.. 1 hour	Pears ..	.. 45 minutes
Currants ..	.. 1 ,,	Plums ..	.. 45 ,,
Cherries ..	.. 30 minutes	Raspberries	.. 35 ,,
Gooseberries	.. 30 ,,	Rhubarb	.. 45 ,,
Loganberries	.. 35 ,,	Strawberries	.. 35 ,,
Peaches ..	.. 1 hour		

PUDDINGS THAT ARE EASY TO MAKE

"Autimo" settings shown in this section represent the temperatures *IN THE CENTRE OF THE OVEN.*

Milk Puddings should be started with hot milk.

SEMOLINA PUDDING
Mark 2

> 1 *oz. castor sugar.*   1 *pint milk.*   1 *oz. semolina.*
> *Strip of lemon rind or little cinnamon.*   1 *egg.*

(1) Put the milk on to boil with the strip of lemon rind or cinnamon, when boiling sprinkle in the semolina. (2) Simmer very slowly until the semolina thickens and is cooked. The time required is about 15 minutes. (3) Remove the lemon rind or cinnamon, add the sugar,

stir in the yolk of egg; whip up the white stiffly and fold into the mixture. (4) Pour the contents of the saucepan into a pie-dish, bake in a moderate oven until slightly brown with the "Autimo" set at 2.

GROUND RICE PUDDING

Mark 1—40 minutes

1½ *ozs. ground rice.*   1 *oz. sugar.*   *Flavouring.*
1 *pint milk.*   1 *egg.*

(1) Mix the ground rice to a paste with a little of the milk. (2) Bring the rest of the milk to the boil. (3) Add the paste, replace over the flame and stir well until thick. (4) Turn into greased pie-dish. (5) Add sugar and flavouring. (6) When cooled slightly, add the beaten egg. (7) Bake for 40 minutes at Mark 1.

RICE PUDDING

Mark 1—1½-2 hours; or
Mark 3—1 hour

¾ *pint milk.*   1 *oz. sugar.*
Little grated nutmeg.   1½ *ozs. rice or soyaghetti.*
½ *oz. butter or margarine.*

(1) Well butter a pie dish, put the well washed rice and sugar in the pie-dish. (2) Pour on the milk, grate a little nutmeg over the top. (3) Bake in an oven with the "Autimo" set at 1, very slowly for 1½ to 2 hours. If less time is available for cooking, pour boiling milk over the rice and set the "Autimo" at 3.

If a milk pudding is cooked with a Complete Dinner, always use boiling milk. It can then be placed in the oven at the time of lighting, on the 3rd runner, and moved down to the 5th runner or base plate when the rest of the dishes are inserted.

DATE AND RICE PUDDING

Mark 3—1¾ hours

1¾ *tablespoonfuls rice or soyaghetti.*   1 *pint milk.*
1 *oz. butter.*   1 *oz. sugar.*
Little grated nutmeg.   10 *or* 12 *dates.*

(1) Stone the dates and cut into two or three. (2) Butter a pie-dish and place the dates in the bottom. (3) Wash the rice and put on top of the dates. Sprinkle on the sugar, and pour on the milk. Grate a little nutmeg on top, if liked. (4) Bake in the oven with the "Autimo" set at 3 for 1¾ hours.

N.B. If the Rice Pudding is cooked as part of an unattended dinner, the milk should be boiled and poured on to the rice immediately as this shortens the length of time required for cooking, and it can be cooked with the "Autimo" set at 5. See Dinner No. 12, page 145.

PLAIN TAPIOCA PUDDING

Mark 2—1-2 hours

1½ or 1¾ ozs. bullet tapioca.　　　1 pint milk.
1 oz. sugar.　　　　　　　　　　　1 egg.

(1) Wash the tapioca and soak it for several hours.　(2) Butter a pie-dish, strain off the soaking water, put the tapioca into the pie-dish, beat up the egg and sugar together into a basin.　(3) Add the milk, mix and pour the custard on top of the tapioca.　(4) If the pudding is to be cooked alone, set the "Autimo" at 2, and bake for 1 hour, or until the tapioca is thoroughly cooked—about 1 to 2 hours.

SAGO PUDDING

Mark 2—1½ hours

¾ pint milk.　　　　　　　　　　1 oz. sugar.
1½ ozs. sago.　　　　　　　　　　½ oz. butter or margarine.

(1) Well butter a pie-dish, wash the sago, and put it in the bottom of the dish.　(2) Add any butter remaining, placing small pieces on top of the sago, and pour on the milk.　(3) Bake in the oven for about 1½ hours with the "Autimo" set at 2.

APPLE AMBER

Mark 3—10-15 minutes

2 lbs. apples.　　　　　　　　Rind and juice of 1 lemon.
4 ozs. sugar.　　　　　　　　　2 or 3 eggs.
2 ozs. butter or margarine. 1 tablespoonful sugar to each white.

(1) Cook the apples with sugar, butter, rind and juice of lemon.
(2) When quite tender beat in the yolks of the eggs with a fork.
(3) Pour into a greased deep dish.　(4) Whip up the whites of eggs and beat in half the sugar, then fold in the remainder of the sugar and pile the meringue on the top of the pudding.　(5) Cook in a cool oven, at Mark 3 for 10 to 15 minutes.

QUEEN OF PUDDINGS

Mark 3—20-30 minutes

½ oz. butter or margarine.　　　1 oz. sugar.
2 dessertspoonfuls jam.　　　　¼ pint breadcrumbs.
2 eggs.　　　　　　　　　　　　The grated rind of half a lemon.
½ pint milk.

FOR THE MERINGUE:
2 large tablespoonfuls castor sugar.　　　2 whites of eggs.

(1) Put the grated lemon rind into a basin, add the crumbs, the sugar, and the butter cut into small pieces.　(2) Warm the milk and pour it over the crumbs, and allow to soak for about ¼ hour.　(3) Separate the yolks from the whites of the eggs, stir the yolks into the soaked

crumbs, put into a buttered pie-dish. (4) Bake in a moderate oven with the "Autimo" set at 3. (5) Spread the top with jam. (6) Beat up the whites of eggs, stiffly, stir in the castor sugar, pile the meringue rockily on the top of the pudding. (7) Return to the baseplate of the oven until the meringue is golden brown.

A variation of this pudding is obtained by using stale cake or biscuit crumbs, or a mixture of bread and cake crumbs.

WEST RIDING PUDDING

Mark 6—50 minutes

Short crust pastry.	*4 ozs. margarine or butter.*
4 ozs. sugar.	*Grated lemon rind or vanilla essence.*
4 ozs. flour.	*½ teaspoonful baking powder.*
2 eggs.	*2 tablespoonfuls jam.*

(1) Line a pudding dish with pastry, decorate the edges with leaves or rounds of pastry, and put a layer of jam at the bottom of the dish. (2) Cream the margarine or butter and sugar together, beat in the eggs, stir in the flour, baking powder and flavouring. (3) Pour into the prepared dish, and bake 50 minutes in the oven with "Autimo" set at Mark 6.

BARLEY KERNEL PUDDING WITH BAKED ORANGES

Mark 2—1¼ hours

2 ozs. barley kernels.	*1 pint milk.*	*1 oz. sugar.*
Grated orange rind.	*1 egg.*	

(1) Put the barley kernels in the bottom of a buttered pie-dish, sprinkle over them a little grated orange rind. (2) Beat the egg and sugar together, add the milk, and pour over the barley kernels. (3) Put in the oven with the "Autimo" set at No. 2. (4) Peel the oranges, remove all pith, and cut into slices of even size, removing the pips. (5) Place in a buttered pie-dish. Sprinkle sugar between the layers of orange slices, adding about 1 or 2 tablespoonfuls of water. (6) Sprinkle the top with sugar. (7) Place in the oven with the Barley Kernel Pudding, with the "Autimo" set at 2, and bake 1 hour and a quarter.

EVE'S PUDDING

Mark 6—1 hour

1 to 1½ lbs. cooking apples.	*4 ozs. sugar.*

MIXTURE:

4 ozs. flour.	*2 ozs. butter.*
4 ozs. sugar.	*1 or 2 eggs.*
1 level teaspoonful baking powder.	

(1) Peel, core and slice the apples. (2) Put them in the bottom of a pie-dish with the sugar sprinkled between them. If the apples are not good cookers, they should be cooked previously, with the sugar, in a

saucepan, and then transferred to the pie-dish. (3) Put the butter and sugar into a basin and cream thoroughly. (4) Beat in each egg separately. Fold in the sieved flour and baking powder. If the eggs are small, a little milk may be required to make it of a thick dropping consistency. (5) Put the mixture on top of the apples in a pie-dish. (6) Bake in an oven with the "Autimo" set at 6 for 1 hour.

BREAD AND BUTTER PUDDING
Mark 3—50-60 minutes

6 *or* 8 *pieces bread and butter.*	4 *ozs. sultanas or currants.*
1 *pint milk.*	1 *oz. candied peel (optional).*
1½ *ozs. sugar.*	2 *eggs.*

(1) Cut the bread and butter into even sized pieces and arrange in a pie-dish, sprinkling the fruit and peel in between. (2) Beat the eggs and sugar together and add the milk, and strain on to the pudding. (3) Leave to soak for 15 minutes, then sprinkle the top with a little nutmeg, if liked, (4) If a shiny sugary top is favoured, sprinkle the top with sugar and put small pieces of butter on top. (5) Bake slowly for 50 minutes to 1 hour in a cool oven, with the "Autimo" set at 3.

BREAD PUDDING

Ingredients and method as above, but using up "leftover" pieces of bread without butter, with the pie-dish well buttered.

BAKED CUSTARD
Mark 1—1 hour

2 *eggs.*	1 *pint milk.*	Pinch *of salt.*
1 *oz. sugar.*	*Little grated nutmeg.*	

(1) Break the eggs into a small basin, beating with the sugar for a minute or two. (2) Put the milk on to boil in a saucepan, and when almost boiling pour it on to the beaten egg, stirring meanwhile. (3) Strain it into a well-buttered pie-dish, and place this in a meat tin containing water. (4) Bake in an oven with the "Autimo" set at 1. If desired, the top of the custard can be sprinkled with a little grated nutmeg, mixed spice, or lemon rind.

BAKED STUFFED APPLES
Mark 6—45 minutes

3 *lbs. apples.*	8 *ozs. dates.*
1 *oz. almonds.*	*A little sugar.*

(1) Wash and core the apples, then cut the skin round the top of each. (2) Stone the dates and blanch the almonds, chop both and mix them together. (3) Half fill each apple with this mixture, then put in a little sugar, and fill with the date and almond stuffing. (4) Place in a

glass fire-proof dish or pie-dish, adding sufficient water to come a quarter-way up the side of the dish. (5) Bake in a moderate oven with the "Autimo" set at 6, till the apples are tender when tested with a skewer.

APPLE DUMPLINGS

Mark 6—About 30 minutes

6 *good cooking apples of medium size.*   6 *ozs. flour.*
3 *ozs. butter or margarine.*   6 *cloves.*
½ *teaspoonful of baking powder.*   *A pinch of salt.*
2 *ozs. castor sugar.*   *Cold water to mix.*

(1) Prepare the pastry by sieving the flour, salt and baking powder into a basin, rubbing in the fat with the tips of the fingers, and mixing to a fairly soft paste with cold water. (2) Divide into six pieces and roll each into a round. (3) Peel the apples and core, using an apple corer. If a corer is not available, the cores can be removed and the apples kept whole by using a sharply pointed knife and scooping the core out with a circular movement. (4) Place one apple in the centre of each piece of pastry, half fill the centre with castor sugar, place a clove in each, and fill up with more sugar. (5) Gather up the pastry to make a tight covering for the apple, moisten the edges so that the pastry will hold together, and place on a baking sheet with the smooth side uppermost. (6) Bake in a moderately hot oven, with the "Autimo" set at 6 until the apples are completely cooked. (The time depending on the size and kind of apple). (7) Remove from the oven, brush over with a little sugar water, dredge with castor sugar and return to the oven for a few minutes.

APPLE CHARLOTTE

Mark 3—40 minutes

Slices of bread.   2 *lbs. cooking apples.*
8 *ozs. castor sugar, or brown sugar.*   5 *tablespoonfuls water.*
2 *tablespoonfuls breadcrumbs.*   2 *ozs. melted butter.*
Pinch of cinnamon.   1 *lemon.*

(1) Butter a pie-dish, cut the bread into strips. Dip each piece of bread in the melted butter, and line the pie-dish with them. (2) Cut another piece of bread to fit the bottom of the dish. (3) Meanwhile cook the apples with the grated lemon rind, sugar, water and cinnamon, until the apples are tender and mashed. (4) Stir in the crumbs to the apple mixture. A little extra water can be added if the apples are very dry. (5) Put the apples into the lined pie-dish, cover with another piece of bread or two, also dipped in butter. (6) Bake on 3rd runner from top for about 40 minutes with the "Autimo" set at 3.

119

APRICOT CHARLOTTE

Mark 4—1 hour

8 *ozs. dried apricots.*	1 *or* 2 *apples.*
½ *lb. Demerara sugar.*	2 *ozs. melted butter.*
2 *tablespoonfuls breadcrumbs.*	1 *lemon.*
Stale bread.	*Little water.*

(1) Wash the apricots and soak them overnight. (2) Butter a pie-dish. (3) Cut the bread into strips of even size, melt the butter, but do not let it get hot; dip each piece of bread in the butter and line a pie-dish with it. (4) Put the sugar, well-soaked apricots, apples, lemon rind, and juice, and a little of the water in which the apricots are soaked, and stew gently until the fruit is thoroughly cooked. Stir breadcrumbs into the mixture. Discretion must be used, and a little more water added, if necessary. (5) Put the fruit mixture in the lined pie-dish, cover the top with pieces of bread dipped in butter. (6) Cook on the third position in the oven.

GOOSEBERRY PIE

Mark 6—40-50 minutes

1½ *lbs. gooseberries.*	4 *ozs. sugar.*
8 *ozs. shortcrust pastry.*	½ *pint water.*

(1) Prepare the fruit in the usual way by topping and tailing and removing stalks. (2) Put gooseberries in a pie-dish, sprinkle with sugar in between. Add just sufficient water to half fill the pie-dish. (3) Roll out the pastry until it is ¼ in. thick. (4) Cut off a rim, moisten the edge of the pie-dish and place it in position. (5) Place the remainder of the pastry on top of the pie, trim off the surplus, tap the edges. (6) Bake in an oven on 3rd runner with the "Autimo" set at 6 for 40 to 50 minutes, according to the time the fruit takes to cook.

CHERRY PIE

Mark 6—40-50 minutes

1½ *lbs. cherries, dark for preference.*	3 *ozs. sugar.*
8 *ozs. shortcrust pastry.*	1 *or* 2 *almonds.*

METHOD.—The same as for Gooseberry Pie.

BLACKBERRY PLATE PIE

Mark 5—50 minutes

8 *ozs. shortcrust pastry.*   1½ *lbs. blackberries*   4 *ozs. sugar.*

(1) Prepare the shortcrust pastry in the usual way. (2) Line a pie-dish or old soup plate, thinly with the pastry. (3) Put the cleaned and picked blackberries in the pie-dish sprinkling each layer with the sugar. Add very little water, 2 or 3 tablespoonfuls should be sufficient. (4) Cover the top with pastry, also rolled out thinly. (5) Decorate the edges, and bake in the oven with the "Autimo" set at 5 for about 50 minutes. The exact time will depend on the thickness of the tart.

TRIFLE

6-8 *sponge cakes.*   1 *packet raspberry jelly.*
3 *tablespoonfuls raspberry jam.*   ½ *pint custard.*
1 *tin pears.*   *Wine, if liked.*
1 *small tin raspberries.*

(1) Split the sponge cakes widthways and spread generously with raspberry jam. (2) Cut into three or four pieces and place at the bottom of a glass dish. (3) Strain the juice from the tinned fruit and pour it over the sponge cakes. The addition of sherry or home-made wine to the fruit is an improvement, but it is not essential. (4) Put the raspberries on top of the sponge cakes, then pour the hot custard over. Put aside to set. (5) Place the pears on top of the custard. (6) Prepare the raspberry jelly in the ordinary way by dissolving it in boiling water. When almost cold and just beginning to set, whisk the jelly vigorously until it is light and frothy and resembling stiffly beaten whites of eggs. (7) Arrange this in pyramids on top of the trifle and decorate with a few glace cherries and a little angelica.

CHOCOLATE BLANC MANGE

1½ *ozs. cornflour.*   1 *pint milk.*   1 *oz. sugar.*
1½ *ozs. plain chocolate.*   4 *tablespoonfuls water.*   ¼ *oz. butter.*

(1) Grate the chocolate coarsely, put it into a saucepan with the water. (2) Heat very gently until it has dissolved. (3) Mix the cornflour with a little of the cold milk, put the remainder on to boil, and when boiling pour it on to the blended cornflour. (4) Return it to the saucepan and simmer very gently for about ten minutes, until the cornflour is thoroughly cooked. (5) Stir in the chocolate and continue to cook for three or four minutes, adding the sugar and butter. (6) Stir well, put the mixture into the wetted bowl and leave in a cool place until set. (7) Turn out and serve with a little cream or custard.

PINEAPPLE CREAM

½ *pint of hot water.*   1 *tablespoonful sugar.*
1 *oz. Cox's Gelatine.*   1 *small tin pineapple, small chunks.*
¼ *pint cream, or condensed milk.*

Dissolve the gelatine in hot water, add sugar and pineapple with juice. Allow to cool, then add the cream, just before setting pour into a wetted mould and leave to set firmly. Turn out into a glass dish, decorate with a few pieces of pineapple and angelica, also whipped cream.

STEWED FIGS

(1) Well wash to remove all dust, put in a basin, add sufficient clean water to cover, and allow to soak for several hours. (2) Put the

soaking water into a saucepan, add 3 or 4 tablespoonfuls of sugar, according to the amount of fruit to be cooked, and if necessary add a little more water. (3) Boil the sugar and water to form a syrup, then add the fruit and simmer very slowly until tender.

If preferred, the cooking can be carried out in the oven. Make the syrup as described above.

(4) Put the fruit into a metal pie-dish or little aluminium basin, cover with the syrup. (5) Stew in the oven with the "Autimo" set at 4 or 5.

N.B. The same method can be adopted for cooking all kinds of dried fruit, e.g., Figs, prunes, fruit salad, apricots, apple rings.

OSBORNE PUDDING

Mark 3—50 minutes

½ *pint milk.*   4 *slices brown bread and butter.*   *Marmalade.*
1 *egg.*   1 *oz. sugar.*   *Pinch of salt.*

(1) Beat the egg and sugar together in a basin, with a pinch of salt, then stir in the milk. (2) Spread the bread and butter with marmalade, and place it in a buttered pie-dish, cutting it to make a better fit. (3) Pour over the custard made from the egg and milk. (4) Place on the 4th runner of the oven.

When cooked separately, remove the pudding as soon as the custard is set.

SPOTTED DOG PUDDING

6 *ozs. flour.*   3 *ozs. suet.*   3 *ozs. sugar.*
⅛ *teaspoonful salt.*   4 *ozs. currants.*   *Milk or water to mix.*
1 *teaspoonful baking powder.*

(1) Sieve the flour into a basin with the baking powder and salt. (2) Add the sugar, cleaned and picked currants, and suet, and mix all dry ingredients together. (3) Mix to a moderately stiff dough with the milk. (4) Have ready a pudding cloth sprinkled very generously with flour, turn the mixture on to the floured cloth, shape into a roll with floured hands, and roll in the pudding cloth. (5) Boil for 1½ to 1¾ hours. (6) Serve with a sweet white sauce if liked, or with sugar only.

LEMON PUDDING (BAKED)

Mark 6—30 minutes

1 *cup breadcrumbs.*   *Grated rind of* 1 *lemon.*
1 *or 2 eggs.*   1 *tablespoonful chopped suet.*
A squeeze of lemon juice.   1 *tablespoonful sugar.*
1 *pint boiling milk.*

(1) Put the breadcrumbs, lemon rind, suet and sugar and lemon juice in a buttered pie-dish, pour over one pint of boiling milk, allow to cool a little. (2) Separate the yolk from the white of egg, stir the

yolk into the mixture, allow to stand about 15 minutes. (3) Bake in a moderate oven half an hour at Mark 6. (4) Beat the white of an egg stiffly, add 1 teaspoonful sugar, pile on top of the pudding. (5) Finish off on lower shelf in the oven with "Autimo" at Mark 3.

PLUM SPONGE

Mark 5—40 minutes

1 *large tin or bottle of plums.*   1 *teaspoonful baking powder.*
2 *eggs—their weight in flour, butter, sugar.*   *A little milk.*

(1) Drain off the syrup from the plums and place them at the bottom of a buttered pie-dish.

Prepare the mixture thus:—(2) Beat the butter and sugar together until they resemble whipped cream. (3) Beat in each egg separately and stir in the sieved flour and baking powder as lightly as possible. (4) Blend all the ingredients thoroughly. (5) Put the mixture on top of the plums and bake for 40 minutes at Mark 5. Hand the warmed syrup from the plums.

STEAMED PUDDINGS

DATE PUDDING

Time—1¼ hours

4 *ozs. flour.*	2 *ozs. breadcrumbs.*
¼ *teaspoonful salt.*	1 *egg.*
3 *ozs. dates chopped finely.*	½ *teaspoonful bicarbonate soda.*
3 *ozs. shredded suet.*	½ *teaspoonful mixed spice.*
1 *tablespoonful treacle.*	*A little milk if necessary.*

(1) Mix the dry ingredients together. (2) Warm treacle and milk, mix to a soft consistency. (3) Put into a greased basin, cover with greased paper. (4) Steam 1¼ hours; serve with custard or white sauce.

VIENNOISE PUDDING

Time—1¾ hours

4 *ozs. bread.*	2 *eggs.*
1½ *ozs. loaf sugar.*	2 *ozs. castor sugar.*
1½ *gills milk.*	4 *ozs. sultanas.*
1 *oz. crystallized cherries.*	*Juice and rind of* 1 *orange.*
Very little grated lemon rind.	1 *oz. candied peel.*

(1) Grease one fancy mould with butter. (2) Put the loaf sugar into a small strong saucepan. Heat slowly at first until the sugar changes colour and becomes caramel. (3) Remove from the heat, and when cool, add the milk and allow it to dissolve the caramel by heating slowly. (4) Cut the bread into very small dice, put into the basin

with all the other ingredients. The cherries should be cut into four, the orange and lemon rind finely grated, and the peel chopped finely. (5) Meanwhile beat the eggs in a basin, with the castor sugar, and stir in the milk containing the dissolved caramel. (6) Then stir the custard into the dry ingredients. Allow it to soak for a few minutes, stir well again, and put into the mould. (7) Steam for 1¾ hours.

SMALL CASTLE PUDDINGS

1 teaspoonful baking powder, and milk to mix, about ¼ pint.
2 eggs—their weight in flour, butter and sugar.

(1) Sieve the flour with the baking powder. (2) Grease six or seven small castle pudding moulds, or, if preferred, a basin or a large mould can be used. (3) Put the butter and sugar into a basin and work with a wooden spoon until creamy. (4) Beat in each egg separately, fold in the flour as lightly as possible, adding a little milk alternately to the flour. (5) When well blended, three parts fill the small moulds or basin with the mixture, cover each with well greased paper and steam until they are well risen and firm. The time naturally depends on the size. If cooked in small individual tins, they will take about 35 to 40 minutes, but if in a big one allow 2 hours. (6) Serve with custard or chocolate sauce, or warmed jam.

STEAMED JAM PUDDING

2 ozs. margarine.	*2 ozs. sugar.*
1 teaspoonful baking powder.	*2 ozs. fine semolina.*
4 ozs. plain flour.	*2 tablespoonfuls milk.*
1 egg.	*2 or 3 tablespoonfuls jam.*

(1) Cream margarine and sugar together, beat in the egg. (2) Stir in the flour, semolina and baking powder, adding enough milk to mix to a stiff consistency. (3) Put 2 or 3 tablespoonfuls of jam in a greased pudding basin, pour in the pudding mixture. (4) Cover the basin with a piece of greased paper, and steam for 1½ hours.

DARK FRUIT PUDDING
(No Sugar required)

4 ozs. plain flour.	*2 ozs. breadcrumbs.*
½ teaspoonful spice.	*6 ozs. sultanas and dates, mixed.*
4 ozs. dripping or suet.	*Breakfast cup grated potato (raw).*
Little milk.	*1 level teaspoonful bicarbonate soda.*
Breakfast cup grated carrot (raw).	

(1) Mix flour, breadcrumbs and spice together, rub in fat, or use finely chopped suet. (2) Add grated potato, carrot and dried fruit. Dissolve soda in 1 tablespoonful warm water. (3) Pour into the pudding mixture with enough milk to mix to a stiff consistency. (4) Three quarters fill a greased pudding basin, cover with greased paper. (5) Steam for 3 hours.

STEAMED MARMALADE PUDDING

4 *ozs. breadcrumbs.*	3½ *ozs. finely chopped suet.*
2 *ozs. flour.*	1 *teaspoonful baking powder.*
2 *tablespoonfuls marmalade.*	1 *egg.*
3 *ozs. sugar.*	*Milk to mix.*

(1) Well grease a pie-dish or pudding mould. (2) Put the breadcrumbs, flour, suet, sugar, and salt into a basin, make a well in the centre, stir in the egg and marmalade, if necessary a little milk may be added; this would depend on the dryness of the flour and crumbs. (3) Blend all the ingredients thoroughly, put into the greased mould, cover with well greased paper. Steam for 2½ hours.

CANARY PUDDING

5 *ozs. flour.*	2 *eggs.*
4 *ozs. butter.*	*Little milk if necessary.*
4 *ozs. sugar.*	*Level teaspoonful baking powder.*

(1) Butter several small moulds or one large one. (2) Put the butter and sugar into a basin and cream well with a wooden spoon. (3) Beat in each egg separately. Fold in the sieved flour and baking powder as lightly as possible. If the eggs are small a little milk may be necessary to make it of a fairly stiff dropping consistency. (4) Three-parts fill the moulds or large mould with the mixture, cover with well greased paper. Steam until firm and set. Large moulds will take about 1 hour 20 minutes, and small ones 50 minutes to 1 hour.

Canary Pudding can be baked in the oven, with the "Autimo" set at Mark 6 for 1 hour.

GINGER PUDDING

4 *ozs. flour.*	4 *ozs. breadcrumbs.*
⅛ *teaspoonful salt.*	1 *egg.*
3-4 *ozs. suet.*	4 *ozs. brown sugar.*
1 *teaspoonful ground ginger.*	2 *ozs. chopped preserved ginger.*
Milk to mix (approx. ¼ pint).	1½ *teaspoonfuls baking powder.*

(1) Butter a basin or mould. (2) Sieve the flour into a basin with the baking powder, salt, ground ginger, add the breadcrumbs and the preserved ginger, cut into pieces, and the finely chopped suet. (3) Make a well in the centre, stir in the beaten egg to which a little of the milk has been added. (4) Add the remainder of the milk gradually, until the mixture is of a stiff consistency. (5) Put into the buttered mould or basin. (6) Steam for 1¾ hours to 2 hours.

This pudding is delicious if served with a syrup from preserved ginger, although this is not necessary.

PLAIN SUET PUDDING
(Without eggs).

8 ozs. flour.   1½ teaspoonfuls baking powder.
4 ozs. sugar.   ¼ teaspoonful salt.
4 ozs. suet.   Milk or water to mix (approx. ¼ pint).

(1) Sieve the flour, salt and baking powder into a basin, stir in the sugar and suet. (2) Make a well in the centre, and mix in just sufficient milk to make a pudding of a fairly stiff dropping consistency. (3) Put into one well-buttered basin or mould, or six individual moulds, filling the basins three-parts full. (4) Cover with greased paper and steam for 2 hours. If small puddings are made, 1½ hours will be sufficient.

N.B. This pudding is improved by the addition of a beaten egg with milk. Serve very hot with brown sugar, golden syrup, marmalade or jam.

COFFEE AND NUT PUDDING

4 ozs. flour.   4 ozs. breadcrumbs.
4 ozs. sugar (castor).   4 ozs. suet.
1½ teaspoonfuls baking powder.   Good pinch of salt.
1 teaspoonful strong coffee essence.   1 egg.
2-3 ozs. chopped Brazil nuts.   5-6 tablespoonfuls milk.

(1) Butter a mould or pudding basin. (2) Sieve the flour, baking powder and salt into a basin. (3) Add the breadcrumbs, sugar, suet, and the chopped nuts. (4) Warm the milk slightly and add the coffee essence to it. (5) Beat up the egg, make a well in the centre of the dry ingredients, stir in the beaten egg and the milk containing the coffee essence. (6) Mix well and put into the prepared mould. (7) Steam for 1¾-2 hours.

CHOCOLATE PUDDING

Small bar chocolate or 1 tablespoonful cocoa.   3 ozs. sugar.
Few drops vanilla essence, if available.   3 ozs. flour.
3 ozs. breadcrumbs.   3 ozs. suet.
Milk to mix (5 or 6 tablespoonfuls).   1 egg.
1 teaspoonful baking powder.

(1) Sieve the flour and baking powder into a basin. If cocoa is used it should be sieved with the flour. (2) Add the breadcrumbs, sugar, and the suet. If bar chocolate is used, it should be cut up roughly and warmed in the milk, until it dissolves. (3) Make a well in the centre of the flour, stir in the beaten egg, and chocolate and milk. (4) Mix well to form a stiff dropping consistency, if necessary, a little more milk can be added. (5) Put into a well-buttered mould or pudding-basin. (6) Steam for 2 hours.

JAM ROLY POLY

4 *ozs. plain flour.*	2 *ozs. breadcrumbs.*
¼ *teaspoonful salt.*	½ *teaspoonful baking powder.*
3 *ozs. shredded suet.*	*Jam.* *Cold water.*

(1) Mix together flour, breadcrumbs, salt, baking powder and suet.
(2) Mix to a stiff paste with water.   (3) Roll out into an oblong shape.
spread with jam and roll up.   (4) Place on a floured cloth, fold over,
tie each end with string.   (5) Place in a steamer over boiling water.
Steam 1½-2 hours.

ORANGE PUDDING

4 *ozs. flour.*	4 *ozs. sugar.*
Grated rind of 2 *oranges.*	2 *eggs.*
3 *ozs. butter.*	½ *teaspoonful baking powder.*
Little milk.	2 *ozs. breadcrumbs.*

(1) Butter a plain round mould, or pudding basin if the former is not
available.   (2) Put the butter and sugar into a basin, and work them
together until they are light in appearance and resemble whipped
cream.   (3) Sieve the flour on to a plate with the baking powder, add
the grated orange rind to the flour and the breadcrumbs.   (4) Beat
in each egg separately to the creamed butter and sugar, and stir in
the flour, etc., adding a little milk as required, to make it of a
moderately soft consistency.   (5) Put it into the greased mould or
pudding basin, and steam for 1½ hours.   (6) Serve with orange
marmalade.

SOUTHPORT PUDDING

2 *ozs. chopped dates.*	*Grated rind of half lemon.*
2 *ozs. flour.*	2 *ozs. shredded suet.*
1 *tablespoonful golden syrup.*	1 *egg.*
A squeeze of lemon juice.	4 *ozs. breadcrumbs.*
1 *teaspoonful baking powder.*	4 *ozs. shredded apples.*

(1) Mix the suet, apples and dates with the dry ingredients.   (2) Add
the beaten egg, and squeeze of lemon juice.   (3) Melt syrup and add
to mixture, mix well.   (4) Press into a greased pudding basin.   (5)
Steam for 1½ hours; serve with custard.

STEAMED CAKE PUDDING

6 *ozs. stale fruit cake crumbs.*	2 *teaspoonfuls sugar.*
½ *pint milk.*	1 *teaspoonful baking powder.*
¼ *teaspoonful mixed spice.*	

(1) Mix together the cake crumbs, milk, spice, sugar and baking
powder.   (2) Put into a greased pudding basin, cover with greased
paper.   (3) Steam for 1 hour; serve with Custard or White Sauce.
(See Recipe page 131).

FIG SPONGE PUDDING

3 ozs. plain flour.
¼ teaspoonful salt.
3 ozs. shredded suet.
3 ozs. chopped figs previously
    soaked in 1 tablespoonful
    warm water for 1 hour.

3 ozs. breadcrumbs.
½ teaspoonful baking powder.
¼ teaspoonful bicarbonate soda.
A little milk.
1 dessertspoonful golden syrup.

(1) Mix together all dry ingredients, then add the figs. (2) Warm the syrup and milk, add to the ingredients, mixing well. The mixture must be rather moist. (3) Put into a well greased pudding mould, or three small ones, and cover with greased paper. (4) If a large pudding—steam for 1½ hours; if small ones—from 40 to 50 minutes. (5) Serve with Custard or White Sauce (page 131).

ECONOMICAL FIG PUDDING

5 ozs. flour.   3 ozs. breadcrumbs.   4 ozs. sugar.
3½ ozs. suet.   1 level teaspoonful baking powder.   4 ozs. figs.
Pinch of salt.   1 egg.   Little milk.

(1) Chop the suet and figs. (2) Put all the dry ingredients into a basin, mix well, make a well in the centre, stir in the beaten egg and sufficient milk to make it of the correct consistency. (For steamed puddings the mixture should drop easily from the spoon). (3) Put the mixture into a well greased basin and cover tightly with greased paper. (4) Steam for 2½ hours.

STEAMED EGG CUSTARD
(Suitable for an invalid).

2 eggs.   ½ pint milk.   Little sugar.   Little lemon rind.

(1) Heat the milk, with a strip of thinly peeled lemon rind, over a low flame. (2) Meanwhile, whisk the eggs with the sugar. (3) Bring the milk to the boil, when boiling, remove the lemon rind, pour the boiling milk on to the eggs, continuing to whisk gently. (4) Pour into a well greased china soufflé case or basin, cover with greased paper and steam until set. Time required about ½ hour to 40 minutes.

OLD ENGLISH PLUM PUDDING

1¼ lbs. raisins.
¾ lb. sultanas.
1 oz. sweet almonds.
4 ozs. breadcrumbs.
½ lb. dark brown sugar.
½ lb. suet.
Brandy or milk to mix.
¼ teaspoonful ground cinnamon.

¾ lb. currants.
6 ozs. peel.
1 oz. bitter almonds.
½ teaspoonful grated nutmeg.
4 eggs.
Rind and juice of 1 lemon.
½ lb. flour.

(1) Prepare the fruit. Chop the suet, raisins, peel and almonds. (2)

Grate the lemon rind and make the breadcrumbs by passing through a coarse wire sieve. (3) Mix all the dry ingredients together in a large basin or crock. (4) Beat the eggs and mix them with the lemon juice. (5) Add to the dry ingredients, with a little brandy, stirring well, and, if more moisture is necessary, add a little milk. (6) Leave the ingredients to blend for 24 hours, then mix thoroughly again before putting into the greased basins. (7) Boil or steam for 7 hours.

SAUCES

ANCHOVY SAUCE

To ½ pint of White Sauce add 1 dessertspoonful of Anchovy Essence.

APPLE SAUCE

1 *lb. cooking apples.*   4 *ozs. sugar.*

(1) Peel and core the apples. Cut into slices. (2) Cook gently with a little water until they fall. (3) Add the sugar and cook for a few minutes. (4) Beat until smooth.

BECHAMEL SAUCE

1¼ *pints of milk or milk and white stock.*		1 *small onion.*
Cayenne.	12 *peppercorns.*	1 *blade of mace.*
1 *bay leaf.*	2 *ozs. margarine.*	1½ *ozs. flour.*
1 *teaspoonful dried herbs.*	*Nutmeg.*	*Salt.*

(1) Heat milk in saucepan, with peeled onion, peppercorns, bay leaf, herbs and mace tied in muslin. (2) Simmer for 15 minutes. (3) Cook together margarine and flour as for White Sauce. Add milk stock strained from the other ingredients. (4) Whisk together and bring to the boil and continue boiling for 10 minutes, whisking all the time. (5) Pour through a very fine strainer, and serve.

BRAIN SAUCE

(1) Wash the brains in salted water, and skin. (2) Tie in muslin and place in a pan of cold water and boil for 10 minutes. (3) Chop up, and add to Parsley Sauce.

BREAD SAUCE
(Hot plate method).

3 *ozs. breadcrumbs.*	¾ *pint milk.*
2 *onions of medium size.*	2 *cloves.*
½ *oz. butter.*	*Salt and pepper.*

(1) Peel the onions, stick the cloves into them, put into the milk, and bring very slowly to simmering point. (2) Allow to remain at this

129

temperature for 20 minutes to extract the flavour from the onions and cloves. (3) Remove the onions, sprinkle in the breadcrumbs, add a little pepper and salt, and the butter. (4) Continue to cook for a few minutes to blend thoroughly all the ingredients. Bread sauce is much enriched by the addition of a tablespoonful of cream or unsweetened evaporated milk.

BREAD SAUCE
(Oven method).

2 ozs. breadcrumbs.	1 oz. margarine.
1 small onion.	½ pint milk.
1 clove.	Pepper and salt.

(1) Put onion stuck with clove, breadcrumbs and seasoning in a small casserole. (2) Cover with milk, replace lid and place in oven. (3) Remove onion before serving, and stir in the margarine.
NOTE. When cooked with complete dinner place on 5th runner or base plate. Mark 7.

BROWN SAUCE

1 oz. dripping.	1 onion.
½ pint stock, or water.	1 carrot.
1 oz. flour.	1 teaspoonful meat essence.

(1) Melt the fat in a pan, slice the onion and carrot. (2) Fry until brown, add flour; mix well, add stock gradually. (3) Stir until it falls, bringing to the boil. (4) Season, and pass through a strainer.

CAPER SAUCE

To ½ pint of White Sauce add 1 tablespoonful capers, and 1 teaspoonful of vinegar from the capers.

CHEESE SAUCE

To ½ pint of White Sauce add 2 ozs. grated cheese.

CORNFLOUR SAUCE

½ pint milk.	½ oz. cornflour.
½ oz. sugar.	Pinch of salt.

(1) Boil the milk, add blended cornflour, stir until it boils. (2) Allow to cook 5 minutes, add sugar, but if too thick, a little more milk should be added.

CURRY SAUCE

2 tablespoonfuls margarine.	1 teaspoonful curry powder.
2 tablespoonfuls flour.	1 cupful stock.

Melt the butter, add flour and curry powder. Mix well but do not allow it to brown. Add stock and simmer 2-3 minutes. Strain and serve.
(This sauce is good with game).

CUSTARD SAUCE

½ *pint milk.* 2 *teaspoonfuls cornflour.* 1 *egg.*
Pinch of salt. 2 *teaspoonfuls sugar.* *A little lemon rind.*

(1) Boil the milk, pour it over blended cornflour, return to pan, and cook a few minutes. (2) Add sugar and flavouring, allow to cool a little, then add well beaten egg. (3) Re-heat again, but do not boil.

EGG SAUCE

To ½ pint White Sauce add 1 hard boiled egg finely chopped, together with seasonings.

FOUNDATION WHITE SAUCE
(Melted Butter Sauce)

1 *oz. margarine.* ¼ *pint liquid, milk, water,*
1 *oz. flour.* *or stock.*

(1) Melt margarine in saucepan, stir in the flour. (2) Cook for a few minutes without browning. (3) Add some of the liquid, stir and boil for a few minutes. (4) Add salt and pepper and flavourings to taste as required.

HORSE-RADISH SAUCE

2 *ozs. horse-radish.* 2 *teaspoonfuls lemon juice or vinegar.*
Salt and Pepper. ¼ *pint cream, or 2 tablespoonfuls cream*
  and 4 tablespoonfuls unsweetened
  evaporated milk.

(1) Wash and grate the horse-radish very finely. (2) Whip the cream and condensed milk, whichever is being used, and blend the two together. (3) Stir in the vinegar or lemon juice, pepper and salt and lastly, the grated horse-radish. (4) Blend thoroughly. Horse-radish Sauce should be made in small quantities so that it can be served fresh.

JAM SAUCE

The same ingredients and method as Cornflour Sauce, page 130, with one tablespoonful of jam added.

MAITRE d'HOTEL BUTTER

(1) Blend 1 oz. of butter or margarine with a teaspoonful of finely chopped parsley and the juice of half a lemon. (2) Put the butter to cool after reshaping into a rectangle. (3) Divide into the required number of portions.

MARMALADE SAUCE

2 tablespoonfuls marmalade.   ¼ pint water.
½ teaspoonful lemon juice (optional).   1 tablespoonful sugar.
1 teaspoonful cornflour or arrowroot.

(1) Boil the marmalade, sugar and water together for 3 or 4 minutes. (2) Stir in the cornflour or arrowroot, previously blended with a little cold water. (3) Cook until the sauce thickens. (4) Add lemon juice and serve.

MAYONNAISE SAUCE

1 teaspoonful made mustard.   1 hard boiled yolk of egg
3 tablespoonfuls cream or condensed milk. ¼ teaspoonful salt.
1 tablespoonful vinegar.   1 tablespoonful sugar.

(1) Beat up yolk of egg, adding mustard, sugar, vinegar and salt. (2) Add cream gradually, stirring well.

MINT SAUCE

2 tablespoonfuls chopped mint.   1 dessertspoonful sugar.
¼ pint vinegar, or lemon juice   1 tablespoonful hot water.
   and water.

(1) Wash and chop mint finely, add sugar and hot water. (2) Allow to cool, lastly add vinegar or lemon juice. (3) Serve with roast lamb.

MUSHROOM SAUCE

To 1 pint White Sauce add 4 ozs. chopped mushrooms, and cook until tender.

MUSTARD SAUCE

To half a pint of White Sauce add 1 tablespoonful of made mustard and 1 dessertspoonful vinegar.

ONION SAUCE

1 pint White Sauce (see page 131), with the addition of 2 large onions, boiled and chopped finely, also seasonings.

PARSLEY SAUCE

(1) Melt 1 oz. butter in saucepan, add 1 oz. flour. Mix well. (2) Add gradually 1 pint of milk and water mixed. Stir until it boils. (3) Add one dessertspoonful chopped parsley, salt and pepper.

RUM SAUCE

1 oz. butter.	1 oz. flour.	½ pint milk.
½ pint water.	1 oz. sugar.	Pinch of salt.
1 tablespoonful rum.		

Melt butter in a saucepan, add flour, mix well, add liquid gradually, stir until it boils, cook a few minutes, add sugar and rum. Pour a little sauce over the Pudding before sending to the table, also put a sprig of holly in top of pudding. Serve the rest of the sauce in a sauce boat.

SHRIMP SAUCE

| ¼ pint picked shrimps. | 1 oz. butter. |
| 1 oz. flour. | ¾ pint milk. |

(1) Melt the ounce of butter, stir in the flour. Add the milk and any liquid that has come from the fish during the cooking, this improves the flavour of the sauce considerably. (2) Simmer for 8 minutes, add the shrimps, continue to cook for a little longer.

SWEET SAUCE

1 pint Foundation Sauce. 1 oz. sugar and suitable flavouring.

TARTARE SAUCE

1 teacupful mayonnaise, or thick salad dressing.
1 tablespoonful chopped gherkins, or capers.
½ teaspoonful finely grated shallot (optional).

(1) Mix the finely chopped capers, or gherkins (and shallots if used) to the mayonnaise. (2) Add a little seasoning (if necessary). (3) Serve quite cold.

WINE SAUCE

| 2 ozs. sugar. | 1 wineglass sherry. | ¼ pint water. |
| 1 dessertspoonful jam. Carmine to colour. | | |

(1) Boil the sugar and water in a pan until a syrup is formed. (2) Add the jam, carmine and sherry. (3) Strain and serve.

HOME MADE SWEETS

MAKING sweets at home not only affords a good deal of pleasure, but effects considerable economy, for sugar, which is the principal ingredient is a cheap commodity, and even when it is combined with chocolate, cream, condensed milk, etc., the cost of home made sweets is very low.

133

There are a number that are very easy to make and do not require the use of a sugar boiling thermometer. Anyone, however, who is ambitious and wants to try a variety of sweets should provide herself with a thermometer, for without one it is almost impossible to ensure success with a large majority of sweets, as a few degrees make an enormous amount of difference.

Sugar boiling thermometers cost about 21/- according to the range of graduations. As, however, they last indefinitely, provided they are not smashed with careless handling, their cost is well worth while.

In addition to a sugar thermometer, a marble slab is very convenient. There is no need to buy a special piece of marble, as most people have the top of an old wash-stand which answers the purpose quite well, and only requires thorough scrubbing to ensure cleanliness. Alternatively, an enamelled topped table can be used if preferred. A scraper is also a convenient little utensil which every sweetmaker should possess. It consists of a flat piece of metal with a handle, and is used for scraping and lifting fondant when it is cooling.

A pair of scissors, shallow tins for turning out toffees, scales, palette knife, pastry brush and one or two strong iron saucepans are all the other utensils that are necessary.

Starch trays and rubber fondant mats would not be required by the amateur sweetmaker.

The saucepan is important. This should be thick and large enough so that the batches of toffee, etc., cooked in it little more than half fill it. Thin aluminium or thin enamelled steel are not suitable; thick iron, copper, or thick aluminium pans should be chosen.

The Boiling of Sugar.

Practically all sweets are made—with few exceptions—by the boiling of sugar to certain definite temperatures. Everyone knows that when sugar is cooked either alone or with water that it gradually changes its character and colour from a colourless clear liquid to corn coloured syrup and through various stages until it becomes dark coffee colour and finally caramel, and if heating is continued it is burned and charred.

The following are the sugar boiling degrees. Syrup containing 1 lb. sugar to $\frac{1}{2}$ pint of water and boiled until the temperature of 225° F. is reached produces a stage called—"The Thread". If heating is continued until 230° F., the "Pearl" stage is reached. If heating is continued to 235° F., the "Blow" stage is reached.

240—245° F., the "Feather".

250—255° F., the "Ball".

310—315° F., the "Crack".

The last temperature is the one at which most toffees have to be cooked, and the syrup forms a piece of toffee or sweetmeat which cracks when knocked. If very hard sweets are required the boiling must be continued a little longer.

Anyone interested in sweet-making should, before commencing to make sweets, experiment once or twice with sugar boiling only, noting the various stages through which the sugar passes and the results obtained at the different temperatures.

There are one or two simple rules that should be remembered.

1. The temperature must be read very carefully, and to read the temperature the eye should be on the level of the mercury and the bulb should remain in the syrup. It is therefore necessary to bend down so that the eye reaches the surface level. In no circumstances should the bulb be removed to do this.

2. Unless directions be given the mixture should not be stirred or shaken unnecessarily as this causes the sugar to candy or crystallize.

3. The sides of the pan must be kept free from particles of sugar which become deposited. To remove these, a brush should be dipped in warm water and the sides of the pan gently brushed.

4. Draughts should also be avoided, as sudden cold is often liable to cause crystallization.

ALMOND PRALINES

½ *lb. granulated sugar.*   1½ *gills water* (4 *gills to pint*).
½ *lb. sweet almonds.*

Put the sugar and chopped blanched almonds into a strong saucepan with the water. Stir until the sugar is dissolved and then heat until a temperature of 260° F. is reached. Warm a teaspoon and drop the mixture from the spoon on to an oiled tin or greased waxed paper. Wrap up and store in an airtight tin.

ALMOND TOFFEE

1 *lb. demerara sugar.*   ¼ *teaspoonful cream of tartar.*
1 *oz. butter.*   2 *or 3 drops acetic acid.*
2 *tablespoonfuls golden syrup.* 3 *ozs. chopped almonds.*
¼ *pint water.*

Put the sugar and water into a thick pan, dissolve and bring to the boil, add the butter, cream of tartar, acetic acid and golden syrup. Put the lid on and boil for a few minutes. Then remove the lid, place the thermometer in the syrup and boil to 300° F. Stir the mixture quietly with the thermometer, pour out the toffee on to a greased slab. Sprinkle with chopped nuts and turn the sides of the toffee to the middle, until it is cool enough to handle. Then pull lightly, having previously rubbed the fingers over with olive oil. Cut into cushion shaped pieces and wrap in waxed paper.

CHOCOLATE TOFFEE

¾ *lb. demerara sugar.*   4 *ozs. grated chocolate.*
11 *ozs. golden syrup.*   2 *ozs. butter.*

Warm the syrup in a strong pan, add the sugar, stir very quietly to prevent burning, and when all the sugar has dissolved, add the butter and grated chocolate. Stir again until they are dissolved, and boil quickly to 290° F. stirring from time to time very gently with the thermometer. Pour into an oiled toffee tin or Yorkshire pudding tin, and when almost cold, mark with a strong knife or caramel cutter into squares. When cold, break and wrap in waxed paper.

GOLDEN TOFFEE

2 *lbs. loaf sugar.*   6 *ozs. butter.*
½ *pint water.*   2 *tablespoonfuls glucose.*

Put the ingredients into a covered saucepan and bring to the temperature of 300° F. Pour into an oiled tin and cool. When cool, mark with a greased knife or caramel cutter, and when quite cold break the toffee into squares and wrap in waxed paper.

COCONUT ICE

2 *lbs. loaf sugar.*   ½ *lb. desiccated coconut.*
½ *pint cold water.*

The sugar and water should be put in a strong pan, dissolve and heat to 240° F. Remove from the fire and stir in the coconut until it thickens. Pour half the mixture into an oiled tin, colour the remaining half pale pink and pour it on top of the white coconut. When cold cut into bars.

PEPPERMINT HUMBUGS

2 *lbs. demerara sugar.*   3 *ozs. butter.*
3 *tablespoonfuls golden syrup.*   ½ *teaspoonful cream of tartar.*
½ *pint water.*   *Little oil of peppermint.*

With the exception of the oil of peppermint put all the ingredients into a pan and boil rapidly for a few minutes without stirring. Remove the lid, put in a sugar boiling thermometer and boil until a temperature of 290° F. is reached. Pour on to an oiled marble slab or enamelled topped table, and leave to cool for a short time. Pour about half a teaspoonful of oil of peppermint on to the toffee, oil the hands and fold the sides of the mixture to the centre. Pull as soon as the toffee is cool enough to handle. Finally, pull it into an even roll, cut into squares or cushions with scissors, and when quite cold, wrap in waxed paper.

BOILED ALMOND PASTE OR MARZIPAN

1 *lb. loaf sugar.*	1 *gill of water.*
¾ *lb. ground almonds.*	*A pinch of cream of tartar.*
2 *whites of eggs.*	3 *ozs. icing sugar.*

Boil the sugar and water until it reaches 220° F., then add the cream of tartar and continue to boil until 240° F. is reached; remove the saucepan from the heat and stir rapidly until the syrup grains. Stir in the ground almonds and the whites of egg, and continue to cook for a few minutes slowly, stirring well. Pour on to an oiled slab of marble, add the sieved icing sugar and work with a palette knife. As soon as the mixture is cool enough, knead with the hands until smooth. Divide into portions, add colour and flavouring according to requirements.

N.B. Marzipan made thus will keep satisfactory for several weeks if wrapped in greaseproof paper and stored in a cool place.

CHOCOLATE FUDGE

1 *lb. granulated sugar.*	1 *oz. butter.*
3 *ozs. walnuts.*	2 *tablespoonfuls cocoa.*
½ *pint condensed milk.*	*A pinch of salt.*
1 *oz. plain chocolate.*	1 *teaspoonful vanilla essence.*

Put all the ingredients except the walnuts and essence into a pan, and bring to a temperature of 238° F., stirring occasionally to prevent burning. Remove from the flame. Have the nuts ready chopped and add them with the essence to contents in the saucepan, beating well until thick and creamy. Pour into a greased tin and cut into squares when cold.

UNBOILED OR PLAIN FONDANT

2 *lbs. best icing sugar.*	*White of egg.*
A good pinch of cream of	1 *dessertspoonful of lemon*
tartar.	*juice.*

Pass the icing sugar through a fine hair sieve. Add the cream of tartar, lemon juice, and sufficient beaten white of egg to make a pliable paste. If necessary, a little more white of egg can be added. Knead the paste thoroughly for five minutes, then leave for an hour before using.

This fondant can be flavoured and coloured to produce a variety of different sweets, of which the following are examples.

137

TANGERINE CREAMS

Prepare the plain fondant, add a few drops of tangerine essence and a very little yellow and red colouring. Knead these in and allow to stand one hour before using. Shape into balls. Roll in yellow castor sugar. Allow to dry for 24 hours.

CHOCOLATE CREAMS—UNBOILED FONDANT

½ *lb. of prepared cream fondant.* 4 *ozs. finely chopped grated*
½ *teaspoonful vanilla essence.* *chocolate.*

Melt the chocolate and knead it and the essence into the fondant and leave for an hour. Roll out, cut into neat squares and decorate with a small piece of crystallized violet, rose leaf or pistachio nut. Stand for 24 hours.

ALMOND CREAMS

4 *ozs. unboiled fondant.* *Green colouring.*
4 *ozs. ground almonds.*

Work the almonds into the fondant, add a very little green colouring and stand for one hour. Roll out and cut into narrow bars, dry for 24 hours. If preferred, the fondant can be shaped into oval cups and each decorated with a blanched nut.

A Series of WHOLE DINNER MENUS which can be COOKED IN

CANNON GAS COOKERS

The amount of food partaken of at a meal necessarily varies with different persons. The following dinners, however, are definitely planned for four to six people endowed with average appetites.

Arrangement of Whole Dinner Menus

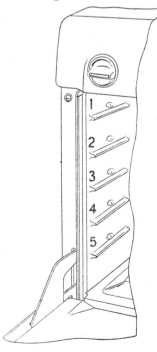

To facilitate the instructions in the following menus, the shelf positions in the oven are numbered, 1st, 2nd, 3rd, etc., from the top downwards. The runners are embossed on the side linings of the oven, as shown on this illustration.

DINNER No. 1

ROAST CHICKEN
SAUSAGES   BREAD SAUCE
ROAST POTATOES   STEWED CELERY
QUEEN OF PUDDINGS

Set the "Autimo" at 7, pre-heat the oven for 20 minutes and arrange the food as follows:—

3rd Shelf Position	Roast Chicken (*page* 41)	2½-3 *lbs.*
	Roast Potatoes (*page* 143)	1½ *lbs.*
5th Shelf Position	Baked Sausages	1 *lb.*
5th Shelf Position	Bread Sauce (Oven method, *page* 130)	
5th Shelf Position	Stewed Celery	1½ *lbs.*

Clean the celery in the usual way, cut into convenient lengths, place it in the bottom of a pie-dish or fire-proof casserole, sprinkle with pepper and salt, add just sufficient milk or milk and water to cover. Cover with greased paper or a lid. When cooked, the milk can be poured off and used for making a White Sauce to serve with the celery.

Base Plate   Queen of Puddings (*page* 116)

When the first course is dished up the white of egg can be beaten, mixed with the castor sugar, put on top of the Queen pudding, and returned to the oven until ready to be served.

Time required: 1 hour 15 minutes.

DINNER No. 2

SOUSED HERRINGS   BAKED POTATOES
STEWED CUCUMBER OR CELERY
BREAD AND BUTTER PUDDING

Set the "Autimo" at 6, pre-heat the oven for 20 minutes. Put in the pudding and potatoes when the oven is lighted, and at the end of 20 minutes arrange the other food as follows:—

3rd Shelf Position	Soused Herrings (*page* 14)	6
5th Shelf Position	Baked Potatoes	8 *of medium size*
	Stewed Cucumber	1 *large one*

Peel the cucumber, and cut into slices ⅛". Put into a pie-dish, sprinkle with pepper and salt, top with a little butter, and cover with water to which one teaspoonful of lemon juice or vinegar has been added. Cover with greased paper or a lid. Serve with White Sauce, made from the strained liquor, if liked, although Stewed Cucumber is often served without a sauce.

Base Plate   Bread and Butter Pudding (*page* 118)

Time required: 1 hour.

DINNER No. 3

HOT POT
CASSEROLE OF ONIONS, TURNIPS AND CARROTS
APPLE CHARLOTTE

Set the "Autimo" at 4, and pre-heat the oven for 20 minutes. Arrange the food as follows:—

3rd Shelf Position	Hot Pot (*page* 54)	1½ *lbs. neck of mutton* 2 *lbs. potatoes* 1 *large onion* ½ *pint water*
5th Shelf Position	Casserole of Vegetables (*page* 55)	2½ *lbs.*
Base Plate	Apple Charlotte (*page* 119)	1½ *pints custard, etc.*

Time required: 2-2½ hours.

DINNER No. 4

TOAD-IN-THE-HOLE
BAKED POTATOES AND TOMATOES
CANARY PUDDING

Set the "Autimo" at 6, and pre-heat the oven for 20 minutes, putting in the dripping for the batter when the oven is lighted.

3rd Shelf Position	Toad-in-the-Hole (*page* 44)	1 *pint batter* 1 *lb. sausages*
5th Shelf Position	Baked Potatoes Baked Canary Pudding (*page* 125)	2 *lbs.* (*medium size*)
Base Plate	Baked Tomatoes	1 *lb.* (*medium size*)

Time required: 1 hour.

DINNER No. 5

WHITING EN CASSEROLE WITH BACON ROLLS AND TOMATOES

CASSEROLE OF POTATOES

STEWED APRICOTS   BAKED CUSTARD

Set the "Autimo" at 5, and pre-heat the oven for 20 minutes.
Arrange the food as follows:—

3rd Shelf Position	Whiting en Casserole (4-6 filleted) (*page* 14)	*Fillets seasoned, laid in buttered dish, half cover with milk and put lid on casserole*
	2 lbs. Potatoes	*Sliced thinly, seasoned, covered with milk and boiling water, and lid put in position*
5th Shelf Position	Tomatoes and Bacon	1 *lb. tomatoes left whole* $\frac{1}{4}$ *lb. streaky bacon rolled and put on skewer. All covered with greased paper.*
	Baked Custard (*page* 118)	1 *pint*
Base Plate	Stewed Dried Apricots	$\frac{1}{2}$ *lb. fruit, sugar and boiling water put into a covered vessel*

Time required: 50 minutes.

DINNER No. 6

(A Vegetarian Meal)

CHEESE PUDDING

TOMATOES AND MARROW EN CASSEROLE

BLACKBERRY PLATE PIE

Set the "Autimo" at 6, and pre-heat the oven for 20 minutes.
Arrange the food as follows:—

3rd Shelf Position	Blackberry Plate Pie (*page* 120)	$\frac{3}{4}$ *lb. pastry* $1\frac{1}{2}$ *lbs. fruit*
5th Shelf Position	Cheese Pudding (*page* 61)	1 *pint milk, etc.*
Base Plate	Tomatoes and Sliced Marrow en Casserole	$\frac{1}{2}$ *lb. marrow, seasoning* $\frac{3}{4}$ *lb. tomatoes*

Time required: 45 minutes.

142

DINNER No. 7

SAVOURY LIVER

BAKED POTATOES   CARROTS AND PARSNIPS

GROUND RICE PUDDING

Set the "Autimo" at 6, and pre-heat the oven for 20 minutes, putting the baked potatoes on the base plate when the oven is lighted. Then arrange the food as follows:—

3rd Shelf Position   Savoury Liver (*page* 44)   ¾ *lb. liver, etc.*

5th Shelf Position   Baked Potatoes   8 *of medium size*

                         Carrots and Parsnips   1½ *lbs., diced and covered with boiling water.*

Base Plate   Ground Rice Pudding (*page* 115)

Time required: 45 minutes.

DINNER No. 8

ROAST SIRLOIN   YORKSHIRE PUDDING

BAKED POTATOES   BRUSSELS SPROUTS

APPLE DUMPLINGS

Set the "Autimo" at 7, and pre-heat the oven for 20 minutes.

Arrange the food as follows, leaving space for the Yorkshire pudding, which only requires baking for the last 20-30 minutes according to thickness. The dripping should be thoroughly heated in the tin before pouring in the Yorkshire pudding batter.

2nd Shelf Position   Yorkshire Pudding (*page* 37)   ½ *pint milk, etc.*
                         (Last 20-30 minutes only).

                         Apple Dumplings (*page* 119)
                         (For first 30 minutes)

4th Shelf Position   Boned and Rolled Sirloin   3 *lbs.*

                         Potatoes around meat   10 *of medium size*

Base Plate   Brussels Sprouts (*page* 20)

Time required: 1¼ hours.

143

DINNER No. 9

STEAK AND KIDNEY PIE   BAKED POTATOES
CASSEROLE OF CARROTS   PLUM SPONGE

Set the "Autimo" at 6, and pre-heat the oven for 20 minutes.
Arrange the food as follows:—

3rd Shelf Position Steak and Kidney Pie 1½ *lbs. steak*
                          (*page* 96) ¼ *lb. ox kidney*
                                       8 *ozs. rough puff pastry*

                        Baked Potatoes 6 *large potatoes scrubbed
                                          and cut through the
                                          skin around the centre*

5th Shelf Position Casserole of Carrots 12 *of medium size* (1½ *lbs.*)
                                             *sliced, seasoned and
                                             just covered with water*

                        Plum Sponge (*page* 123) *Bottled plums,* 2 *eggs,
                                                  their weight in butter,
                                                  sugar, and flour, made
                                                  into cake mixture and
                                                  put on top of fruit*

The juice of the plums should not be used in this recipe.
First stew meat on hot plate for about 1 hour before putting into
pie-dish.   Time required: 1 hour.

DINNER No. 10

ROAST LOIN OF PORK   SAGE AND ONION STUFFING
APPLE SAUCE   ROAST POTATOES
CARROTS AND CELERY EN CASSEROLE   OSBORNE PUDDING

Set the "Autimo" at 7, and pre-heat the oven for 20 minutes.
Arrange the food as follows:—

3rd Shelf Position Roast Loin of Pork 2½ *lbs.*
                        Roast Potatoes 1½ *lbs.*
5th Shelf Position Apple Sauce
                        Carrots and Celery 1½ *lbs. carrots sliced thin-
                          en Casserole ly, celery heart sliced
                                        thinly, salt, pepper,
                                        butter and water*

Base Plate Sage and Onion Stuffing ¼ *lb. breadcrumbs*
                                         1 *large onion,* 1 *lemon,
                                         salt, cayenne,* 1 *dessert-
                                         spoonful sage,* 1 *tea-
                                         spoonful parsley,
                                         beaten egg to mix*

                Osborne Pudding 1 *pint milk*
                          (*page* 122) 1 *egg, etc.*
                (Bread and Butter and
                Marmalade)

Time required: 1½ hours.

144

DINNER No. 11

BRAISED NECK OF MUTTON
BAKED POTATOES   STEWED FIGS
TAPIOCA PUDDING

Set the "Autimo" at 5, and pre-heat the oven for 20 minutes.
Arrange the food as follows:—

3rd Shelf Position	Braised Neck of Mutton (*page* 46)	2½ *lbs.*
	Baked Potatoes Place on Grid Shelf, outside casserole	2 *lbs. in jackets*
5th Shelf Position	Stewed Figs (*page* 121) and Tapioca Pudding (*page* 116) Place in cold oven	½ *lb. figs* 1¾ *Tablespoonfuls tapioca* 1 *pint of boiling milk Sugar*

Time required: 1¼ hours.

DINNER No. 12

STUFFED SHEEP'S HEART WITH SAVOURY BALLS
DATE AND RICE PUDDING

Set the "Autimo" at 6, and pre-heat the oven for 20 minutes.
Arrange the food as follows:—

3rd Shelf Position	Stuffed Sheep's Heart (*page* 42)	3, *or as many as required. Veal or sage and onion stuffing*
5th Shelf Position	Potato and Tomato Casserole	½ *lb. tomatoes,* 1 *lb. potatoes, pepper, salt, boiling water*
Base Plate	Date and Rice Pudding (*page* 115) Insert in cold oven, 5th Runner for 20 minutes	1¾ *ozs. rice,* 1 *pint milk, sugar. Put dates at bottom of rice and pour boiling milk over*

Time required: 1¼ hours.

DINNER No. 13

SHEPHERD'S PIE

BAKED YOUNG CARROTS   GREEN PEAS

BAKED STUFFED APPLES

Set the "Autimo" at 6, and pre-heat the oven for 20 minutes.
Arrange the food as follows:—

3rd Shelf Position   Baked Young Carrots   *A bundle of young carrots*
          and Green Peas   *2 lbs. peas, a little sugar,*
                                      butter, pepper and salt.

Scrape the young carrots but do not cut them beyond removing the green stalks, shell the peas. Melt ½ oz. of butter in a saucepan, and toss the peas and carrots in the butter. Transfer them to a pie-dish or casserole, sprinkle with a little pepper, salt and sugar, add just sufficient stock to prevent the vegetables from burning. It is not necessary to cover them completely with the stock. Put greased paper or a lid on top of casserole, and cook on the 3rd shelf. Serve with the liquor in which the vegetables have been cooked.

5th Shelf Position   Shepherd's Pie (*page 58*)   1¼ *lbs. cooked potatoes*
                                             8 *ozs. minced cold meat*

          Baked Stuffed Apples   6 *apples, etc.*
               (*page* 118)

Time required: approx. ¾ hour.

DINNER No. 14

BAKED HADDOCK WITH MUSHROOM STUFFING

BAKED TOMATOES   POTATOES IN JACKETS

STEWED RHUBARB AND MILKY RICE

Set the "Autimo" at Mark 5, pre-heat the oven for 20 minutes, and arrange the food as follows:—

3rd Shelf Position   Baked Haddock (*page* 10)

          Baked Tomatoes   4 *medium size, around*
          Potatoes in Jackets (small) 1½ *lbs.*   [*the fish*
          Insert when lighting oven.

5th Shelf Position   Stewed Rhubarb and   *Cook the rice in water*
            Milky Rice   *for* 10 *minutes, then*
                                  strain and put into a
                                  pie-dish, cover with
                                  boiling milk

Prepare rhubarb by stringing it, cut into 1" lengths. Prepare a heavy syrup from 3 tablespoonfuls water and 3 ozs. sugar, by boiling it in a saucepan on top of the stove. Put the rhubarb into the basin, pour over the syrup, cover with a saucer and seal tightly with grease-proof paper.

Time required: ¾ hour.

DINNER No. 15

STUFFED BREAST OF MUTTON
ROAST POTATOES, CARROTS AND TURNIPS EN CASSEROLE
CHERRY PIE

Set the "Autimo" at Mark 7, pre-heat the oven for 20 minutes, and arrange the food as follows:—

3rd Shelf Position   Stuffed Breast of Mutton 2½ -3 *lbs. mutton*
                              (*page* 46)
                          Roast Potatoes (around
                            meat)
5th Shelf Position   Cherry Pie (*page* 120)   1 *lb. cherries*
                                           8 *ozs. short pastry*
Base Plate   Carrots and Turnips   1 *lb. together. Prepare*
                      en Casserole   *and cut into dice, put*
                                           into saucepan or cas-
                                           serole with 1 *oz. butter*
                                           and sufficient boiling
                                           water to cover barely

Remove Cherry Pie after 45-50 minutes.
Time required: 1¼ hours.

DINNER No. 16

MEAT SHAPE   RUNNER BEANS
POTATOES IN JACKETS   GINGER PUDDING

Set the "Autimo" at Mark 7, and pre-heat for 20 minutes.   Arrange the food as follows:—

3rd Shelf Position   Meat Shape (*page* 43)
                          Potatoes   2 *lbs. potatoes*
5th Shelf Position   Baked Ginger Pudding
                              (*page* 125)
                          Runner Beans (*page* 20) 1½ *lbs. runner beans*
Time required: 1¼ hours.

DINNER No. 17

CORNISH PASTIES
CASSEROLE OF MIXED VEGETABLES
APRICOT CHARLOTTE

Set the "Autimo" at 6, and pre-heat the oven for 20 minutes. Arrange the food as follows:—

3rd Shelf Position   Cornish Pasties (*page* 95)
5th Shelf Position   Apricot Charlotte (*page* 120)
                         Casserole of Mixed
                           Vegetables
Time required: 1 hour.

DINNER No. 18

ROAST RABBIT   FORCEMEAT BALLS
ROAST POTATOES   STEWED PARSNIPS
EVE'S PUDDING

Set the "Autimo" at 6, and pre-heat the oven for 20 minutes.
Arrange the food as follows:—

3rd Shelf Position   Roast Rabbit (*page* 45)   *Bake the forcemeat balls*
Forcemeat Balls (*page* 42)   *and potatoes around*
and Potatoes   *the rabbit*

5th Shelf Position   Eve's Pudding and Parsnips (*page* 117)
Time required: 1¼ hours.

DINNER No. 19

SAVOURY ROAST   FORCEMEAT STUFFING
ROAST POTATOES   PEAS OR CARROTS
CRANBERRY AND APPLE PIE

Set the "Autimo" at Mark 6, pre-heat the oven for 20 minutes, and arrange the food as follows:—

3rd Shelf Position   Savoury Roast   2 *lbs. steak. Beat steak*
Forcemeat Stuffing   *thoroughly, lay on*   •
stuffing, roll up and tie
with tape. Put some
dripping into the tin,
also over the meat

2 lbs. Potatoes   *Place potatoes around*
the meat

5th Shelf Position   Fruit Pie (*page* 90)   1 *lb. apples, etc.*
Peas or Carrots
Time required: 1 hour.

DINNER No. 20

ROAST STUFFED VEAL WITH BACON ROLLS
ROAST POTATOES   CAULIFLOWER
BARLEY KERNEL PUDDING WITH BAKED ORANGES

Set the "Autimo" at 6, and pre-heat the oven for 20 minutes.
Arrange the food as follows:—

3rd Shelf Position   Roast Veal   3 *lbs.*
Roast Potatoes, around   2 *lbs.*
meat

5th Shelf Position   Cauliflower   *Cover with boiling water,*
add salt, and a table-
spoonful of milk.

Base Plate   Barley Kernel Pudding with
Baked Oranges (*page* 117)
Time required: 1¾ hours.

DINNER No. 21
BEEF STEAK AND ONIONS EN CASSEROLE
BAKED POTATOES IN JACKETS
RICE OR TAPIOCA PUDDING

Set the "Autimo" at Mark 4, and pre-heat the oven for 20 minutes.
Arrange the food as follows:—

3rd Shelf Position Beef Steak and Onions in
Casserole (*page* 43)
2 lbs. Potatoes baked in
jackets, or peeled and
cut in halves and cooked
in the Casserole with
the meat

5th Shelf Position Rice or Tapioca Pudding
using boiling milk

Time required: 1¾ hours.

DINNER No. 22
ROAST BRISKET OF BEEF
ROAST POTATOES   CARROTS AND PARSNIPS EN CASSEROLE
MILK PUDDING

Set the "Autimo" at Mark 5, and pre-heat the oven for 20 minutes.
Arrange the food as follows:—

3rd Shelf Position 3 lbs. Brisket of Beef   *Wrap the meat in grease-*
proof paper. Place in
2 lbs. Potatoes around   *the tin, put potatoes*
Beef   *around the meat.*
(Before cooking, the
Brisket may be boned
and rolled, if desired).

5th Shelf Position 1½ lbs. Carrots and   *Cut into very small dice.*
Parsnips en Casserole
Milk Pudding

Time required: 2 hours.

DINNER No. 23
STEWED RABBIT (No. 2)
BAKED POTATOES IN JACKETS.   PARSNIPS EN CASSEROLE
QUEEN OF PUDDINGS

Set the "Autimo" at Mark 4, and pre-heat the oven for 20 minutes.
Arrange the food as follows:—

3rd Shelf Position Stewed Rabbit (No. 2)
(*page* 31)
2 lbs. Potatoes in Jackets

5th Shelf Position 1½ lbs. Parsnips en   *Cut parsnips into small*
Casserole   *pieces*

Base Plate Queen of Puddings
(*page* 116)

Time required: 1¾ hours.

149

DINNER No. 24

COD STEAKS   STUFFED TOMATOES

SCALLOPED POTATOES   PLATE APPLE TART

Set the "Autimo" at Mark 6, and pre-heat the oven for 20 minutes. Arrange the food as follows:—

3rd Shelf Position   Plate Apple Tart (*page* 92)

5th Shelf Position   Cod Steak (*page* 14) with
Stuffed Tomatoes (*page* 47).

Scalloped Potatoes   1 *lb. potatoes, 1 tablespoonful flour, Pepper and salt, ½ pint milk, 1 oz. margarine, Browned breadcrumbs.*

Cut potatoes into ¼" slices. Line a pie dish with potatoes, sprinkle with flour and seasoning. Pour in the milk and add small pieces of margarine together with browned crumbs.

Time required: 45 minutes.

(It is not intended that the two Special Dinners which follow should be cooked without attention, or at the same time).

CHRISTMAS DINNER

Oysters		
Palestine Purée	*For recipe see page*	3
Roast Turkey, with accompaniments, 1 lb. Sausage, 3 slices Bacon		
Forcemeat. Bread Sauce	*For recipe see page*	129
Roast Potatoes		
Brussels Sprouts	*For recipe see page*	21
Old English Plum Pudding	*For recipe see page*	128
Rum Sauce	*For recipe see page*	133
Mince Pies	*For recipe see page*	98
Pineapple Cream	*For recipe see page*	121
Cheese Straws	*For recipe see page*	63

HORS D'ŒUVRES

Oysters should be served on the shell, four neatly arranged on a small plate with a section of lemon, thin brown bread and butter should be handed.

TURKEY

Prepare and truss the Turkey, fill the crop with forcemeat, skewer the bacon over the breast, place the sausage over the wings and legs, cook at Mark 7 for 2-3 hours, according to size. Baste frequently. Remove bacon and sausage when cooked and allow the breast to brown.

Send the gravy and bread sauce to the table in sauce boats.

N.B.—A 24 lb. English bird requires about 3 hours.

An 18 lb. English bird requires about 2 hours 20 minutes.

A 12 lb. English bird requires about 1 hour 45 minutes.

A 6 lb. English bird requires about 1 hour 15 minutes.

(See remark on page 36).

FORCEMEAT

½ lb. breadcrumbs.   ¼ lb. shredded suet.
1 teaspoonful salt.   1 tablespoonful chopped parsley.
Egg to bind the mixture.   A good dust of pepper.
Rind of ½ a lemon.

(If liked, ¼ teaspoonful mixed herbs may be added to the stuffing).

RUM SAUCE

For recipe see page 133.

PINEAPPLE CREAM

For recipe see page 121.

CHEESE STRAWS

For recipe see page 63

A SUMMER DINNER MENU

Cream of Corn Soup, or Grape Fruit, Sole
   Farci, Chicken in Casserole   ..   ..   For recipe see page 5
Duchess Potatoes   ..   ..   For recipe see page 53
Roast Loin of Lamb, 3½ lbs.   ..   ..   For recipe see page 35
Green Peas, New Potatoes, Mint Sauce ..
Raspberry Flan, Cream   ..   ..   ..   For recipe see page 93
Cheese and Watercress   ..   ..   ..
Coffee   ..   ..

SOLE FARCI

Mark 6—20 minutes

6 *fillets of sole.*   ½ *oz. butter.*
½ *oz. flour.*   ¼ *pint stock.*
Yolk of egg.   *Lemon juice.*
2 *ozs. cleaned shrimps.*

Melt butter in saucepan, add flour, mix well, add stock, stir until it boils. Allow to cool a little, then add shrimps, seasonings and a squeeze of lemon juice. Roll fillets and place in a buttered dish, coat with the sauce, cover with greased paper, then bake 20 minutes.

CHICKEN IN CASSEROLE

Mark 6—1½-2 hours

1 *chicken.*   3 *ozs. streaky bacon.*   2 *ozs. butter.*
1 *oz. flour.*   1 *shallot chopped finely.*   *Seasonings.*
2 *tablespoonfuls mushrooms, coarsely chopped.*   *Stock.*

Divide chicken in neat joints, heat 1 oz. butter in pan or casserole, fry the bacon, then put in the chicken, shallots and mushrooms, put lid on pan and cook gently, turn the pieces over and when slightly browned on both sides add the stock to cover barely; add seasonings, mix together the flour and remaining ounce of butter, add the mixture in small pieces about 15 minutes before serving.

The chicken should be served in casserole, or may be turned out on to a hot dish.

MINT SAUCE

For recipe see page 132.

COFFEE (WHITE)

Allow 1 dessertspoonful coffee to each ½ pint water. Put coffee in a muslin bag then place in a saucepan with cold water and a pinch of salt. Bring to boil and simmer 5 minutes. Pour into coffee pot and serve with equal quantity of hot milk.

Or, using percolator and the above ration of coffee to water, heat percolator and measure the coffee into strainer and pour correct quantity of boiling water through coffee. Stand over a low flame and allow to infuse 5 minutes. Serve with hot milk.

ALPHABETICAL INDEX

Continued

Continued

Continued

Continued

Continued

ALPHABETICAL INDEX—*continued*

For reference to the various sections see page iii.

PUBLISHED BY CANNON (G A) LTD.
HEAD OFFICE: DEEPFIELDS, BILSTON, STAFFS.
PRINTED BY CRAFTON PRESS LTD., LEICESTER